SAC & FOX - SHAWNEE

GUARDIANSHIPS, PART 1

(UNDER THE SAC & FOX AGENCY, OKLAHOMA)

1892 - 1909

VOLUME XII

TRANSCRIBED BY

JEFF BOWEN

NATIVE STUDY
Gallipolis, Ohio
USA

Originally published:
Santa Maria, California
2019

Reprinted by:

Native Study LLC
Gallipolis, OH
www.nativestudy.com

Library of Congress Control Number: 2022900261

ISBN: 978-1-64968-141-6

Made in the United States of America.

Other Books and Series by Jeff Bowen

Compilation of History of the Cherokee Indians and Early History of the Cherokees by Emmet Starr with Combined Full Name Index
(Hardbound & Softbound)

1901-1907 Native American Census Seneca, Eastern Shawnee, Miami, Modoc, Ottawa, Peoria, Quapaw, and Wyandotte Indians (Under Seneca School, Indian Territory)

1932 Census of The Standing Rock Sioux Reservation with Births And Deaths 1924-1932

Census of The Blackfeet, Montana, 1897- 1901 Expanded Edition

Eastern Cherokee by Blood, 1906-1910, Volumes I thru XIII

Choctaw of Mississippi Indian Census 1929-1932 with Births and Deaths 1924-1931   Volume I
Choctaw of Mississippi Indian Census 1933, 1934 & 1937, Supplemental Rolls to 1934 & 1935 with Births and Deaths 1932-1938, and Marriages 1936-1938 Volume II

Eastern Cherokee Census Cherokee, North Carolina 1930-1939
Census 1930-1931 with Births And Deaths 1924-1931 Taken By Agent L. W. Page Volume I
Eastern Cherokee Census Cherokee, North Carolina 1930-1939
Census 1932-1933 with Births And Deaths 1930-1932 Taken By Agent R. L. Spalsbury   Volume II
Eastern Cherokee Census Cherokee, North Carolina 1930-1939
Census 1934-1937 with Births and Deaths 1925-1938 and Marriages 1936 & 1938 Taken by Agents R. L. Spalsbury And Harold W. Foght Volume III

Seminole of Florida Indian Census, 1930-1940 with Birth and Death Records, 1930-1938

Texas Cherokees 1820-1839 A Document For Litigation 1921

Starr Roll 1894 (Cherokee Payment Rolls) Districts: Canadian, Cooweescoowee, and Delaware Volume One
Starr Roll 1894 (Cherokee Payment Rolls) Districts: Flint, Going Snake, and Illinois   Volume Two
Starr Roll 1894 (Cherokee Payment Rolls) Districts: Saline, Sequoyah, and Tahlequah; Including Orphan Roll   Volume Three

Cherokee Intruder Cases Dockets of Hearings 1901-1909 Volumes I & II

Indian Wills, 1911-1921 Records of the Bureau of Indian Affairs
Books One thru Seven

Other Books and Series by Jeff Bowen

Native American Wills & Probate Records 1911-1921

Turtle Mountain Reservation Chippewa Indians 1932 Census with Births & Deaths, 1924-1932

Chickasaw By Blood Enrollment Cards 1898-1914 Volume I thru V

Cherokee Descendants East An Index to the Guion Miller Applications Volume I
Cherokee Descendants West An Index to the Guion Miller Applications Volume II (A-M)
Cherokee Descendants West An Index to the Guion Miller Applications Volume III (N-Z)

Applications for Enrollment of Seminole Newborn Freedmen, Act of 1905

Eastern Cherokee Census, Cherokee, North Carolina, 1915-1922, Taken by Agent James E. Henderson   *Volume I (1915-1916)*
        Volume II (1917-1918)
        Volume III (1919-1920)
        Volume IV (1921-1922)

Complete Delaware Roll of 1898

Eastern Cherokee Census, Cherokee, North Carolina, 1923-1929, Taken by Agent James E. Henderson   *Volume I (1923-1924)*
        Volume II (1925-1926)
        Volume III (1927-1929)

Applications for Enrollment of Seminole Newborn Act of 1905 Volumes I & II

North Carolina Eastern Cherokee Indian Census 1898-1899, 1904, 1906, 1909-1912, 1914 Revised and Expanded Edition

1932 Hopi and Navajo Native American Census with Birth & Death Rolls (1925-1931) Volume 1 - Hopi
1932 Hopi and Navajo Native American Census with Birth & Death Rolls (1930-1932) Volume 2 - Navajo

Western Navajo Reservation Navajo, Hopi and Paiute 1933 Census with Birth & Death Rolls 1925-1933

Cherokee Citizenship Commission Dockets 1880-1884 and 1887-1889 Volumes I thru V

Applications for Enrollment of Chickasaw Newborn Act of 1905 Volumes I thru VII

Other Books and Series by Jeff Bowen

Cherokee Intermarried White 1906 Volume I thru *X*

Applications for Enrollment of Creek Newborn Act of 1905
Volumes I thru *XIV*

Applications for Enrollment of Choctaw Newborn Act of 1905 Volumes I thru *XX*

Choctaw By Blood Enrollment Cards 1898-1914 Volumes I thru *XX*

Oglala Sioux Indians Pine Ridge Reservation 1932 Census Book I
Oglala Sioux Indians Pine Ridge Reservation Birth and Death Rolls 1924-1932
Book II

Census of the Sioux and Cheyenne Indians of Pine Ridge Agency
1896 - 1897 Book I
Census of the Sioux and Cheyenne Indians of Pine Ridge Agency
1898 - 1899 Book II

Northern Cheyenne Tongue River, Montana 1904 - 1932 Census
1904-1916 Volume I

Northern Cheyenne Tongue River, Montana 1904 - 1932 Census
1917-1926 Volume II

Identified Mississippi Choctaw Enrollment Cards 1902-1909 Volumes I, II & III

Sac & Fox - Shawnee Estates 1885-1910 (Under Sac & Fox Agency)
Volumes I-VIII
Sac & Fox - Shawnee Estates 1920-1924 (Under The Sac & Fox Agency,
Oklahoma) & Wills 1889-1924 Volume IX
Sac & Fox - Shawnee Deaths, Cemetery, Births, & Marriage Cards (Under The Sac
& Fox Agency, Oklahoma) 1853-1933 Volume X
Sac & Fox - Shawnee Marriages, Divorces, Estates Log Books Volumes 1 & 2, Log
Book Births & Deaths (Under Sac & Fox Agency, Oklahoma)1846-1924 Volume XI

Visit our website at **www.nativestudy.com** to learn more about these
and other books and series by Jeff Bowen

Portrait of Tecumseh from Lossing's
The Pictorial Field-Book of the War of 1812
is a pencil sketch drawn by Pierre Le Dru,
a young French trader at Vincennes, circa 1808.

This series is dedicated to
Tanner Tackett
the Constant Gardner
and Friend
and
In memory of
Raina Mae Fulks.

Ab·sen·tee

noun: **absentee**; plural noun: **absentees**

> 1. a person who is expected or required to be present at a place or event but is not.

(According to Webster)

Shawnee

noun, plural Shaw-nees, (especially collectively) Shaw-nee.

> 1. a member of an Algonquian-speaking tribe formerly in the east-central U.S., now in Oklahoma.

(According to Dictionary.com)

Shawnee Teaching

"Tagi nsi walr mvci-lutvwi mr-pvyaci-grlahkv, xvga mytv inv gi mvci-lutvwv, gi mvci-ludr-geiv. Walv uwas-panvsi inv, wa-ciganv-hi gi gol-utvwv u kvgesakv-namv manwi-lanvwawewa yasi golutv-mvni geyrgi.

"Tagi bemi-lutvwi walr segalami mr-pvyaci-grlahkv, xvga mvtv inv gi bemi-lutvwv, gi bemi-ludr-geiv gelv. Wakv vhqalami inv, xvga nahfrpi Moneto ut vhqalamrli nili yasi vhqalamahgi gelv!"

Translation:

"Do not kill or injure your neighbor, for it is not him that you injure, you injure yourself. But do good to him, therefore add to his days of happiness as you add to your own.

"Do not wrong or hate your neighbor, for it is not him that you wrong, you wrong yourself. But love him, for Moneto loves him also as He loves you!"

Thomas Wildcat Alford
circa 1936

Special Note

You will notice throughout these volumes the author has attempted to duplicate from the original documents places on the page that were destroyed due to water damage. Whole sections of a page could be missing or torn into multiple pieces. In order to duplicate the damage you will find various shapes with a white format to try to represent the damage and the loss of the ability to completely transcribe many of the pages.

TABLE OF CONTENTS

INTRODUCTION

The history of the Shawnee is fascinating. Naturally the most famous Shawnee known would be Tecumseh, born circa. 1768, after four other siblings before him. His father was Puckeshinwa, a Shawnee war chief from Ohio. Puckeshinwa crossed the Ohio close to what is now Gallipolis with his fourteen year son Chiksika by his side. As they followed the lead of Chief Cornstalk during the fall of 1774. Tecumseh's famous father was mortally wounded during the fight they would soon encounter. The Shawnees were unexpectedly discovered by a couple of early morning turkey hunters from the settlement called Point Pleasant. These hunters ran as fast as possible back to where the Ohio and Kanawha Rivers meet and sounded the alarm that the Shawnees were coming, the fight lasted most of the day but not without loss to both sides. The Shawnees were badly outnumbered. Pucheshinwa was carried back across the Ohio or as the Shawnees called it the *Spaylaywitheepi*, with the intention to take him back to his village. He must have known his time was short as he laid there telling Chiksika to make sure he devoted his time not only to Tecumseh's but also his younger brothers training in becoming warriors. Pucheshinwa succumbed to his wounds shortly after that request and was secretly buried deep in the forest that day. Chiksika saw his father mortally wounded while defending their home. He had a reverence for his father as a great warrior. He wanted to follow his father's path and not die an average death. In his heart, it had to be on the battlefield as a warrior. Tecumseh followed his brother's every step and planned to die defending his land as his father and brother had. There was no surrendering or giving in to the Americans.

There are several descriptions out there of Tecumseh from his contemporaries, but David Edmunds found one during his research that seems to be the most commanding of any found. "Captain John B. Glegg, Brock's aide-de-camp, who was present at the meetings between Brock and Tecumseh, recorded one of the most vivid descriptions of the Shawnee. According to Glegg, in August 1812 Tecumseh still was in the prime of his life, giving the impression of a man ten years younger. Tecumseh's appearance was very prepossessing; his figure light and finely proportioned; his age I imagined to be about five and thirty [he actually was forty four]; in height, five feet nine or ten inches; his complexion, light copper; countenance, oval, with bright hazle eyes, beaming cheerfulness, energy, and decision. Three small silver crowns, or coronets were suspended from the lower cartilage of his aquiline nose; and a large silver medallion of George the Third, which I believe his ancestor had received from Lord Dorchester, when governor-general of Canada, was attached to a mixed coloured wampum string, and hung around his neck. His dress consisted of a plain, neat uniform, tanned deer-skin jacket, with long trousers of the same material, the seams of both being covered with neatly cut fringe; and he had on his feet leather moccasins, much ornamented with work made from the dyed quills of the porcupine."[1]

There were approximately 39 years that passed between Tecumseh's and his father's deaths.

It is hard to believe that the Shawnee's history being as extensive as it was during the early stages of the United States that their descendants' records were so closely guarded under the care of a vegetable bind in an leaky attic. Not only the Shawnee's but also the Sac & Fox, the Pottawatomie and the Kickapoo. There are also many other tribal affiliates to be found in this series, not to mention someone like Jim Thorpe and his family members of the Sac and Fox tribe. Not only was he a gold metal Olympian and multiple sport competitor, but at the time one of America's favorite sons. Thank goodness someone was finally conscious of the situation. The description in the next paragraph explains the neglect of these important documents as given by the Oklahoma Historical Societies Microfilm Catalog.

"In 1933 a survey of Indian tribal records in Oklahoma revealed that the files of the Shawnee and the old Sac and Fox agencies had been sadly neglected, and the lack of space for storing them properly had resulted in much loss. Charles Eggers, Superintendent of the Shawnee Agency, reported that most of the non-current records of his agency were boxed in a storehouse. The papers of the old Sac and Fox Agency were in the loft of a warehouse which was also used for storing vegetables. The roof of the building leaked and the papers were in danger of destruction from moisture. Following the passage of the Congressional Act of March 27, 1934 (H.R. 5631 Public No. 133) which placed the tribal records in the custody of the Oklahoma Historical Society."

As described above the history of the Shawnee people isn't an ordinary history but an extraordinary time in all of our ancestors' lives. Reading Allen W. Eckert's extensive studies taken from what is known as the Draper Papers, a historical record meticulously documented beginning circa 1830. Though Draper covered an approximate time between the 1740's to the 1810's, his collection covered documents and transcriptions concerning Boone, Kenton, Rogers Clark and Joseph Brant, not to mention a considerable amount of Shawnee history from the entirety of the Ohio and Mississippi Valley's. Other authors such as Colin G. Calloway and R. David Edmunds provide an in depth study of the Shawnee people as well as Tecumseh and his life leaving no rock unturned in their research.

As you read different references you find diverse opinions on Tecumseh's mother as to what tribe she came from. Eckert through Draper's work says, "This was

---

[1] Tecumseh, R. David Edmunds Pg. 162-163, Para. 3-4

when Pucksinwah, then twenty-six, led the war party against the Cherokees that had resulted in the capture of Methotasa."[2] Indicating Tecumseh's mother might have been Cherokee. Yet, R. David Edmunds writes, "In 1768, while the Iroquois were selling Shawnee lands at the Treaty of Fort Stanwix, a Creek woman married to a Shawnee man gave birth to a son at Old Piqua, a Shawnee village on the Mad River in Western Ohio. The woman had a difficult labor before giving birth in the small lodge especially constructed for that purpose, some distance from the family's wigwam. The mother, Methoataske (Turtle Laying Its Eggs), had grown up among the Creek villages in Alabama and had met her husband when some of the Shawnee sought refuge among the Creeks during the 1750s. The father Puckeshinwa, remained with his wife's people until about 1760, when the family left Alabama and migrated to Ohio."[3]

You also will find different opinions on how they dressed back then or wore their hair. In Edmunds' book *Tecumseh*, his brother the Prophet Tenskwatawa states, "Warriors should again shave their heads and wear the scalp locks worn by their ancestors." And yet in Thomas Wildcat Alford's *Civilization*, he says, "We boys wore our hair short, very much as the girls of today wear their hair bobbed. This is the way Shawnee men always have worn their hair. Never did they braid it, as some other tribes do."

Alford's book *Civilization* out of the many resources read was likely one of the most informative and enjoyable references in the study. Thomas Wildcat Alford was born in 1860 and belonged to the Absentee Shawnee tribe. He states that he was a descendant of Tecumseh. He spoke about when his family slept under the stars each night and that he never had an English name until his father had him go to school at a Quaker mission. Mr. Alford also talks about two things with real clarity. Alford educates us about clans in the sixth chapter, expounding upon the active history of the Shawnees and the different responsibilities of each as well as divisions among the clans that created tribal changes. These dissensions were nothing new. Anyone that has read extensively about the Shawnee will realize that Alford understood his people and their history. When he wrote about tribal clashes or divisions during the early days, he managed to translate on paper their strength and character. He showed for generations they literally believed they were given an ability to make themselves self-reliant when it came to survival. They traveled far and wide following their own path while installing their own way of life that made them powerful adversaries whether it be against the British, the French or the Americans moving west. Other tribes found them to be awful enemies or potent allies. Then he compares their tribal government

---

[2] A Sorrow in Our Heart, Allen W. Eckert Pg. 22, Para. 3

[3] Tecumseh, R. David Edmunds, Pg. 17 Para. 1

and the clan leaders to being quite similar to the U.S. Presidency and the different government entities. Alford also brings up business committees for the tribe.

He starts with a concise description of the clans, "Originally there were five clans composing the Shawnee tribe, including the two principle clans, Tha-we-gi-la and Cha-lah-kaw-tha, from one of which came the national or principal chief. The remaining three, the Pec-ku-we, the Kis-pu-go, and the May-ku-jay, each had its own chief who was subordinate to the principal chief in national matters, but independent in matters pertaining to the duties of his clan. Each clan had a certain duty to perform for the whole tribe. For instance the Pec-ku-we clan, or its chief, had charge of the maintenance of order and looked after the celebration of things pertaining to religion or faith; the Kis-pu-go clan had charge of matters pertaining to war and the preparation and training of warriors; the May-ku-jay clan had charge of things relating to health and medicine and food for the whole tribe. But the two powerful clans, the Tha-we-gi-la and the Cha-lah-kaw-tha, had charge of political affairs and all matters that affected the tribe as a whole. Indeed, the tribal government may be likened to the government of the United States, in which each state (clan), with it governor (chief), is sovereign in local matters, but subordinate to the president of the United States (principal chief) in national matters. The difference is that the president of the United States must be elected, and may be changed with each election, while the principal chief came to his office by heritage and held it for life, or during good behavior.

At the time of which I write the Shawnee tribe had been divided for many years, and only the Tha-we-gi-la, the Pec-ku-we, and the Kis-pu-go clans were represented in the Absentee Shawnee band. These three clans always had been closely related, while the Cha-lah-kaw-tha and the May-ku-jay had always stood together, and were represented in the group that I have mentioned as living in Kansas at the time of the Civil War."[4]

As referenced earlier Thomas Wildcat Alford brought up their present Indian agent, Thomas, on September 13, 1893, wanting him to present a list of prominent men in their tribe to hold positions on a business committee. This presented a whole new world for the tribe with new pressures through white change so to speak. The government was instilling in their world the destruction of their heritage in tribal customs and culture all to control Indian land through allotment. When he was being told to help form this committee, he was actually being told, what we are doing is we are wiping out your way of life forever. The Congress of the United States was presenting the abolition of all tribal governments so the land could be manipulated through the Curtis Act of 1898. They said, we are splitting the land up. They were allotting so many acres to each tribal member. How much they got depended on

---

[4] Civilization, Alford; Pg. 44, Para. 1-2

whether they planned to farm or raise cattle. If they were building herds they were given double the land for grazing. Alford said, "It was on the thirteenth day of September, 1893 that Agent Thomas informed the Shawnees that he had been directed by the Commissioner of Indian Affairs to submit for approval the names of seven of the most prominent men of the tribe who would constitute a Business Committee to supersede the chiefs and councilors of the old tribal government. The Business Committee was to represent the Absentee Shawnees as a tribe in all dealings with the United States and to act in an advisory capacity to the individual members of the tribe. They were to certify to the identity of grantors of sales of land and to act for the tribe in other matters.[5]

During the study it was noticed that the Curtis Act being enacted on June 28, 1898 and Alford's mentioning its initiation during 1893 became a point of interest or at least premature. It was found that Congress had actually started working in this area of seizure approximately five years prior to the agent's notification, "In 1893 Congress began a special allotment process for the Five Tribes, enacting a number of laws that affect the governmental powers of the tribes. Some of these laws, like the 1889 and 1890 Acts, extended certain Arkansas laws over Indian Territory and expanded federal court jurisdiction; they are relevant today only insofar as they may indirectly affect tribal judicial powers."[6]

Their mention of these laws only being relevant today, though actually not spoken, plead plausible deniability while coinciding with the Indian Reorganization Act of 1934. The government was on a mission. Land and control. The allotment had to take place. They were wanting statehood. They were wanting the Native people to be under one umbrella with everyone else. Tribes were nations. Just like a foreign nation, they were their own government. Originally our constitution was modeled after the Iroquois model, had to start somewhere? So what we did was split up the land among the people that already owned it. Then we took what was left, approximately 90 million acres and sold it at a profit. Who got the money? Only the politicians at the time know? But years after taking the chiefs and councils away there was likely mass chaos like a town hall today. So the government likely was wanting out of the tribal control business. At least enough that they could just control it without being in the bullseye so to speak. Congress and the state had already achieved its goals. So this act was written with the statement that it was a model to make all think we do this for you. "The IRA was intended to provide a mechanism for the tribe as a governmental unit to interact with and adapt to a modern society, rather than to force the assimilation of individual Indians.

---

[5] Civilization, Alford; Pg. 161, Para. 2

[6] Federal Indian Law, Cohen; Pg. 781, Para. 3

The IRA was also an attempt to improve the economic situation of Indians. The Act was intended to stop the alienation of tribal land needed to support Indians, and to provide for acquisition of additional acreage for tribes. Tribes were encouraged to organize along the lines of modern business corporations; a system of financial credit was included to reach this economic objective."[7] Interestingly enough Cohen and Alford both mention this same organizational technique, only one as law and another as a tribal member.

It is disconcerting just in reading a reference from Senator Charles Curtis as he mentioned in his biography that by the time Congress finished rewriting the bill he had submitted he hardly recognized it. "Officially titled the "Act for the Protection of the People of Indian Territory", the Act is named for Charles Curtis, congressman from Kansas and its author. He was of mixed Native American and European descent: on his mother's side -Kansa, Osage, Potawatomi, and French; and on his father's - three ethnic lines of British Isles ancestry. Curtis was raised in part on the Kaw Reservation of his maternal grandparents, but also lived with his paternal grandparents and attended Topeka High School. He read law, became an attorney, and later was elected to the United States House of Representatives and Senate. He served as Vice-President under Herbert Hoover. In the usual fashion, by the time the bill HR 8581 had gone through five revisions in committees in both the House of Representatives and the Senate, there was little left of Curtis' original draft. In his hand-written autobiography, Curtis noted having been unhappy with the final version of the Curtis Act. He believed that the Five Civilized Tribes needed to make changes. He thought that the way ahead for Native Americans was through education and use of both their and the majority cultures, but he also had hoped to give more support to Native American transitions."[8]

The records within this series concern The Absentee Shawnee as well as many other people with different tribal affiliations. Also within these pages are closely related tribes that were under the same agency (The Sac & Fox Agency, Oklahoma) for many years like the Sac & Fox, the Pottawatomie and the Kickapoo. There are likely state recognized Shawnee tribes in the United States, but, "The Absentee Shawnee Tribe of Indians of Oklahoma (or Absentee Shawnee) is one of three federally recognized tribes of Shawnee people. Historically residing in the Eastern United States, the original Shawnee lived in the areas that are now Ohio, Indiana, Illinois, Kentucky, Tennessee, Pennsylvania, and other neighboring states. It is documented that they occupied and traveled through lands from Canada to Florida, from the Mississippi River to the eastern continental coast. In contemporary times, the Absentee Shawnee Tribe headquarters in Shawnee, Oklahoma; its tribal jurisdiction

---

[7] Federal Indian Law, Cohen; Pg. 147 Para. 1-2
[8] Curtis Act of 1898, Wikipedia

area includes land properties in Oklahoma in both Cleveland County and Pottawatomie County." [Today] "There are approximately 3,050 enrolled Absentee Shawnee tribal members, 2,315 of whom live in Oklahoma. Tribal membership follows blood quantum criteria, with applicants requiring a minimum of one eighth (1/8) documented Absentee-Shawnee blood to be placed on its membership rolls, as set forth by the tribal constitution. Though it is not a formal division, there is a social separation within its current tribal membership between the traditionalist Big Jim Band, which kept cultural traditions and ceremonies and has its primary populace in the Little Axe, Norman area, and the assimilationist White Turkey Band, which adopted European ways of the European majority, with many families based in the Shawnee area. Regardless of historical viewpoints, the bands cooperate for the future of the tribe."[9]

When this study was first pursued an old Xerox copy of a catalog that sat on the shelf for twenty five years was the first place searched for a viable source. It was titled, "Catalog of Microfilm Holdings in the Archives & Manuscripts Div. Oklahoma Historical Society 1976-1989". As mentioned in the description from this catalog's Introduction for the Sac and Fox Indian Agencies, it states, "In 1901 the Sac and Fox Agency was divided. The Sac and Fox Agency itself remained at the old site near Stroud with jurisdiction over the Sac and Fox and the Iowa. The Shawnee, Potawatomi and Kickapoo Agency (sometimes simply called the Shawnee Agency) was established about two miles south of Shawnee, Oklahoma. The agencies continued their separate existence until 1919 when they were merged becoming the Shawnee Agency.

Of course today in 2018, everything is digital and on the computer. You have to be thankful for having an old catalog and books on a shelf. There is nothing like the feel of holding a book in your hand. You can pick it up when you want and let your eyes travel to anywhere or any time in history. It has solid print that nobody can manipulate or change. It's just yours to wrap yourself up in without any glowing distractions as Native Americans call them, "Talking Leaves".

Jeff Bowen
Gallipolis, Ohio
NativeStudy.com

---

[9] Absentee-Shawnee Tribe of Indians Wikipedia

Sac and Fox-Shawnee – <u>ADOPTIONS</u>

December, 1906 and September, 1923

Sac & Fox – Shawnee
1892-1909 Volume XII

[Transcriber's Note: This note is a courtesy because we realize that adoptions are so difficult to find. There is no last name with the first adoption for the child (William), but in reading a little further it mentions an Alex Jefferson in relation to William. There is reference to a William H. Jefferson in Vols'. VI, X and XI Indexes. The second adoption concerns the name Anna Bassett. There is reference to Anna and Mary Ford Bassett in Vol. IX's Index. Adoptions weren't titled on this Volume's cover because there are only two adoptions in the whole series. A heading for adoptions was placed in the Table of Contents.]

Stillwater, Okla.

Box 561   Dec-10-06

RECEIVED

DEC 12 1906

W.C. Kohlenberg

Sac & Fox, Okla.

SAC & FOX AGENCY,
OKLAHOMA.

Dear Sir:-

I have tried to get you by telephone, that I might talk with you about William. I would like to have him with me - if - I could legally adopt him - which I would like very much to do. Otherwise I would not feel at liberty to rear him as I thought best. If this cannot be done - why not send the child to Carlisle?

Everything is so sanitary there- and daily exercise in and out of doors compulsory - which I think would be of great benefit to the boy.

He would pass the necessary examination wouldn't he?

The "Outing System" at Carlisle might be of use as it would at least place him with some cultured family in the country. If you would like to take with me personally we might arrange to come down or meet you in Stroud--

I would like to meet you and talk with you more fully about William.

Very truly
Fannie H Banister

****

3

RECEIVED

DEC 29 1906

**SAC & FOX AGENCY,
OKLAHOMA.**

W. C. Kohlenberg
  Sac & Fox, Okla.

Dear Sir:-

Since our return Mr. Banister and I have talked matters over about William and we have both decided that if Alex Jefferson cannot or rather will not consent to our adopting William that we would like to have him anyway - that is if we can so arrange with you.

I am alone so much that I am afraid that I need William about as much as he needs our care - If this will be alright with you, Mr Banister will come down and have William return with him. Just as soon as you think best.

Please let us know just when to come down. I would like so much to have him up here on New Year's day - if possible - as I shall have a turkey dinner - We were invited out on Xmas Day - so our turkey escaped that time.

Very truly

(Phone 195)?   Fannie H. Banister
                                              Stillwater
                   Dec-28-06   Box 561   Okla.

Shawnee Indian Agency,
Shawnee, Oklahoma,
Sept. 26, 1923.

Mr. J. W. Reece,
  Attorney at law,
    Stillwater, Okla.

Dear Mr. Reece:-

This will acknowledge the receipt of your letter of the 25th inst. with reference to Robert Small and his wife adopting one, Anna Bassett, the daughter of Mary Bassett Springer.

In reply you are advised that this matter was brought to my attention by Robert Small and his wife and as far as I can see there are no objections on the part of this office, and it is believed that this adoption will be for the best interests of the little girl. I am personally acquainted with Robert Small and his wife and as far as I know they are good people. They live a clean moral life and it is believed that the little girl would be surrounded by the proper environment.

With reference to the fee of $10.00 which Robert promised to pay you, and said that same would be paid you from this office; I have to advise that at the present time Anna Bassett has no money to her credit, however she received funds from time to time and it has been directed that the proper hypothecation of the amount necessary--viz $10.00--be set aside and just as soon as it is received a check will be sent to you from this office.

Very truly yours,

J. L. Suffecool,
Superintendent.

JLS:EV.
cc to Robert Small
    Perkins, Oklahoma,
    R#1.

Sac and Fox-Shawnee – <u>GUARDIANSHIPS</u>

Undated and August, 1892 – August, 1914

RECEIVED

W. N. MABEN
PROBATE JUDGE,
POTTAWATOMIE COUNTY.

MAR 23 1905

SAC & FOX AGENCY,
OKLAHOMA

Tecumseh, Okla. Mch 22nd   190__

Hon. W.C. Kohlenberg,
　　　　Sac and Fox Agency, O.T.

My Dear Sir:-

　　　　Your letter of the 15th inst. received and contents carefully noted. In reply I beg to say that I was not aware of the stringent rules of the Secretary of the Interior, in regard to the distribution of the money of these Indians. I of course can appreciate the position that you are placed in and shall gladly do anything in my power to assist you, to the end that we both may discharge our official duty in accordance with law. It is sometimes a very difficult matter to take up with you, the matter of appointment of administrators and guardians, for the reason, that relatives will petition the court to appoint parties, who in all probabilities are competent, yet, parties whom you would not approve and parties whom I do not in all cases regard as the best persons to appoint. However this may be, I have reached the conclusion, that I will instruct all guardians and administrators, under my jurisdiction, to co-operate with you, and we will take up each case of distribution of funds, on their respective merit.

　　　　Assuring you that I should be glad to hears from you at any time, on matters pending in this court. I am,

　　　　　　　　　　Yours very truly,
　　　　　　　　　　W. N. Maben

Sums paid to guardians of Indian Minors since 1901

Name of Guardian			Amount
John Foster	Payne		$9387.86
H.C. McGaughy	Lincoln		497.67
A.D. Wright	Lincoln		4989.76
H.C. Brunt	Lincoln		4278.69
Milton Bryan	Pottawatomie		3361.04
Mary Goodell	~~gdn for her son~~ Lincoln		1166.67
Fannie Nadeau	Indian	Lincoln	800.00
P.S. Hoffman		Lincoln	2422.00
Stephen S. Rains	Pottawatomie		507.11
Herman Josey	Lincoln		2820.01
George L. Rose	Pottawatomie		1396.67

L.T. Sammons			500.80	
HG Beard				
Samuel L. Moore	Indian	Lincoln	2468.01	
John O. Arnold	Lincoln		33.32	
Hiram Holt	Pottawatomie		55.61	
Lee Patrick	Lincoln		1550.00	$36283.22

Simpson?	Pottawatomie			
F.G. [Illegible]	Lincoln			
Laura Carter	Lincoln			
Walter Battice	Lincoln			
Henry C. [Illegible]	Pottawatomie	EE Jones	7/31/05	12.50
John A. [Illegible]			5/16/05	12.50
			7/9/06	12.50

****

Sums paid to guardians of Indian Minors since 1901

Name of Guardian	Amount
John Foster	$9387.86
H.C. McGaughy	497.67
A.D. Wright	4989.76
H.C. Brunt	4278.69
Milton Bryan	~~3350.62~~ 3361.04
Mary Goodell	1166.67
Fannie Nadeau	800.00
P.S. Hoffman	2422.00
Stephen S. Rains	507.11
Herman Josey	2820.01
George L. Rose	1396.67
L.T. Sammons	500.80
Samuel L. Moore	2468.01
John O. Arnold	33.32
Hiram Holt	55.61
Lee Patrick	1550.00 ~~$36224.81~~ 36336.22

Various sums paid to John Foster as legal guardian of the
following minor Indians since 1901

Names of Wards	Land Money	Lease Money	Total
George Perry	$ 816.00		$ 816.00
Rachel Hall	9/9/04 4/20/04 }641.62	2/23/05 $ 22.50	664.12
Clara Ellis	4/8/04 250.00		250.00
Laura Ellis	4/8/04 250.00		250.00
Maude Kakaque	4/8/04 1075.00		1075.00
Maude Bigwalker	4/30/04 176.19		176.19
Esther Bigwalker	4/30/04 176.19	8/7/06 12.50	176.19
Harrison Hunter	4/20/04 111.37	2/23/05 5.00	116.37
Gertrude Hunter	4/20/04 111.37	2/23/05 5.00	116.37
Daniel S. Hunter	4/20/04 111.37	2/23/05 5.00	116.37
Isadore Neal	4/20/04 680.01	2/23/05 17.53	697.54
Cora Bass	2/9/04 [387.22		387.22
Lee Bass	{387.22		387.22
Ione C. Bass	3/31/04 [387.23		387.23
Walter Kakaque	3/5/04 400.00		400.00
Mary Mansur	2/25/04 [1433.32		1433.32
Silas Hawk	2/25/04 {1016.56		1016.56
Stella Hawk	12/9/03 [868.00	8/8/05 125.	868.00
Charley Mohee		2/23/05 37.50	37.50
Robert Tohee		5/27/04 16.66	16.66
Ben Hull			9387.86
Henry Hull			152.50
Wm Pennock		2/8/06 15⁰⁰	9540.36
			9540.36

****

Various sums paid to H.C. McGaughy as legal guardian of
Fullwood Lincoln since 1901

Name of Ward	Land Money	Lease Money	Total
Fulwood[sic] Lincoln	9/19/03 11/30/0 }$ 497.67		$497.67

497.67
136.66
360.01

****

Various sums paid to A.D. Wright as legal guardian of the
following minor Indians since 1901

Name of Ward	Land Money	Lease Money	Total
Thomas Morris	9/14/04 $ 720.00	2/23/05 $ 24.94	$ 744.94
Susan Morris	9/14/04 720.00	2/23/05 34.94 ⓧ	754.94
Grover Morris	9/14/04 720.00	8/24/04 2/23/05 } 124.94	844.94
Edward Morris	9/14/04 720.00	2/23/05 24.94	744.94
Harvey Madison	9/14/04 1900.00		1900.00
			4989.76
			133
			5122.76

ⓧ Susan Morris   5/22/05 73⁰⁰
                                              5/7/06 60⁰⁰

754.94
73
827.94

****

Various sums paid to H.C. Brunt as legal guardian of the
following minor Indians since 1901

Name of Ward	Land Money	Lease Money	Total
George Butler	11/4/04 $2000.00	2/23/05 $139.34	$2139.34
Jane Butler	11/4/04 2000.00	2/23/05 139.35	2139.35
			4278.69

****

Various sums paid to Milton Bryan as legal guardian of the
following minor Indians since 1901

Name of Ward	Land Money	Lease Money	Total
James Littlebear	4/20/04 $ 402.91	3/5/04 $ 20.74	$ 423.65
Lillie Littlebear	402.91	20.74	423.65
Jessie Chisholm	201.45	8/18/04 10.42	211.87
Nellie Chisholm	4/2/04 201.45	10.42	211.87

12

Bertha Pattequa	2/24/04 462.50			462.50
Addie Pattequa	2/24/04 462.50			462.50
Dickson Duncan	2/10/04 577.50	2/23/05 5.00		582.50
Allen G. Thurman	2/10/04 577.50	2/23/05 5.00		582.50
				3361.04

****

Various sums paid to Mary Goodell as legal guardian of
John Isaac Goodell Indian

Name of Ward	Land Money	Lease Money	Total
John Isaac Goodell	5/3/04 $1166.67		$1166.67

Various sums paid to Fannie Nadeau as legal guardian of
Guy Whistler   Indian

Name of Ward	Land Money	Lease Money	Total
Guy Whistler	3/1/04 $ 800.00		$ 800.00

****

Various sums paid to P.S. Hoffman as legal guardian of the
following minor Indians.

Name of Ward	Land Money	Lease Money	Total
Martha Baker	6/6 2/27 04 ⎫ $1206.00 3/2 ⎬		$1206.00
Paul Randall	3/19/04 166.67	2/23/04 $ 9.18	175.85
(x) Stephen Harrison	3/19/04 166.66	2/23/04 9.17	175.83
Edward Tohee	440.00		440.00
Rachel Smith	237.16		237.16
Charley Smith	237.16		237.16
			2472.00

(x) W Battice L.G. after 3/1/06   3/20/16   15⁰⁰

****

13

Various sums paid to Stephen S. Rains as legal guardian of the
following minor Indians

Name of Ward	Land Money	Lease Money	Total
Mamie Morton	4/30/04 3/24/04 } $ 484.53	2/23/04 $22.58	$507.11

****

Various sums paid to Herman Josey as legal guardian of
Sadie Ingalls

Name of Ward	Land Money	Lease Money	Total
Sadie Ingalls	4/16/04 $2614.34	2/23/04 $205.67	$2820.01

****

Various sums paid to George L. Rose as legal guardian of the
following minor Indians since 1901

Name of Ward	Land Money	Lease Money	Total
Geo. O. Morton	4/30/04 {$643.33	8/25/03 12/14/0 }$60.00	$703.33
Clifford H. Morton	2/24/04 { 643.34	8/25/03 50.00	693.34
			1396.67

****

Various sums paid to L.T. Simmons as legal guardian of
Etta Shaw since 1901   Resigned Pres. Gdn H.G. Beard

Name of Ward	Land Money	Lease Money	Total
Etta Shaw	4/6/04 $500.80		$500.80

****

Various sums paid to Samuel L. Moore as legal guardian of the
following minor Indians since 1901   Indian

Name of Ward	Land Money	Lease Money	Total
Albert Moore	3/8/04 [$1234.00		$1234.00
Clifford H. Morton	2/10/04[1234.01		1234.01
			2468.01

****

Various sums paid to John O. Arnold as legal guardian of the
following minor Indians since 1901

Name of Ward	Land Money	Lease Money	Total
John Crane		5/9/05 $16.66	$16.66
Clifford H. Morton		5/9/05 16.66	16.66
			33.32
Theresa Logan			

J. Crane		5/9/05 16.66	
		9/14/05 50.	
		9/14/05 16.68	
		1/31/06 9.72	
		7/12/ " 2.78	
		1/31/06 16.66	112.50
H. Crane		5/9/05 16.66	
		9/14/05 50.	
		9/14/05 16.68	
		1/31/06 9.72	
		7/12/ " 2.78	
		1/31/06 16.67	112.51
Theresa Logan		9/14/05 50.	
		9/14/05 8.32	
		1/31/06 5.56	
		7/12/ " 2.78	
		1/31/06 16.67	93.33

318.34

****

Various sums paid to Hiram Holt as legal guardian of the
following Indian Minors since 1901

Name of Ward	Land Money	Lease Money	Total
Mary Thorp		3/7/05 $43.87	$43.87
Adeline Thorp		3/7/05 5.87	5.87
Edward Thorp		3/7/05 5.87	5.87
			55.61
James Thorpe			
Charlotte Thorpe			
Mary Thorp		7/31/05 8.75	
		9/7/ " 6.66	
Adeline Thorp		7/31/05 8.75	
		9/8/ " 6.67	
James Thorp		7/31/05 8.75	
		9/8/ " 6.67	
		9/11/ " 25.88 41.30	
Edward Thorp		7/31/05 8.75	
		9/8/ " 6.67	

****

Various sums paid to Lee Patrick as legal guardian of the
following minor Indians since 1901

Name of Wards	Land Money	Lease Money	Total
Pearl Conger	3/20/04 $1200.00		$1200.00
Fannie Keokuk		10/22/04 }$350.00 3/23/05 }	350.00
		8/18/05 187.50	
		1/5/06 600.00	
		7/30/ " 30.00	
		" " 12.51	
		1180$\frac{01}{}$	
Wm H Jefferson		7/30/06 45$\frac{04}{}$	

****

16

Statement of funds paid to S.C. Huber, Tama, Iowa,
as legal guardian for the following
minor Indians since 1901.

Name of ward	Lease Money.		Total
Nellie Davenport	Aug. 11, ' 05	$16.67	
	Jan. 31, '06	16.67	$33.34
Seba Davenport	Aug. 11, '05	16.67	
	Jan. 31, '06	16.67	
	Aug. 4, "	33.33	$66.67
			$100.01

****

Statement of amounts paid to George L. Rose,
Tecumseh, Okla., as legal guardian,
of the following Indian minors, since 1901.

Name of Wards	Land Money		Lease Money		Total
George O. Morton	Mar. 9, '04	$643.33	Aug. 25, '03	$60.00	$703.33
			(Dec. 14, "		
Clifford H. Morton	Feb. 24, "	643.33	Aug. 25, '03	50.00	693.34
					$1396.67

****
[The above statement given again]

****

Statement of amounts paid to H. C. McGaughy
Chandler, Okla., as legal guardian of
Fulwood Lincoln, since 1901.

Sept. 19, '03)		
Nov. 30, ")	$497.67	(Land money)

497.67
136.66
363.01 Rec
170.10 Bal
$192.90 Exp

17

****

[The above statement given again]

****

Statement of funds paid to John O. Arnold, Cushing,
Oklahoma, as legal guardian of the following minor Indians since 1901.

Name of ward.	Land Money	Lease Money		Total
John Crane		May 9, '05	$16.66	
		Sep.14, "	50.00	
		" " "	16.68	
		Jan.31, '06	9.72	
		" " "	16.66	
		Jul. 12, "	2.78	$112.50
Harry Crane		May 9, '05	$16.66	
		Sep.14, "	50.00	
		" " "	16.68	
		Jan.31, '06	9.72	
		" " "	16.67	
		Jul. 12, "	2.78	$112.51
Theresa Logan		Sep.14, '05	50.00	
		" " "	8.32	
		Jan.31, '06	5.56	
		" " "	16.67	
		Jul. 12, "	2.78	$ 93.33

$318.34

****

[The above statement given again]

****

Sac & Fox – Shawnee
1892-1909   Volume XII

Statement of funds paid to S.C. Huber, Tama, Iowa,
as legal guardian for the following
minor Indians since 1901.

Name of ward	Lease Money.		Total
Nellie Davenport	Aug. 11, ' 05	$16.67	
	Jan. 31, '06	16.67	$33.34
Seba Davenport	Aug. 11, '05	16.67	
	Jan. 31, '06	16.67	
	Aug. 4, "	33.33	$66.67
			$100.01

****

Statement of Funds paid to Legal Guardians of
Indian Minors since 1901.

Guardian :	Ward :	Amount :	Total:
Lee Patrick,	Pearl Conger	$1200.00	
	Fannie Keokuk	1180.01	
		45.04	$2425.05
F. G. Dennis,	Peyton Keokuk	8.34	8.34
Chief McKosito	Ira Walker	145.00	145.00
John O. Arnold,	John Crane	112.50	
	Harry Crane	112.51	
	Theresa Logan	93.33	318.34
John Foster,	George Perry	816.00 Sarah Mansur	
	Racheal Hall	664.12 Harry Davis	
	Clara Ellis	250.00 Frank Davis	
	Laura Ellis	250.00 Ben Hull	
	Maude Kakaque	1075.00	
	Maude Bigwalker	176.19	
	Esther Bigwalker	176.19	
	Harrison Hunter	128.87	
	Gertrude Hunter	116.37	
	Daniel S. Hunter	116.37	
	Isadore Neal	697.54	
	Cora Bass	387.22	
	Lee Bass	387.22	
	Ione C. Bass	387.23	

	Walter Kakaque	400.00	
	Mary Mansur	1433.32	
	Silas Hawk	1016.56	
	Stella Hawk	868.00	
	Charley Mohee	162.50	
	Robert Tohee	16.66	
	~~William~~ David Pennock	15.00	9540.36
John A. Jenson,	Charley Lightfoot	40.00	40.00
S. C. Huber,	Nellie Davenport	33.34	
	Seba Davenport	66.67	100.01
Samuel L. Moore,	Albert Moore	1234.00	
	Ruth Moore	1234.01	2466.01
H. C. McGaughey[sic],	Fulwood Lincoln	497.67	497.67
A. D. Wright,	Thomas Morris	$744.94	
	Susan Morris	887.94	
	Grover Morris	884.84	
	Edward Morris	744.94	
	Harvey Madison	1900.00	$ 5122.76
H. C. Brunt	George Butler	2139.34	
	Jane Butler	2139.35	4278.69
P. S. Hoffman,	Martha Baker	1206.00	
	Paul Randall	175.85	
	Stephen Harrison	175.83	
	Edward Tohee	440.00	
	Racheal Smith	237.16	
	Charley Smith	237.16	2472.00
Walter Battice	Stephen Harrison	15.00	15.00
Mary Hurr	Orlando Johnson	88.89	88.89
Fannie Nadeau	Guy Whistler	800.00	800.00
Mary Goodell	John Isaac Goodell	1166.67	1166.67
Herman Josey	Sadie Ingalls	2820.01	2820.01

Milton Bryan	James Littlebear	423.65	
	Lillie Littlebear	423.65	
	Jessie Chislom[sic]	211.87	
	Nellie Chislom	211.87	
	Bertha Pattequa	462.50	
	Addie Pattequa	462.50	
	Dickson Duncan	582.50	
	Allen G. Thurman	582.50	3381.04
George L. Rose,	George O. Morton	703.33	
	Cliff H. Morton	693.34	1396.67
L. T. Sammons,	Etta Shaw	500.80	500.80
Stephen S. Raines	Mamie Morton	507.11	507.11
Hiram Holt,	James Thorp	$41.30	
	Mary Thorp	59.28	
	Adeline Thorp	21.29	
	Edward Thorp	21.29	$ 143.06
Henry C. Jones,	Ellen Easley Jones	37.50	37.50

****

Statement of amounts paid to Milton Bryan, Shawnee, as
legal guardian of the following Indian minors
since 1901.

Name of wards	Land money		Lease money		Total
James Littlebear	Apr. 20, '04	$402.91	Mar. 5, '04	$20.74	$423.65
Lillie Littlebear	" " "	402.91	" " "	20.74	423.65
Jessie Chisholm	" 2, "	201.45	Aug.18, "	10.42	211.87
Nellie Chisholm	" " "	201.45	" " "	10.42	211.87
Bertha Pattequa	Feb. 24, "	462.50			462.50
Addie Pattequa	" " "	462.59			462.50
Dickson Duncan	" 10, "	577.50	Feb. 23. '05	5.00	582.50
Allen G. Thurman	" " "	577.50	" " "	5.00	582.50
					$3361.04

Letters of Guardianship of Minors -   Aug-7-1892
The Territory of Oklahoma Cleveland Co } ss

The Territory of Oklahoma Cleveland County
All whom it may concern and especially to Winnie G. Williams, George Williams,
Minor heirs of deceased and it appearing to the Court that it is necessary to appoint a
guardian to said Winnie G. Williams and Geo. Williams and the said Wm W. Williams
having been approved for said trust by the Court, and having given Bond as required
by law which has been approved, filed and recorded in said Court:- Now therefore
trusting in you[sic] care and fidelity, We have appointed and do by these presents
appoint you the said William W Williams as such guardian hereby authorizing and
empowering you to take and to have the custody of said minors and the care of their
education, and the care and management of their estate until they arrive at the age of
thirty one years, or until you shall be discharged according to Law:- And require you
to make a true inventory of all the estate, real and personal of said Ward, that shall
come to your possession or knoledge[sic], and to return the same into the Probat[sic]
Court within three months from the date of these letters, or at any other time the Court
shall direct, to dispose of and manage all such estate according to Law, and for the
best interest of the Wards. and faithfully to discharge your trust in relation thereto and
also when required in relation to the care, custody and education of wards to render an
account on oath of the property, real and personal of the said Wards in your hands-
and all proceeds and interests derived therefrom and of the management and
disposition of the same within one year after your appointment, and annually
thereafter, and at such other times as the proper Court shall direct and at the expiration
of your trust to settle your account with the Probate Court or with the wards if they
shall be of full age or their legal reprasentatives[sic] and to pay over and deliver all the
property, real and personal, remaining in your hands or due from you in such
settlement to the person lawfully entitled thereto.   In testimony whereof we have
caused the seal of our said Probate Court to be hereto affixed
Witness F. Please
Judge of our said County at
Norman in said County this 7" day of August A.D. 1892
Frank Please
Probate Judge

****

Copy

Territory of Oklahoma ⎱
Cleveland County ⎰ ss-

In the Probate Court of Cleveland County
Territory of Oklahoma-

In the matter of the Guardianship of Willie Williams and Geo. Williams- Minors-

Oath of Office of Guardian

I, Wm W. Williams, being duly sworn, on oath do say, that he will faithfully perform the duties of guardian to the above named minors as described in my letters of guardianship, and according to Law and to the best of my ability so help me God

Witness   his mark
Albert [Illegible]   William W X Williams

Subscribed and sworn to before me, and in my presence this 7" day of August, 1892
Frank Please
Probate Judge

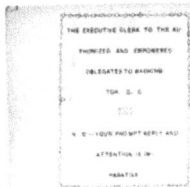

WALTER H. SHAWNEE,

General Secretary and Interpreter for the

Absentee Shawnee Indians of Okla. Ter.

Tecumseh, Okla.   June 29.....189 4

Gen E L Thomas
   U. S. Indian Agent
      Sac and Fox Agency, O.T.
Sir,
      We the undersigned parties, members of Big Jim band of Absentee Shawnee Indians of Oklahoma Territory and Councilors and Head Men of said tribe or band, do hereby certify on our honor that we are personally acquainted with Iuaw Cumpsey, and that she is the daughter of Leaw-wah- Cumpsey and Billy Williams (deceased) and are certain that she has reached the full age of 19 years.

She has requested us to ask of you for her money in full, and we would think that she is lawfully and rightly entitled to the same; We beg to state in obedience to her request that we have selected our Principal Chief to be Trustee for the said Iuaw Cumpsey and to receive and hold this money for her exclusive benefit.

In your reply to her letter of May 28 bearing date of June 2, you state that she would be paid her money in the sum of Three Hundred and Fifty Dollars (350\frac{00}{}$) when she arrived at the age of 21 years.

In her behalf, we wish to call your attention to the fact that we have always understood and are informed from various sources that the legal age of the female was (18) years and of the male (21) years.

We have therefore to request for the said Iuaw Cumpsey that he wish be accepted.

We further certify our entire disinterestedness in this matter this 29th day of June, A.D. 1894. In presence of

Walter H. Shawnee

Wm Shawnee

Little his x mark Creek

Bob His x mark White

Big His x mark Jim

Joe His x mark Billy

Long His x mark Man

John His x mark Taylor

John His x mark Scott

John His x mark Welsh

John His x mark Pecan

OFFICE OF : : :
GEO. B. CAMPBELL
ATTORNEY-AT-LAW

ROOM 34 BANK BLOCK.

DENVER, COLORADO.   Dec. 22d. 1892,

Hon S. L. Patrick,

Sac, & Fox Agency, O. Terr.

Dear Sir:--   In reply to yours of the 16th. inst asking for information regarding the ages of the Children of Eleanora Alley, in reply will say that Suella Loder is 23 years of age, Gertie Cook 20, Charles Miller 18, Clara May Freeland 7. Geo.

B. Campbell has been appointed guardian for the two minor children.   If you desire an affidavit setting forth their ages I will furnish the same.

Respectfully yours,

Geo.B.Campbell

Econtuchka I.T.
July 9 1894
J. T. Peyton

Asking for his
Guardian Papers

****

[The note below typed as given]

Econtuchka I T
July 9 1894

sac & fox agent
Sac & fox agency
Sir is my guardian Papers in your offes yet if so Pleas send them to me just as soon as you can as I will need them in a few days   O Blige
J T Peyton

Norman Ok Ty
Aug 27 - 1894
J H Goodin

Wanting to know how he
can get possession of John Goodin
his work & land now illegally held
by Wall

****

[The letter below typed as given]

ᴮᴱᴿᴿᵞ ᴮᴿᴼˢ.,

DEALERS IN

EVERYTHING IN OUR LINE IN STOCK.

Dry Goods, Notions, Boots, Shoes, Hats and Caps.

Groceries, Flour and Feed.

Sumner, Okla   July 27ᵗʰ   *1894.*

E L Thomas
US Indian Agt
Sac & Fox Agency OT

Dear Sir. The alotment agent allotted to John Gooden a piece of Land, Rachael <u>Wall</u> by her husband & self has taken possession of the same by puting a fence arround it & puting into cultivation a part of it. I am the natural and legaly appointed guardian of John Gooden who holds <u>Indian patent</u> from Goverment for same - Wall refuses to give up possession- Now I appeal to you for information or assistance in geting possession of the land covered by Patent issued to John Gooden and ask that you inform me when & how to proceed

Yours
J H Gooden
Guardian John Gooden
Minor

OFFICE OF—
JOHNSON WHILES,
Probate Judge, Payne County,
STILLWARTON, OKLAHOMA.

Stillwater, Oklahoma,   Aug 15ᵗʰ   *1894*

U.S. Indian Agt.

Sir:

I issued Letters of Guardianship today of the person and estate of Jake Dole, to a Mrs. Josie Springer who is the mother of said minor and formerly widow of Willie Dole, father of said minor.

I also married her and a Mr. Springer, to day.

They informed me that you wished a copy of Letters of Guardianship which I herewith inclose.

Yours Respectfully,
Johnson Whiles

Territory of Oklahoma   ⎫
County of Pottowatomie[sic] ⎬ ss
                         ⎭

I W.A. Ruggles Probate Judge in and for the County and Territory aforesaid hereby certify that Lillie Va[illegible] is the duly appointed Guardian of the person and property of Hilda Irene Canalas according to law.

given under my hand and the official seal of the Probate Court this the 6th day of May 1895

W.A. Ruggles
Probate Judge

In the Probate Court of Pottowatomie[sic] County Oklahoma Territory
In the matter of the Guardianship of Angeline View

I W.A. Ruggles Sole Judge and Ex officio clerk of the Probate Court of Pottowatomie[sic] County Oklahoma Territory hereby certify that W.R. Asher is the duly appointed Guardian of Angeline View, that he has filed his Bond, which has been duly approved by the Court.

Given under my hand and the seal of the Probate Court this the 1st day of January 1896

W.A. Ruggles
Probate Judge

[The letter below typed as given]

Kansas City Kansas
February 18, 1896

U.S. Indian Agent
Sox[sic] and Fox Agency
I.T.

Dear Sir
Inclosed
find my affidavid as to Guardianshipp of Zane children. Which I send if It will be satisfactory to you. My papers are in Washington

D.C. at present if you can get along with this. It will save me great expence. If not will get another copy of papers and send you.

Please let me hear from you immediately as I understand the money will be sent to Washington if not paid by 1st of March,

Yours respectfully
Rebecca A. Zane

1312 N. 8th Street
Kan. City
Kansas

Irvin P Zane
Rebeca Zane
Maude B Zane
Jenne M Zane
Mary Zane

Territory of Oklahoma } ss
County of Pottowatomie[sic] }

In Probate Court in and for said County and Territory

Before W A Ruggles Probate Judge.

In the matter of the Guardianship

of

Che-we-quay

I W.A. Ruggles sole Judge and Ex officio clerk of the Probate Court of Pottowatomie[sic] County Oklahoma Territory, hereby certify that White Turkey is the duly appointed and legally constituted Guardian of Che-we-quay, that he has filed his Bond as required by law which Bond has been duly approved by this Court, that he has complied with all the requirements of law as shown by the Records of this Office and the papers now on file herein.

In testimony whereof I have hereunto set my hand and affixed the seal of the Probate Judge at my office in Tecumseh Oklahoma Territory this the 4th day of August 1896.

W A Ruggles
Probate Judge

CERTIFICATE.

TERRITORY OF OKLAHOMA,
LINCOLN COUNTY, } SS.

I, ___W L Harvey___ *Judge of the Probate Court of Lincoln County, Territory of Oklahoma, do hereby certify that the records of my office show that* _____

___Charles Crane___*is the duly appointed, qualified and acting*

___Guardian___ *of* ___the estate of___

___Alice Morris, a minor___

WITNESS my hand and Official seal affixed at my office in Chandler, Lincoln County, Territory of Oklahoma, this ___3rd___ *day of* ___December___ *1896.*

___W L Harvey___

Probate Judge

[Statement below typed as given]

December 8th 1896

We the undersigned members of the National Council of the Sac & Fox Indians certify that following named person are the ~~Lawful~~ Natural and lawful guardian of the minors for which they have signed and that U.S. and Ulyses S Grant is one and the same person

Nos 172 173 & 174	R Shanon Moore, Father
" 185 & 186	Thos P Miles husband & father
" 215	US Grant - Guardian

being the daughter of his [illegible] No 214

314 & 530.	Jennie Hamilton	Mother

530   being the daughter of her minor daughter
No 314.

CERTIFICATE.

o o o ———•—•— o o o

Territory of Oklahoma,⎫
Lincoln County,   ⎬ SS.
                     ⎭

I, ___ S A Cordell ___ *Judge of the Probate Court of Lincoln County, Territory*

of Oklahoma, do hereby certify that the records of my office show that ___ Isaac ___

___ McCoy _____ *is the duly appointed, qualified and acting*

_____ Guardian _____ *of* _____ the person and _____

_____ estate of Lorenzo Dora _____

_____

> *WITNESS my hand and Official seal affixed at my office in*
>
> *Chandler, Lincoln County, Territory of Oklahoma, this*
>
> ___ 1" ___ *day of* _____ March _____ *1897.*
>
> _____ S A Cordell _____
>
> *Probate Judge*

Refer in reply to the following:
"A"
19461-97

Department of the Interior.

OFFICE OF INDIAN AFFAIRS

Washington,   June 1, 1897.

E. L. Thomas,
    U. S. Indian Agent,
        Sac and Fox Agency, Oklahoma.

Sir:

I am in receipt of a petition from a number of the Sac and Fox Indians of Oklahoma, under date of the 14th ultimo, requesting that "all annuity moneys belonging to orphan Indian children, who have legal guardians, be turned over to the Indian Agent for the future benefit of such orphan children, or in event of the marriage of such orphan children or in cases of actual necessity of such orphan children, the legal guardian, who is an Indian, can apply to Agent and draw such sums from said funds as circumstances of such minor orphan children demand at the time."

In reply you are advised that this office cannot permit money of the Indians to be placed in the hands of the Agent to be disposed of at his will. If there is any good reason for withholding moneys payable to guardians, the Agent is at liberty to withhold the same, giving his reasons therefor, depositing the same to the credit of the United States for the benefit of such minor children upon their arrival at the age of maturity.

Respectfully, Tho P Smith

W.S.O. (ELG)   Acting Commissioner.

In Probate Court,

County of _____

In the Matter of the Estate of
Guardianship of
Winnie & Geo Williams

Certificate of Transcript.

Filed the _____ day of _____
A.D. 189__

_____
Judge of Probate.

Refer in reply to the following:

Land
40923-1900

Department of the Interior.

OFFICE OF INDIAN AFFAIRS

Washington,   August 31, 1900.

Lee Patrick, Esq.,
    U. S. Indian Agent,
        Sac and Fox Agency,
            Oklahoma.

Sir:-

    Enclosed, herewith, for investigation and report, is a communication dated August 18, 1900, from Joe Vetter of Perkins, Oklahoma, who states that he is the Second Chief of the Iowa Indians and guardian of Theresa Rubidoux.

    Vetter complains that one, Wm. A. Knipe, of Perkins, Oklahoma, entered upon the allotted lands of said ward and took therefrom a large quantity of building stone, without the consent of the guardian or allottee, and without making payment therefor.

    An early report is desired.

Very respectfully,
A.C. Tonner
Acting Commissioner.

E.B.F.

C

_____Please return enclosure_____

Territory of Oklahoma
County of Pottawatomie   ss

    I, J. Jennings Clerk of The Probate Court with in and for said County and Territory aforesaid do hereby certify the reports of J. S. Mills, S. S. Davis, S.W. Jones, and B. H. Mills as Guardians and Administration in these definant[sic] and [illegible] Estates, as they appear hereto attached [illegible] complete and correct copies of the original as appears on file and record of this Court.

    Witness my hand and The official seal of this office this 24" day of Dec A.D. 1900

J Jennings Clerk of the Probate Court
County and Territory aforesaid

Territory of Oklahoma ⎱ ss
County of Pottawatomie ⎰

In The Probate Court in and for said
County and Territory aforesaid-

In the Matter of The ⎱
Estate of Thos. Nona ⎰
Deceased

Report of S.W. Jones Administrator

Now on this 29" day of Sept. 1900 comes S W Jones administration of
The Estate of Thos. Nona, Deceased and makes this his report for 1898,
1899 and 1900, as follows to wit:

Sept. 15" 1897	Paid court fees to Judge JDF Jennings		$3.20
" " "	" Printers fees		2.00
" " "	" Court " for certificate		.50
" " "	" " " " "		50
Oct "	" Medicine bill on Andy Morrison		7.50
Nov "	" Store bill on Dr. Craves		6.50
July and August "	To board and taking care of said Deceased, who was an invilad[sic] for 2 months		24.00
Aug. 1897	To Funeral expenses		18.00
Sept 23 "	To[sic] trips to Tecumseh, in interest of said Deceased		2.00
Mch 9 "	" " " " " " " " "		2.00
Nov 6 "	" " " " " " " " "		2.00
		mark	68.70

SW x Jones
his
Witness: W R Asher

Subscribed and sworn to before me this
15" day of Sept. 1898

In the matter of the
estate of Mohska
J.S. Milles[sic]
Guardian

Report of J.S Mills
Filed and approved this
24" day of Dec AD 1900
J.D.F. Jennings Probate Judge
By J. Jennings-Clerk

****

In the Matter of The ⎱
Estate of Mohska   ⎰
 J.S. Mills
  Guardian

Report of J.S. Mills
Guardian

Now on this 24" day of Dec. AD 1900 comes J. S. Mills Guardian of said Estate or ward, and presents this his report as follows to wit:

Mch 29" 1894-	Paid Probate J.H. Daugherty as court fees	$3.20
" " "	CC Chase Atty, in interest of ward	5.00
May "	Paid Liverybill to "Big Janes" Crossing in the interest of said ward	3.00
Aug "	Paid Liverybill and board on trip to Sac and Fox Agency in interest of ward	7.50
Dec. 24" 1900	Paid J.D.F. Jennings Probate Judge and Sheriff fees on citation and hearings in said estate	4.00
	Total Amt paid out by Guardian	$22.70

And I further more state that I have not rec'd. from said estate any benefit, nor compensation whatever owing to the fact that I was compelled to refund $40^{00} that was paid me as Lease money from G.N. Gephart as ~~money~~ The Lessee. Hence there is now due me as money paid by me in the interest of said estate the above amount of $22.70.

Jacob S. Mills
Guardian

Territory of Oklahoma ⎱
County of Pottawatomie ⎰ ss

(Seal)

Subscribed and sworn to before me this
24" day of Dec AD 1900

J Jennings Clerk of The Probate Court
County and Territory aforesaid

34

In The Matter of The Guard-
ianship of Geo. Clifford
and Mamie Morton
Minor Heirs of
Ollie Morton
Deceased

Report of S S Rains
Filed and approved by
The Court this day of
Dec, 1900
JDF Jennings Probate Judge
By J Jennings
Clerk

****

Copy

Territory of Oklahoma
County of Pottawatomie } ss

In The Probate Court in and for said
County and Territory aforesaid-

In the Matter of The
Guardianship of
Geo Clifford and
Mamie Morton heirs
S.S. Rains
of Ollie Morton
Deceased

Report of Guardian
S.S. Rains

Now on this day, Sept 28" 1900 comes SS Rains Guardian of said wards and makes this his report as follows to wit:- Was on the 2nd day of Sept 1895 appointed Guardian of said wards and from that date up to present time, (Sept 28" 1900) have transacted the following business only

Sept 2" 1895	Paid Probate Judge WA Ruggles	$ 3.20
1896	" " " " "	2.50
1896	" " " " "	3.00
"	" To trip to Shawnee in interest of said wards	3.50
"	" Liverybill in interest of estate	2.00
Dec. 23 "	" " " and board to Sac and Fox Agency in interest of said ward	7.00

Dec. 24" 1900	To Court fees in interest of ward	3.00
	For personal services " " "	15.00
	Total Amt due Guardian	$39.20

Subscribed and sworn to before me this 24" day of Dec AD 1900

J Jennings Clerk of Probate Court
County and Territory aforesaid

In the Matter of The
Estate of Tho's Nona
Deceased

S.W. Jones
Administrater[sic]

Copy of Report

****

Territory of Oklahoma ⎰
County of Pottawatomie ⎱ ss

In The Probate Court in and for said
County and Territory aforesaid-

In the Matter of The
Estate of Thos. Nona
Deceased

Report of
S.W. Jones
Administrator

Now on this 29" day of Sept. 1900 comes S W Jones administration of
The Estate of Thos. Nona, Deceased and makes this his report for 1898,
1899 and 1900, as follows to wit:

Sept. 15" 1897	Paid court fees to Judge JDF Jennings	$3.20
" " "	" Printers fees	2.00
" " "	" Court " for certificate	.50
" " "	" " " " "	50
Oct "	" Medicine bill on Andy Morrison	7.50
Nov "	" Store bill on Dr. Craves	6.50

36

July and		
August "	To board and taking care of said Deceased, who was an invilad[sic] for 2 months	24.00
Aug. 1897	To Funeral expenses	18.00
Sept 23 "	To[sic] trips to Tecumseh, in interest of said Deceased	2.00
Mch 9 "	" " " " " " " " "	2.00
Nov 6 "	" " " " " " " " "	2.00
	mark	68.70

SW x Jones

Witness: W R Asher   his

Subscribed and sworn to before me this

15" day of Sept. 1898

In the matter of the
estate of Mohska
J.S. Milles[sic]
Guardian

Report of J.S Mills
Filed and approved this
24" day of Dec AD 1900
J.D.F. Jennings Probate Judge
By J. Jennings-Clerk

****

Copy

In the Matter of The   Report of J.S. Mills
Estate of Mohska   Guardian
JS Mills Guardian

Now on this 24" day of Dec. AD 1900 comes J. S.
Mills Guardian of said Estate or ward, and presents this his report as follows
to wit:

Mch 29" 1894-	Paid Probate J.H. Daugherty as court fees	$3.20
" " "	CC Chase Atty, in interest of said Ward	5.00
May "	Paid Liverybill to "Big Janes" Crossing in the interest of said ward	3.00
Aug "	Paid Liverybill and board on trip to Sac and Fox Agency in interest of ward	7.50
Dec. 24" 1900	Paid J.D.F. Jennings Probate Judge and Sheriff fees on citation and hearings in said estate	4.00
	Total Amt paid out by Guardian	$22.70

And I further more state that I have not rec'd. from said estate any benefit, nor compensation having been compelled to refund ~~$20⁰⁰~~ $40⁰⁰ that was paid me as Lease money from G.N. Gephart The Lessee. Hence there is now due me as money paid by me in the interest of said estate the above amount of $22.70.

Territory of Oklahoma }
County of Pottawatomie (ss

                                          Jacob S. Mills
Subscribed and sworn   Guardian
to before me this 24"
day of Dec AD 1900

                    J Jennings
                    Clerk of The Probate Court
                    County and Territory aforesaid

In the Matter of The
Estate of John White
Deen, Deceased

B.H. Mills
Administrater[sic]

****

Copy

In The Matter of The (
Estate of John White }
Deed, Deceased.   )

        Report of B.H. Mills
        Administrator of said Estate

Dec 17th 1900 comes B. H. Mills adm. of said Estate and [illegible] having been duly sworn upon oath deposes and says: That he was appointed administrator of said estate (as per The record of this office) in the [illegible] of and from the time of his appointment to the present time, he has never had control of any funds of said estate and has never in any way receid[sic] any benefits by said appointment, but that he has expended $3⁵⁰ in behalf of said estate

                    B.H. Mills

Subscribed and sworn to before me this 17ᵗʰ day of Dec. 1900

        (Seal)   J Jennings Clerk of The Probate Court
                      County and Territory aforesaid.

In The Matter of The
Estate of We-se-ke-pea
a minor child

Report of J.S. Mills
Guardian

Filed and approved
By The Court this
24" day of Dec. 1900

J.D.F. Jennings
Probate Judge
By J Jennings
Clerk

Copy

In The matter of The
Estate of We-se-ke-pea
a minor child

Report of J.S. Mills
Guardian

Now on this Dec 24" 1900 Comes J.S. Mills and presents this his report as
Guardian of said estate as follows to wit:

Mch 29 1894-	Paid Probate Judge Daugherty as Court fees	$ 3.20
" " "	" C. Chase as Atty in the interest of said estate	5.00
May "	" Livery bill to go to "Big Janes" Crossing	3.00
Aug 8 "	" Expenses Livery bill and board to Sac & Fox	
	agency in the interest of said Estate	7.50
Dec 24" 1900	" J.D.F. Jennings Probate Judge and Sheriff fees	
	on citation and hearing	4.00
	Total Amt. paid	$22.70

And I further state that I have not rec'd from said estate any benefits, nor
compensation, having been compelled to refund the $20.00 that was paid to

me ~~to~~ as Lease money from G. N. Gephart the Lessee. Hence there is now due me as money paid by me in the interest of said estate the above amount.

Jacob S. Mills

Territory of Oklahoma ⎫ ss
County of Pottawatomie ⎭

Subscribed and sworn to before me this 24" day of Dec. AD 1900

(Seal)   S[sic]. Jennings Clerk of the Probate Court
County and Territory aforesaid

In the Matter of The
Estate of Tho's Nona
Deceased

―――

S.W. Jones
Administrater[sic]

Copy of Report

****

Territory of Oklahoma ⎫ ss
County of Pottawatomie ⎭

In The Probate Court in and for said
County and Territory aforesaid-

In the Matter of The ⎫
Estate of Thos. Nona ⎬
Deceased ⎭

Report of
S.W. Jones
Administrator

Now on this 29" day of Sept. 1900 comes S W Jones administration of The Estate of Thos. Nona, Deceased and makes this his report for 1898, 1899 and 1900, as follows to wit:

Sept. 15" 1897	Paid court fees to Judge JDF Jennings		$3.20
" " "	" Printers fees		2.00
" " "	" Court " for certificate		.50
" " "	" " " " "		50
Oct "	" Medicine bill on Andy Morrison		7.50
Nov "	" Store bill on Dr. Craves		6.50

July and
August   "   To board and taking care of said Deceased, who
                   was an invilad[sic] for 2 months   24.00
Aug. 1897   To Funeral expenses   18.00
Sept 23   "   To trips to Tecumseh, in interest of said Deceased   2.00
Mch 9   "   "   "   "   "   "   "   "   "   "   2.00
Nov 6   "   "   "   "   "   "   "   "   "   "   2.00
                              mark   68.70
                          SW x Jones
Witness: W R Asher   his
                          Subscribed and sworn to before me this
15" day of Sept. 1898

****

In the Matter of The Estate $\big\}$
of Thos. Nona. Deceased

            Report of S.W. Jones
                    Admin. of Tho's Nona #state for
        1898, 1899 & 1900-
                    In The years of 1898 and 1899 did not transact
        any business whatever pertaining to said estate

Sept 2" 1900-   To Shawnee in behalf of Estate as follows to wit:
                 To transportation and board for Lee Cook, Aaron Brgell[sic]
                 and Wash Hardin to Shawnee to lease land   10.00
Sept 2" 1900   To personal service on said trip   2.50
                          For the year 1900 Total am't   12.50
                              (1897-1898-1899   68.70
                          Total am't due for 1900) $81.20
                          mark
                      SW x Jones
Witness: John Jones   his
                      Subscribed and sworn to before me this
24" day of Sept. 1900

          (Seal)   J. Jennings Clerk of the Probate Court
                       County and Territory aforesaid

DEPARTMENT OF THE INTERIOR

UNITED STATES INDIAN SERVICE

Pawhuska, Okla., January 26, 1901.

Maj. Lee Patrick, Agent,

Sac and Fox Agency, Okla.

Dear Major:

Wah-shun-gah, the governor of the Kaw tribe, is guardian of Lizette Bertrand, a member of the Pottawatomie tribe of Indians, who has been allotted the following land: The South West   Quarter (S. W. 1/4) of Section Twenty-three (23); Township Six (6); Range Four (4) East of the Indian meridian.   I wish, when convenient, that you would locate this land, and, if it is of any value, make a lease to some one who will place the land under cultivation for the use of it, for a period of say three or four years.   Any kind of a lease that you may make for the improvement of the farm will be approved by the guardian.

Kindly give this your attention and let me know at an early date what the prospects are, so that I can inform Wah-shun-gah.

Yours truly,

O.A. [Illegible]
U. S. Indian Agent.

W. S. PENDLETON,
PROBATE JUDGE.

JAMES E. SIMPSON,
CLERK.

*Tecumseh, Oklahoma,*____Feb. 11____*1901.*

Hon Lee Patrick
Sac & Fox Agency,

Dear Sir:

Enclosed I send you letter which will explain itself.   There are two minor heirs of the Bullfrom[sic] estate   They could have a guardian appointed and this partition could be made with small expense.

The old lady, Jennie Bullfrog is anxious to get her interests separated.

If, after examination you think this a fair proposition for Tyner & the others I should be glad to have you forward it to him.

Yours Truly,

W. S. Pendleton

J. H. Maxey, President　　　　*C. M. Cade, Vice Pres.*　　　　*Willard Johnston, Cashier*

No. 5095

First National Bank

Capital Stock $50,000⁰⁰
Surplus $10,000⁰⁰
Shawnee, O.T.　　May 24, 1901.

Lee Patrick, U. S. Indian Agent,
　　　　Sac & Fox, O.T.

Dear Sir:-

　　Nancy Wilson was in today and informed me that the deed from her and her children, of whom I am guardian, to W. H. Brown, for the N. E. 1/4 of 21-10-3 had been approved, and I wish you would please send the deed and certificates of deposit here to this bank as she don't want to go to the agency, and I am sure I don't.

　　I suppose some of the merchants at the Agency have an account against her that you want her to pay, so if you will send the account with the deed and instruct me to collect it, I will do so for you before I pay her over the money.

Respectfully yours,

Willard Johnston

J. H. Maxey, President   *C. M. Cade, Vice Pres.*   *Willard Johnston, Cashier*

No. 5095

First National Bank

Capital Stock, $50,000⁰⁰
Surplus $10,000⁰⁰
Shawnee, O.T.   June 11, 1901.

Lee Patrick, U. S. Indian Agent,

Sac & Fox, O.T.

Dear Sir:-

I understand that the deed from the Thomas Goodboo heirs to Ogee, has been approved. As I am guardian for the Goodboo children, and the money will all be paid to me except what goes to the mother, and I understand that she will be here next week, so please send the papers to this bank or, if you are coming down soon, bring them down with you, and greatly oblige me. Your clerk told me that he would leave the Na-num-nuk-skuk deed here at the bank for me, but I guess he forgot it.

Yours truly,

_____Willard Johnston_____
Cashier.

**SIX MONTHS
TO SIX YEARS**   **EVERYTHING
EXACTLY AS AGREED**

W. H. RIGGS. Farm Loans.

GEO. D. BARNARD & CO, ST. LOUIS   *Shawnee, O.T.*____ June 15th,____ *190*1.

Lee Patrick,
    U.S. Indian Agent,
        Sac and Fox, O.T.

44

Sac & Fox – Shawnee
1892-1909   Volume XIIsegment>

Dear Sir:-

I herewith enclose to you a letter from the Interior Department dated June 10th, asking for evidence showing appointment of Mary C. Williams as guardian of James Rock, minor heir of Ellen Delaware deceased, and also showing that she made this conveyance in accordance with the order issued by the Probate Court.

If there is any thing more needed please let me know at once, and oblige,

Yours truly,

W. J. Riggs c.

J.D.F. JENNINGS,
PROBATE JUDGE.

J. JENNINGS,
CLERK.

Tecumseh, Okla. _____June 15_____1901.

Hon. Lee Patrick
    Sac & Fox
Dear Sir:

In the matter of the guardianship of James & Lillie Little Bear, - Shawnee Little Bear, guardian- I am informed that the deed of the guardian to Jas. W. Turner for a part of the land sold by order of the Probate Court, has been approved by the Secretary. Some of the sureties on Shawnee Little Bear's bond feel [illegible] and prefer to have him give another bond. So I thought best to request you to hold the money in your possession until all the deeds are acted on by the Dep't. When I can require him to give another bond or appoint another guardian. Kindly advise me whether any money has been paid over by you to the guardian yet.

Yours Truly,

W.S. Pendleton
P.J.

Sac & Fox – Shawnee
1892-1909   Volume XII

DEPARTMENT OF THE INTERIOR

UNITED STATES INDIAN SERVICE

Sauk and Fox Agency, Oklahoma Territory,
June 22, 1901.

First National Bank,
    Tecumseh, Okla.

Sirs:-

Inclosed you will find your C/D # 462 for $30.84 payable to the heirs of Anna Wilson, deceased, upon the approval of an easement for right of way through her allotment.

Said easement has been approved and is forwarded herewith for delivery.

Please send me a draft for $6.16 payable to Maggie Wilson and one payable to me for $18.52 for shares of Che-we-qua, Sam Wilson and Jeptha Wilson paid to them here.

Take receipts in duplicate on blanks inclosed from Thomas Alford, Legal Guardian and return them to me.

Very respectfully,

Lee Patrick
U. S. Indian Agent.

MA

[The letter below typed as given]

National
OKLAHOMA STATE BANK,
SHAWNEE, OKLA.

C. J. BENSON, PRESIDENT.
H. B. DEXTER, VICE-PRESIDENT.
F. B. REED, CASHIER.

July 6th, 1901.

Hon. Lee Patrick Ind. Agt.
    Sac & Fox Agency Okla.
Friend Lee:-

Old man Fullen stuck a deed under my nose to-day requesting me to sign as adminstrator for the heirs of White Turkey for the N / 1/2 of

NE 1/4 of Sec 22 Twp 10 N of Range 4 East IM he offers $560.00 I dont know who had me appointed admstr. but I want sign that deed for any one at that price. He told me that Tanksley had intimated that he would appraise the land at that price. I told him I did not believe it. The land is only 3 miles from town and on th south side of the road just beyond the bridge over the Canadian river east of Shawnee. I can get an offer of $1000.00 for it. Fullen was hot and said I had no right to ask more than the dept. would approve it for. I give you the facts so you will be prepared to judge when he makes a call on you.

Yours Very Truly

CJ Benson

·Nº 5115·

H.T DOUGLAS. PRESIDENT   J.T. PEDIGO. CASHIER
J M AYDELOTTE. VICE PRESIDENT   JOE BOWERS. ASST. CASHIER.

Shawnee National Bank.
Capital and Surplus $75,000.00.
Shawnee, Oklahoma Territory.

JUL 29 1901

Mr Lee Patrick
    Sauk & Fox
Dear Sir
    We enclosed receipt and duplicate from A.B. Jones, Guardian, for consideration of $160^{00} paid by J.G. Hendrickson for a deed to W^2 of NE^4 Sec 19-6-4 E.
    Mr. A.B. Jones, will send deed to Hendrickson and get receipts and forward to you.

Yours truly
J.T. Pedigo
Cas.

47

OFFICE OF

PROBATE JUDGE

OF POTTAWATOMIE
COUNTY OKLAHOMA.

TECUMSEH, OKLA., _____ Aug. 7 _____ 1901.

Hon. Lee Patrick
    Sac & Fox
My Dear Sir:
    Mr. Willard Johnson has been appointed guardian of the minors, James and Lillie Little Bear, vice Shawnee Little Bear removed. Please forward to him the monies in your hands belonging to said minors. I should be pleased also if you would deposit with him any sum coming to Shawnee Little Bear himself. Shawnee has promised the sureties on his bond to make good to the present guardian, the sums belonging to the minors already spent by him, and I will get an order from him for that purpose. If you cannot forward old Shawnee's money, please hold it till I send his order.

Yours Truly,
W.S. Pendleton
Probate Judge

J. H. MAXEY, Prest.   C. M. CADE, Vice-Prest.   WILLARD JOHNSTON, Cashier

No. 5095

First National Bank

CAPITAL STOCK, $50,000.00

Shawnee, O.T.   Sept 7, 1901

Lee Patrick,
            Sac & Fox Agency, O.T.
Dear Sir:-

Wm. H. Dill bought the S.E. 1/4 of the N.W. 1/4 16-10-3 the first of last April. John King was guardian for the Beaver heirs. We are interested a little bit, and would like to know if the deed will be approved, or what has become of it.

Yours very truly,

_____ C. M. Cade

[The letter below typed as given]

Reily & Adams
Attorneys at Law

F. H. REILY,
JOE M. ADAMS, JR.

Fort Worth, Texas   September 12th, 1901.

Shawnee, O.T.

Hon. Lee Patrick,
    Sac and Fox Agency,
        Oklahoma Ter.
My dear Sir:-
        Enclosed you will please find certified copy of order made by the Probate Court of this County in the Matter of the Guardianship of the Person and Estate of James Washington, Minor, in which we are allowed the sum of fifteen dollars attorneys fees. We had a conversation with your Mr. Daniels when here last in which he informed us that it was his opinion that said money had not been turned over to the Guardian, and if this be the case, we presume that that the money is still in your hands, and if so, we would be please if you would remit us the amount stipulated in said order. This, we recognise, is for necessaries, and is subject to be paid by you.
Anxiously awaiting your reply, we ber to remain,
                            Yours very Respectfully,

                            Reily & Adams

[The letter below typed as given]

C. J. Benson President.   *H. B. Dexter Vice-President.*   *F. B. Reed Cashier.*

N° 5875

THE OKLAHOMA NATIONAL BANK

CAPITAL $50,000.

Shawnee, Okla.   Oct. 12, 1901.

W. R. Gallick, Clerk in chg.,
    Sac & Fox Agency, O.T.
Dear Sir:-
        I beg to acknowledge receipt of your favor of Oct. 9th. enclosing Certificate for $800. and deed to Geo. C. Arnold with instructions to send you $266.67 as Susan Shak-kah's portion and $177.77 as Geo. Coons portion and pay Geo. McKinnis, Gaurdian $444.44

The parties appeared at the Bank today and the first two endorsed the Certificate of Deposit; Geo. McKinnis presented for payment a check for $73.75 signed by Geo. Coons and one for $115.00 signed by Susan Shak-kah and demanded payment thereon, which we refused. There was also presented a bill of costs from the Probate Court for administration fees as follows:

Court costs.................................$6.76
publication fees............................ 4.00
Administrators fees.........................10.00

with an order from the Probate Judge to deduct these amounts from the Certificate of deposit and to pay the balance as follows:
Mrs. Susan Shak-kah one-third of the estate.
Geo. Coons one third of the remainder and Geo. McKinnis, Guardian the balance, after deducting Court costs.

Geo. E. Mckinnis, Guardian refuses to endorse the Certificate of deposit unless these checks are paid as given him by the other two parties. What is your instructions in the matter.

As our certificate is made payable to these three parties it could not be paid out until this certificate is properly endorsed.

Yours very truly,

CJ Benson
President.

Shawnee, Okla.,   Dec. 16th   190 2

Indian Agt.
Sac and Fox O.T.
Dear Sir:-

I was appointed guardian for the four Brown children and want to know if their land is [illegible]. I can base it out now if you will let me know about it.

Please send me the number of their land.

Thomas Brown - Son - age   11 yrs
Harry   "   "   "   8 "
Beulah   "   Dau   "   6 "
Mary   "   "   "   3 "

Kindly let me hear from you at once.

Respectfully

L. T. Sammons

State of Oklahoma   :

ss.

County of Oklahoma :

In the Probate court in and for said county and state. In the matter of the guardianship of Nah-ah-che-thot.

Affidavit.

State of Oklahoma

ss.

Oklahoma County :

Nah-ah-che-thot, of lawful age, being duly sworn, upon his oath, says that he is a Mexican Kickapoo Indian and a member of the Mexican Kickapoo tribe of Indians; that he was born upon the Kickapoo Indian reservation in the state of Oklahoma; that said Indian reservation lies partly in Oklahoma, partly in Pottawatomie and partly in Lincoln counties; that he is over the age of 18 years; that during the greater part of his life he lived upon said Kickapoo reservation hereinbefore described; that while he was living in the now state of Oklahoma, one M.J. Bentley was up on the 11th day of December, 1901, by the Probate court of Oklahoma county, appointed a general guardian for this affiant; that said M.J. Bentley is not related to this affiant in any way neither did any of the relatives of this affiant indicate a wish that said Bentley be appointed guardian; neither did this affiant indicate to said Bentley a wish to have him appointed guardian; neither did he know that said Bentley was appointed guardian; that at the time said Bentley was appointed guardian he was not the trustee of any fund to be applied to the child's support; in short, said Bentley had no interest in the welfare of this affiant or any interest in any of the property of this affiant. This affiant further says that as a member of said tribe of Indians he was by the Government of the United States allotted from the Mexican Kickapoo tribe of Indian reservations a tract or parcel of land, to-wit; the west 1/2 of the northwest 1/4 of Section 24, township 12 range 1 east, in Oklahoma county, state of Oklahoma; and that at the same time his brother, Leonard Lunt, was allotted the West 1/2 of the

51

northeast 1/4 of said section, town and range and that at the same time his mother, Wah-pe-nah-qua-ne-quah, was allotted by the Government of the United States the east 1/2 of the northwest 1/4 of said section of land hereinbefore mentioned. Affiant further says that long prior to the time when said Bentley was appointed guardian, this affiant's said mother and brother died leaving this affiant and his father, Quen-ne-po-thot, as sole surviving heirs; that immediately after the appointment of said Bentley as a general guardian as hereinbefore mentioned, said Bentley, without the knowledge or consent of this affiant assumed to and did take control of said real estate and after taking control of the same made and executed a lease to one Levi J. Piper[sic] and as such guardian put said Piper in possession if said lands; that said Bentley ever since his said appointment and at this time assumes to exercise control and authority over said property. That said guardian never has at any time since his said appointment made a report to the above named court of any of his actions and by his action of placing said Piper in possession of said property he has caused same to be farmed and cultivated most of the time by said Piper from which farming he should have received large sums of money for his ward's interests in the crops; whether he has received any rents or not this affiant does not know; that he should have received rents this affiant believes.

Affiant further states that at the time of making the said lease by the said Bentley hereinbefore set out, the Government of the United States had made and executed and approved a certain lease to said described real estate and had put the persons to whom said lease was made in possession of said property and they were at the time said lease was made by said guardian farming and caring for the property and paying to this affiant regularly a lease rental for the same. Said guardian, under his appointment, dispossessed the persons who were in possession by authority of the Government; by this act the property was taken from the possession of the friends of this affiant and turned over to his enemies. The result of this act brought on a series of law suits and involved this property in litigation which has extended over all the time since the appointment of this guardian. That by this act of dispossessing his tenants which has resulted in continuous litigation, the farming and cultivating of said land as it should have been farmed and cultivated was made impossible. The question of lease and to whom the lease belonged was unsettled and the farms were permitted to go to waste; that out of the income from the farms which this guardian should have received if he had given proper attention to his trust has not given to this affiant one dollar of money nor the equal of one dollar in any kind of property; neither has he made any improvements thereon but as this affiant is inclined to believe, he has used all of the funds of this client in defending and instituting unnecessary and vexatious law suits, subjecting and making this affiant liable to great sums for costs and attorneys[sic] fees.

Affiant states that the said Levi J. Piper is at this time claiming possession of said real estate by reason of a verbal lease made between him and said Bentley for the period of one year, and this affiant believes that said Bentley and said Piper have conspired together to dissipate entirely all of his said property and that they are at this time endeavoring to do so.

This affiant further says that he is at this time a resident of the Republic of Mexico; that he moved to the Republic of Mexico about six years ago; that after moving to the Republic of Mexico as aforesaid and taking up his residence there he, after having attained the age of sixteen years, became and was married and that he has never been divorced from his said wife; that at this time she is in the Republic of Mexico where they make their home; that soon after his said marriage aforesaid he made and executed a deed for his interest in the real estate hereinbefore set out to one Martha A. Grimes, thereby deeding and transferring to her all of his right, title and interest in and to said lease. That said deed was made for valuable consideration and in which affiant warranted the title to be free and clear of all encumbrances; that said Bentley is at this time prosecuting suits in the courts of this county in the name of this affiant in which this affiant has no interest of any nature or character and which only tend to cloud the warranty of this affiant and make him liable to large sums as costs and expenses.

This affiant further says that said guardian has never given any attention to the property of this affiant; neither has he at any time provided for the welfare of this affiant in any direction; neither has he at any time manifested any interest in this affiant's welfare.

By reason of the statements hereinabove made, this affiant desires that said Bentley be brought into court and made to account for the things he has done and that he be discharged.   Nah-ah-che-thot   His
                                                                                          x
                                                                                        mark

Witnesses to signature by mark and his mark:

J.D. Brazeel

T.C. Honea

Subscribed and sworn to before me this 20th day of March, 1909.

E.D. Guffy,
Notary Public
My commission expires July 8th, 1909.

(Endorsed)

No. 200.

Oklahoma Probate court.

In the matter of the guardianship of Nah-ah-che-thot,

Filed in County court, Oklahoma county[sic], Oklahoma, March 25th, 1909.

E.M. Hurry, Clerk of County Court.

Contents: Affidavit

Guthrie, Day & Bernston[sic], Attorney-at-law.

Oklahoma City, Oklahoma.

****

State of Oklahoma   :
ss.
County of Oklahoma :

In the County court in and for said county and state.

In the matter of the guardianship   :
ORDER
of Nah-ah-che-thot   :

Now, to-wit, on this 10th day of April, 1909, the above entitled matter came regularly on to be heard before the above named court, upon the motion hereinbefore filed by Nah-ah-che-thot, and the affidavit filed therewith in support thereof.

The said Nah-ah-che-thot was present and represented by his attorney, Ledru Guthrie. The guardian of the said Nah-ah-che-thot, M.J. Bentley, was not present, neither was there present in the court any one representing him, neither had he filed any pleading or paper in his behalf, but is at this time default of any defense to said motion, whereupon, the hearing of the same was proceeded with, and after an examination of the service of the citation heretofore issued out of said court, the court was satisfied that the said Martin J. Bentley had had due and legal notice of the pendency of said motion, and that the same was to be and would be heard and determined upon this date.

Whereupon the said Nah-ah-che-thot introduced his proof in support of allegations in his motion. The Court, after hearing the evidence introduced on behalf of the said Nah-ah-che-thot, and the argument of his counsel, and being otherwise fully advised in the premises, is of the opinion that his motion should be sustained.

It is therefore by the county court of Oklahoma county, Oklahoma, considered, ordered and adjudged that the said Bentley ne[sic] and he hereby is discharged and removed as the guardian of said Nah-ah-che-thot, and his right to exercise directly or indirectly any control over the person or the property of the said Nah-ah-che-thot is hereby terminated. And the said Martin J. Bentley is hereby ordered and directed to make and file in the above entitled court an account of the monies received and expended during the whole of the time that he has been acting as the guardian of the said Nah-ah-che-thot, and that he make and file said report within thirty (30) days from this date. That upon the making and filing of his said report, a time shall be set for the hearing of the same at which time evidence will be received with a view to determining the question of the amount of money due the estate or trust:

That a citation issue commanding said Bentley to conform to and comply with this order.

Sam Hooker,

Judge of the Probate court.

(Endorsed)

200 Probate Court.

In the matter of the guardianship of Nah-ah-che-thot.

(Copy of order.

Filed in County court, Oklahoma County, Okla. May 28, 1909.

C.O. Offutt, Clerk of county court

Ledru Guthrie, Atty at law.   3-304

****

Guardian's report.

State of Oklahoma   :
                                    ss.
County of Oklahoma :

To the Judge of the County court of said county. The undersigned, guardian of Nah-ah-che-thot (Joseph Johnson), an Indian minor child of Wah-pe-nah-qua-no-quah, deceased, would respectfully submit to the court the following report and final showing of his acts and doings as such guardian from the 11th day of December, 1901 to the present time, to-wit:

Your guardian shows that at the time of his said appointment his said ward was the owner of the following described real estate and as alleged and claimed for him, to-wit

The Northwest quarter and the west half of the northeast quarter of section 24, township 12, range 1 east in the county of Oklahoma and state of Oklahoma, then territory, containing 240 acres; the west half of the northwest quarter above described being the allotment of the said ward; the remainder of said described real estate being at said time claimed by said ward and contested by diverse persons which was then in controversy and has ever since been a matter of legal controversy and is still pending in the court. That said was had no other property of any character whatever and no money or property or other things of value has ever come into the possession of this guardian as the property of said ward[sic] That immediately after his appointment as aforesaid this guardian was directed by the court to lease said real estate to one L.J. Pipher for five years at a rental sum $277.00 per annum for the entire three eighty acre lots aforesaid, subject to the approval of the court. That in pursuance of said order of the court, this guardian entered into a lease [end of report]

****

State of Oklahoma   :
                                    ss.
County of Oklahoma :

In the county court.

The guardianship of Nah-ah-che-thot.   ORDER.

Now, to-wit, on this the 26th day of June, 1909, comes Martin J. Bentley and files his verified report and final showing in the guardianship estate and trust of Nah-ah-che-thot and Indian minor and the court, having examined said report together with the exhibits and showing of said guardian and being fully advised in the premises, finds that said guardian has no money in his hands nor other thing of value belonging to said ward and that he has paid out and expended from his own funds in the administration of his said trust, $590.00 of his own money and said trust has been fully administered and said report is hereby approved by the court and said guardianship is discharged and the guardian, together with all his bondsmen and sureties thereon, are hereby released and discharged free of liability in that behalf, all of which is hereby ordered, adjudged and decreed.

Sam Hooker,

Judge County court.

(Endorsed)

No.200. Guardianship Nah-ah-che-thot, Indian minor, M.J. Bentley, gdn.

Order approving final report.

Filed in County court, Oklahoma county, Oklahoma, June 26th, 1909.

C.P. Offutt, Clerk of county court.

3-331.

****

State of Oklahoma   :
                 ss.
Oklahoma County   :

In the County court of said county and state.

In the matter of the guardianship of Nah-ah-che-thot.

NOTICE.

The above named Nah-ah-che-thot will take notice that Martin J. Bentley, guardian, has filed his final report and settlement of his trust in the matter of the above named guardianship in the County court of said county and the came[sic] will come up for hearing and approval in said court on the 26th day of June, 19019, at 9 o'clock in the forenoon, and if you are not present in person or by attorney, said report will be taken up and disposed of in your absence.

Witness my hand this the 15th day of June, 1909.

_____Guardian.

By _____, his attorney

This writ served on the above named defendant by delivering him a true copy of the original summons this the 17th day of June, 1909.

L.J. Pipher.

(Endorsed)

No.200.

Guardianship, Nah-ah-che-thot.

Notice of hearing report.

Filed in County court, Oklahoma county, Oklahoma, June 19th, 1909.

_____, Clerk of County court.

****

State of Oklahoma   :
                                    ss.
Oklahoma County   :

In the probate court in and for said county and state. In the matter of the guardianship of Nah-ah-che-thot.

AN ANSWER.

Now comes the above names Nah-ah-che-thot and for his answer to the report of the guardian filed herein says:

That he admits that Martin J. Bentley was heretofore by the above entitled court appointed guardian and that he was the owner of the property set out and described in the guardian's report, and that the guardian made the lease mentioned and set out in his report.

The said Nah-ah-che-thot denies each and every allegation in said report, not hereinbefore admitted, or controverted.

Wherefore, he asks that hearing be had upon said report and the same be corrected so as to conform to the facts.

(Signed) Guthrie, Day and Bernstein.

Attorneys for Nah-ah-che-thot.

(Endorsed)

No.200

Oklahoma Probate court.

In the matter of the guardianship of Nah-ah-che-thot.

Filed in County court Okla. Co., Okla. Jul. 30, 1909.

Inez M. Murshott,

Clerk of Co. Court.

Contents: Answer.

Guthrie, Day and Bernstein.

****

M.R. Lee - $5000.   J.O. Pipher, $5000.

Subscribed and sworn to before me this 28th day of September, 1901.

J.J. Buell, Notary Public.

My Commission expires June 11th, 1906.   (Seal)

The Territory of Oklahoma, Oklahoma County. In Probate court. This lease having been presented to the Probate Judge of said county for his approval on the 28th day of September, 1902, the Judge not being satisfied as to price offered for said lots of land and continued the hearing for the purpose of obtaining evidence as to value and afterwards, to-wit, on the 7th day of November, the lessee submitted affidavits of three disinterested parties as to price agreed to be paid as being fair and reasonable and in their opinion they believed that it was to the interest of the minor that said lease be made/ the Probate Judge in pen[sic] court after carefully considering said application for lease and the evidence submitted is satisfied that the lease is to the interest of the minor and that the same should be allowed and approved. It is therefore considered, ordered and adjudged by the court that said lease be in all things approved allowed and confirmed. This 10th day of November A.D. 1902.

J.P. Allen, Probate Judge.   (SEAL)

(Endorsed on exhibit A)

200. Filed the 28th day of September, A.D. 1902. J.P. Allen Probate Judge.

Refiled August 15th, 1904. E.M. Hurry, Probate clerk.

(On back)

No.200. Guardianship of Nah-ah-che-thot, Indian minor. M.J. Bentley, guardian.
Final report. Filed county court, Oklahoma county, Oklahoma, June 19th, 1909.
O.P. Offutt, clerk of Probate court.

****

[Pages out of sequence]

receivership and law suits growing out thereof; and said tenant at this time is in possession of said real estate and is permitted to cultivate the same by reason of an injunction issued from the District court of said county which is now in full force and effect.

That suit has been pending for the purpose of determining the title of said real estate of said ward wherein Everest & Smith, attorneys, were employed by this guardian and said lawyers have defended the guardian herein in his suits and also the tenant in nearly all of said numerous law suits to which he refers in this report..

He further says that by reason of the enormous costs of litigation and numerous attorneys[sic] fees, transportation and fees of witnesses paid and assumed by the lessee of said land, there is at this time nothing justly due from said lessee to this estate.

But he says there is justly due this guardian for moneys actually laid out and expended by him the sum of $590.00, not taking into account the value of his services as such guardian or advances made for the support of his ward.

That on the 10th day of April, 1909, this guardian by order of the county court was duly discharged and removed as the guardian of his said ward upon the petition of said ward and he was directed by said order of the court to make and file his report and he now tenders this as his final report and asks that he be finally discharged from said trust and that his sureties upon his bond be also discharged and released from all liability thereon.

I, Martin J. Bentley, being duly sworn according to law, depose and say that I have read over and heard the foregoing report and exhibits read over and know the contents thereof and that the same are true in substance and in fact and that said report is a full, true and complete report of his said trust so far as he is at this time able to make for the reason that his vouchers, books and memorandums relating to said trust were burned in a recent fire when his house and effects thereof were consumed by fire.

Martin J. Bentley,

Guardian.

Subscribed and sworn to before me this the 15th day of June, A.D., 1909.

Stella Roberts, Notary Public.

My commission expires on the 21st day of April, 1913.

(Exhibit A)

Indian allotments Nos. 71, 72 and 73.

Farming lease.

Indenture of lease made and entered into this the 23rd day of September, 1902, A.D., by and between Martin J. Bentley, legal guardian of Nah-ah-che-thot, of Shawnee, Oklahoma, and Levi J. Pipher, of Harrah, Oklahoma, party of the second part:

Now this indenture Witnesseth that the said party of the first part for and in consideration of the sum of $1.00 paid him by the said party of the second part, receipt of which is hereby acknowledged, and in consideration of the rents to be paid as hereinafter specified and of the covenants, stipulations and conditions hereinafter contained and hereby agreed to be paid, kept and performed by the said party of the second part, his executors, administrators and assigns, hereby lets and leases to the said party of the second part, his executors, administrators and assigns, the following described tract of land, to-wit: the northwest quarter and the west half of the northeast quarter of section 24, township 12, range 1 east in the county of Oklahoma in the territory of Oklahoma, 240 acres more or less, for the full term of five years from January 1st, 1903 for farming purposes, with the right to use and occupy said land and premises herein leased for said period.

In consideration of which the party of the second part hereby agrees and binds himself, his executors, and administrators, and assigns and sublessees[sic] to pay or cause to be paid to party of the first part at the First National Bank of Oklahoma City the sum of $277.00 per annum, the same being at the estimated rate of two and .50 dollars per acre for the 111 acres now in cultivation on said tract, to be paid annually on the first day of July, and the said party of the second part further covenants and agrees that he will break up and clear and put in cultivation enough additional land to make the total cultivated area on the aforesaid tract at the expiration of this lease not less than 200 acres and that for the last and fifth year of this lease he will pay the sum of 2 and .50 dollars per acre for the additional 89 acres aforesaid and that during the continuance of this of this lease he will cultivate and improve said land in good and husbandmanlike[sic] manner and if at any time any portion of the lease money should be due and unpaid that portion unpaid shall be a lien on the crop grown on said land as security for the payment of rents.

This indenture and lease shall be valid and binding only after the approval of the Probate Judge of the county of Oklahoma, Oklahoma territory inscribed thereon.

In witness whereof, parties of the first and second part have hereunto set their hands and seals this the day and year first above written.

M.J. Bentley.

L.J. Pipher.

In consideration of the letting of the premises described in the foregoing indenture and lease and the sum of $1.00 to each of us in hand paid, the receipt whereof is hereby acknowledged, we, the undersigned, J.O. Pipher and M.R. Lee, in the county of Oklahoma, territory of Oklahoma, hereby become sureties for the punctual payment of all the rents and the performance of all the covenants and agreements in the above indenture of lease to be paid and performed by Levi J. Pipher, the party of the second part named therein, and if any default shall be made therein, that we hereby promise and agree to pay such sum or sums of money as will be sufficient to make up such deficiency and fully satisfy all the conditions, covenants and agreements contained in said indenture of lease without requiring any notice of nonpayment or proof of demand being made and we do hereby bind ourselves, our heirs, executors and administrators jointly and severally and firmly by these presents.

Signed and sealed this 28th day of September, 1902.

J.O. Pipher.

M.R. Lee

Verification of sureties.

Territory of Oklahoma
County of Oklahoma

The sureties to the foregoing indenture of lease being duly sworn and examined by me state that they signed the foregoing obligation as sureties for the lessee in the annexed lease and that they and each of them respectively own and possess property over and above all debts, liabilitis[sic] and legal exemptions of the value, worth and sum placed opposite their names:

[Pages out of sequence]

contract in writing with said L.J. Pipher, a copy of which lease contract, marked Exhibit A, is attached hereto and made a part hereof.

That thereafter, and on the 10th day of November, 1902, said lease contract was duly submitted to the Judge of the Probate court of said county and state or territory and was duly approved by J.P. Allen, Probate Judge thereof.

That from the time said guardian took Letters of guardianship, there began litigation over the title to and possession of said real estate and the cases were almost innumerable, beginning with Justices of the Peace and going through the County court, the District court and the Supreme court of the territory; long tedious and expensive suits were had in the District court of the county and the litigation was interminable, so much so that the guardian did not get possession of said real estate until some time in the year 1904 which possession was thereafter contested in the courts of the county, all of which litigation has cost the tenant and lessee aforesaid a sum largely in excess of the rental values of said real estate besides a large amount of costs and expenses laid out and expended by the guardian in that behalf in the ahhregate[sic] sum of $590.00 and in consequence thereof this guardian has never received any rentals from said tenant nor any one else and the tenant has had such irregular and uncertain possession of said real estate that he has been unable to cultivate said lands with any certainty of profit; the contestors[sic] from time to time and from year to year breaking said close and taking possession of the houses, plowing up the crops, turning their stock upon the crop and destroying it and the last year's crop being at this time in the hands of a receiver and the value thereof being almost eaten up by costs of said receivership and law suits growing out thereof; and said tenant at this time is in possession of said real estate and is permitted to cultivate the same by reason of an injunction issued from the District court of said county which is now in full force and effect.

That suit has been pending for the purpose of determining the title of said real estate of said ward wherein Everest & Smith, attorneys, were employed by this guardian and said lawyers have defended the guardian herein in his suits and also the tenant in nearly all of said numerous law suits to which he refers in this report.

He further says that by reason of the enormous costs of litigation and numerous attorneys[sic] fees, transportation and fees of witnesses paid and assumed by the lessee of said land, there is at this time nothing justly due from said lessee to this estate.

But he says there is justly due this guardian for moneys actually laid out and expended by him the sum of $590.00, not taking into account the value of his services as such guardian or advances made for the support of his ward.

That on the 10th day of April, 1909, this guardian by order of the county court was duly discharged and removed as the guardian of his said ward upon the petition of said ward and he was directed by said order of the court to make and file his report and he now tenders this as his final report and asks that he be finally discharged from said trust and that his sureties upon his bond be also discharged and released from all liability thereon.

I, Martin J. Bentley, being duly sworn according to law, depose and say that I have read over and heard the foregoing report and exhibits read over and know the contents thereof and that the same are true in substance and in fact and that said report is a full, true and complete report of his said trust so far as he is at this time able to make for the reason that his vouchers, books and memorandums relating to said trust were burned in a recent fire when his house and effects thereof were consumed by fire.

Martin J. Bentley,

Guardian.

Subscribed and sworn to before me this the 15th day of June, A.D., 1909.

Stella Roberts, Notary Public.

My commission expires on the 21st day of April, 1913.

(Exhibit A)

Indian allotments Nos. 71, 72 and 73.

Farming lease.

Indenture of lease made and entered into this the 23rd day of September, 1902, A.D., by and between Martin J. Bentley, legal guardian of Nah-ah-che-thot, of

Shawnee, Oklahoma, and Levi J. Pipher, of Harrah, Oklahoma, party of the second part:

Now this indenture Witnesseth that the said party of the first part for and in consideration of the sum of $1.00 paid him by the said party of the second part, receipt of which is hereby acknowledged, and in consideration of the rents to be paid as hereinafter specified and of the covenants, stipulations and conditions hereinafter contained and hereby agreed to be paid, kept and performed by the said party of the second part, his executors, administrators and assigns, hereby lets and leases to the said party of the second part, his executors, administrators and assigns, the following described tract of land, to-wit: the northwest quarter and the west half of the northeast quarter of section 24, township 12, range 1 east in the county of Oklahoma in the territory of Oklahoma, 240 acres more or less, for the full term of five years from January 1st, 1903 for farming purposes, with the right to use and occupy said land and premises herein leased for said period.

In consideration of which the party of the second part hereby agrees and binds himself, his executors, and administrators, and assigns and sublessees[sic] to pay or cause to be paid to party of the first part at the First National Bank of Oklahoma City the sum of $277.00 per annum, the same being at the estimated rate of two and .50 dollars per acre for the 111 acres now in cultivation on said tract, to be paid annually on the first day of July, and the said party of the second part further covenants and agrees that he will break up and clear and put in cultivation enough additional land to make the total cultivated area on the aforesaid tract at the expiration of this lease not less than 200 acres and that for the last and fifth year of this lease he will pay the sum of 2 and .50 dollars per acre for the additional 89 acres aforesaid and that during the continuance of this of this lease he will cultivate and improve said land in good and husbandmanlike[sic] manner and if at any time any portion of the lease money should be due and unpaid that portion unpaid shall be a lien on the crop grown on said land as security for the payment of rents.

This indenture and lease shall be valid and binding only after the approval of the Probate Judge of the county of Oklahoma, Oklahoma territory inscribed thereon.

In witness whereof, parties of the first and second part have hereunto set their hands and seals this the day and year first above written.

Sac & Fox – Shawnee
1892-1909   Volume XII

M.J. Bentley.

L.J. Pipher.

[Copy of original last page of document on page 59]

1102
8841

Office of Indian Affairs
Rec, FEB 7 1903

Stroud, Oklahoma.
Jan. 30/03

W.L. Harris

In matter of

guardianship

of his grandson

Department of the Interior,
FEB 7 1903

Respectfully referred to
the Commissioner of Indian
Affairs, for reply to writer.

Assistant Secretary.

****

[Transcription of letter on page 67]

STROUD, OKLAHOMA, _____Jan 30_____ 1903

hon Sec ter of   Washing D. Co.
I will say to you that my grant son Willim Moses Jeferson there has not right gardian
apontmt yet in this reason I am his grandfather rased him Explain the mater is this
grandfather would save money but the father would spend his money but grandfather
would save his money the boy is going [giving] to [illegible]

but the council did not apoint a gardian yet the council has a right to pont for a gardian
for the boy   Mr W.L. Harris his grandfather ouaght to be gardian for the the boy.

Court gives my daughter of cusday of child living to Aunt so I want
from W.L. Harris   Rest E Stroud Ok

66

[Copy of original letter on Page 66]

STROUD, OKLAHOMA, Jan 30 1903

Hon. Dealer of Washington D.C.

I will say to you that my Great son
William Moses [...] there has not
right - Gardian a [...] yet in this
reason I am his grandfather. Please
him Explain the mater is this grand
father could [...] in [...] but the
father would spur [...]
but gran father would [...]
The boy is going to [...]

but the Council did not appoint
a gardian yet - the council has a
right to point for a [...] for the boy
[...] W.L. Harris his grand father
ought to be Gardian for the [...]

Court give my daughter of [...]
of child [...]
of cont washin [...] so I want [...]
from W.L. Harris Best to [...]

****

Refer in reply to the following:
Land.
8841-1903

Department of the Interior.

OFFICE OF INDIAN AFFAIRS

WASHINGTON,   Feb. 13, 1903.

Ross Guffin, Esq.,
  U. S. Indian Agent,
    Sac & Fox Agency, Okla.

Sac & Fox – Shawnee
1892-1909   Volume XII

Sir:

There is enclosed herewith, for report, a letter from W. L. Harris,

dated Stroud, Okla., January 30th, last, complaining of the appointment of a

guardian, who is unsatisfactory, for his grand-son, William Moses Jefferson,

supposed to be a Sac and Fox or Iowa Indian.

Very respectfully,

A.C. Tonner
Commissioner.

J. L. D.
L.

S. C. HUBER
ATTORNEY AT LAW

OFFICE OF
COUNTY ATTORNEY,
of TAMA COUNTY, IOWA.

OFFICES:
COURT HOUSE, TOLEDO, IOWA.
SOLEMAN BLOCK, TAMA, IOWA.

Tama, Iowa, March 21, 1903.

Mr. Ross Guffin,

U. S. Indian Agent,

Sac & Fox Agency, Oklahoma.

My Dear Sir:-

I hereby acknowledge receipt of your favor of March 19th,
enclosing check for Twenty Dollars, in payment of rent due my wards, the
Davenport children. I also return herewith receipt duly witnessed.

Yours truly,

S.C. Huber

Guardian

HOFFMAN & EMBRY,

ATTORNEYS-AT-LAW.

ROY HOFFMAN.

JOHN EMBRY.

CHANDLER, OKLA.,   3-27-1903

Maj. Ross Guffin,
U. S. Indian Agt.,
Sac & Fox Agency,

Dear Sir:-

Your favor of the 23rd received containing petitions for guardianship which will be given proper attention.

Very truly,

Roy Hoffman

[The letter below typed as given]

Sugar Grove
Arkansas
June 1 1903

Mr. Ross Guffin
Sac and Fox Agency

Dear Sir

I would like to know how my nephew William Jefferson is getting along. I want to know if Johnny Dave Harris and William Jefferson have a Gardine. If not my husband and I would like to be thear Gardine So let us know Soon please.

From Julia Brown

Geo. L. Rose.
Loans.

Tecumseh, Okla.   June 9, 1903.

Hon. Ross Guffin,

Sac and Fox Agency, O. T.

Dear Sir:

Replying to your letter of the 23rd ult., I beg to herewith enclose you triplicate receipt for $10.00, as Legal Guardian for George Morton. I note in your letter that you state that you have returned to me the letter from George Morton, which I had sent you. This letter was not enclosed. Will you kindly return the same to me so that I may place the same on file.

Yours very respectfully,

Geo. L. Rose

LAW OFFICES OF
MILTON BRYAN.

Shawnee, Oklahoma, July 1, 1903.

Hon. Ross Guffin,

Sac & Fox Agency, Okla.

Dear Major:

I enclose you herewith an order of the Probate Judge for the payment to Bertha and Addie Pattequa of $10.00 each, out of any funds in your hands belonging to them. If the payment is made, you will please to advise me of the same, that I may make report thereof in my annual accounting to the court.

Very respectfully yours,

Milton Bryan
Gdn

****

Territory of Oklahoma,)
) ss.
Pottawatomie County.   )

In the Probate Court in and for said County

and Territory.

In the matter of the guardianship
of Bertha Pattequa and Addie Pattequa, minors.

Now on this day came Milton Bryan as guardian of Bertha Pattequa and Addie Pattequa, minors, and made application to the court for an order authorizing him to pay to said minors to sum of ten dollars ($10.00) each, for the purpose of purchasing clothing and other necessaries of live, and,

It is thereupon ordered by the court that the said Milton Bryan be and he is hereby authorized and directed to pay and turn over to the said minors said sum of ten dollars ($10.00) each out of any funds in his hands or control, or the U. S. Indian Agent at the Sac and Fox Agency, or any other person holding the same in trust for him as such guardian, or for said minors, and report the same in his next annual account as such guardian.

_____WL McFall_____, Judge.

****

Milton Bryan
Shawnee O. Ty
July 30-03
Asks for ruling
to leasing Land of
Minors &c.

****

LAW OFFICES OF
MILTON BRYAN.

Shawnee, Oklahoma, July 30, 1903.

Hon. Commissioner of Indian Affairs,

Washington, D. C.

Sir:

I am the legal guardian for certain Sac and Fox minors, and have given large bonds with the American Surety Company of New York as surety for the same, and am held to strict accountability for the management and preservation of the property and revenues arising therefrom belonging to my wards. In some instances, these minors have a living parent, who has been leasing the lands of the minors and appropriating the proceeds arising therefrom to his or her own personal use--and that, too, in cases in which they do not have the care, custody and expense of of[sic] living of said minors. Such, if permitted, would be unjust to both the legal guardian and the ward: compelling the legal guardian to account for (and perhaps to stand the loss of) funds which never come into his hands, but for which he is legally bound to account to a court having jurisdiction of him and his wards, while the ward's lands are being impoverished without benefit or profit to him, either present or future.

I should be greatly obliged to you for the ruling of your department in this matter, with instruction as to whether the legal guardian or parent should lease the lands and handle the revenues arising therefrom.

I have the honor to be, very respectfully,

Milton Bryan

****

Refer in reply to the following:
Land.
48. 942-1903.

Department of the Interior.

OFFICE OF INDIAN AFFAIRS

WASHINGTON,   August 20, 1903.

Ross Guffin, Esq.,
            Supt. Sac and Fox Agency,
                Oklahoma.

Sir:

The office is in receipt of a letter from Milton Bryan, dated Shawnee, Oklahoma, July 30 last, stating that he is legal guardian for certain Sac and Fox minors and has given large bonds to the American Surety Company of New York as surety for the same and is held to strict accountability for the management and preservation of the property and revenues arising therefrom and belonging to his wards; that in some instances these minors have living parents who have been leasing the lands of the minors and appropriating the proceeds arising therefrom to his or their own personal use and that too in cases in which they do not have the care, custody and expense of looking after said minors, and that if such is permitted it would be unjust to both the legal guardian and the ward compelling the legal guardian to account for (and perhaps to stand the loss of) funds which never come into his hands but for which he is legally bound to account for to the court having jurisdiction of him and his wards while the wards' lands are being impoverished without benefit or profit to them, either present or future.

The letter is enclosed, herewith, for investigation and report.

Very respectfully,
A.C. Tonner
(J.LD.)   Asst.   Commissioner.
P.

****

Refer in reply to the following:
Land.
57513-1903.

Department of the Interior.

OFFICE OF INDIAN AFFAIRS

WASHINGTON,   September 17, 1903.

Ross Guffin, Esq.,
    Supt. Sac and Fox Agency,
        Oklahoma.

Sir:

The office is in receipt of your letter of August 20th last reporting on the complaint of Milton Bryan of Shawnee, Oklahoma, that he is the duly appointed guardian of certain Sac and Fox minors, and that their living parents in some instances have been leasing their lands and withholding the proceeds therefrom, etc. It is shown by your report that Mr. Bryan had particular reference to the Pattequa children; that Mr. Bryan was appointed about a year ago for the purpose of executing a deed to the land then to be sold under the act of May 27, 1902; that their father, William Pattequa, is a full-blood Indian, has had the benefit of a few years schooling, is a good farmer, of good habits, industrious, and one of the best Indians in the tribe; that the mother is dead and the children are named Bertha and Ada Pattequa, aged 12 and 9 years respectively, and are in school; that their father has always been recognized as their natural guardian, has transacted their business at the agency, receipted for and drawn their annuities and lease money, and has leased their lands and drawn the portion of their lease money heretofore disbursed; and that their annuity money has been used for their maintenance, all except the last payment, which was covered into the United States Treasury at the suggestion of the father, the children not needing it.

The account as shown by your books is a follows:

Due Bertha Pattequa. Annuity money collected and

    deposited in the U. S. Treasury, - - - - - - - - - - - - - - $33.39

Lease money collected in your office, - - - - - - - - - - - - - 541.75

Lease money placed to her credit (in sub-treasury) - - - - 505.50
Lease money paid to her guardian, William Pattequa, - - 36.25
Total - - - - -$538.89 deposited.

Due Ada Pattequa. Annuity money collected and
    deposited in the U. S. Treasury, - - - - - - - - - - - - - - $33.39
Lease money collected in your office, - - - - - - - - - - - - - 351.75
Lease money placed to her credit (in sub-treasury) - - - - 326.75
Lease money paid to her guardian, William Pattequa, - - 25.00
Total - - - - -$360.14 deposited.

This money, you state, as near as you can understand, is the principal difference between the legal and natural guardian. The question is which one of them should control this money; that Mr. Bryan claims a right to do so, and Pattequa wants to leave it where it is until the children become of age; that another difference between Bryan and Pattequa is about the leasing of the minors' land; that Bertha has an allotment of her own, which is and has been under lease executed by her father as natural guardian; that Ada has no allotment of her own (having been born since the allotments were made), but has an interest in her deceased mother's allotment, which is and has been under lease for a term of years; that both these allotments have been fairly treated by the lessees, and valuable improvements have been made thereon; that there is no impoverishment of the soil beyond what is usual to the constant cultivation thereof with proper treatment, which is little or nothing; that the leases on both of these pieces expire on the 31st of December, 1903, and the lessees seek renewal thereof; that the question arose there a little over a month ago when application for renewal of leases was made at your office as to which of the parties legal or natural guardian was the proper one to renew the leases; that both Mr. Bryan and Pattequa were at the office at the time, and the matter was talked over but not definitely settled; the leases were not then renewed, nor have they been since; that Mr. Bryan claimed that as legal guardian he should control the land, while Pattequa claimed that as natural guardian he should control; and that as they did not settle the question among themselves Mr. Bryan wrote his letter of July 30th.

Replying thereto you are hereby instructed to allow the lease money belonging to these children to remain to their credit where it is in the sub-treasury. If Mr. Bryan was appointed guardian of the estate of these two minors he should be recognized as such when said lands are to be again leased, but on the contrary if he was appointed for the purpose of executing a deed to certain lands that were to be then sold his guardianship should be limited to that specific purpose.

You will be further advised in another letter in regard to the disposition of the annuity moneys of these children.

Very respectfully,

WA Jones
Commissioner.

JLD-CGC   NGT

****

Refer in reply to the following:

Land.
57513-1903.

Department of the Interior.

OFFICE OF INDIAN AFFAIRS

WASHINGTON,   September 23, 1903.

Mr. Ross Guffin,
    Superintendent, &c.
        Sac and Fox Agency, Okla.

Sir:

Referring to the closing paragraph of office letter, "Land," of 17th instant, wherein you were informed that you would be instructed in another letter concerning the disposition to be made of the annuity moneys of Bertha and Addie, minor children of William Pattequa, I now have to advise you that inasmuch as Mr. William Bryan, of Shawnee, Oklahoma, appears to have been appointed as guardian of these children for the specific purpose of executing a deed to certain land to be sold under the Act of May 27, 1902, it is neither necessary nor permissible, in the opinion of this office, to recognize him as their guardian with respect to the payment of annuities.

You are, therefore, directed to either pay their annuity money to their father and natural guardian or deposit it in the U. S. Treasury, whichever he directs, he being according to your report the proper and only person entitled to receive it. The annuity money which is so deposited, including the sum which you state is already on deposit, will be paid to William Pattequa, if he make claim therefor, otherwise it will remain in the Treasury until the children become of age and are competent to receipt for it themselves.

Very respectfully,

A.C. Tonner

(K)   NT Commissioner.

Refer in reply to the following:
Accounts,
59849-1903.

Department of the Interior.

OFFICE OF INDIAN AFFAIRS

WASHINGTON,   September 24, 1903.

Mr. Ross Guffin,
        Superintendent, &c.
                Sac and Fox Agency, Okla.

Sir:

Replying to your letter of 14th instant, concerning the desire of George L. Rose, of Tecumseh, Oklahoma, to obtain possession and control of certain annuity and lease moneys belonging to Clifford H. and George O. Morton, as their legal guardian, you are advised that the decision in the case of Milton Bryan, guardian of Bertha and Addie Pattequa, contained in office letter of yesterday, will apply with equal force to the present and all other similar cases. Inasmuch as Mr. Rose was appointed as guardian of Clifford H. and George O. Morton for the specific purpose of effecting a sale of their lands, it is held that he cannot properly claim the right to possession and control of their annuity and lease moneys.

Very respectfully,

A.C. Tonner

(K)   Asst. Commissioner.

Shawnee, Oklahoma, December 10, 1903

Mr. Horace Guffin, Financial Clerk,

Sac and Fox Agency, Okla.

Dear Horace:

I send you herewith, as requested, certified copy of my letters of guardianship of James Little Bear and Lily Little Bear, and send you also certified copy of my letters of guardianship of Jesse Chisholm and Nellie Chisholm, as you will probably have need of the same for the same purpose as that in case of the Little Bears.

Yours truly,

Milton Bryan

Refer in reply to the following:

Finance.

13971-1904.

Department of the Interior.

OFFICE OF INDIAN AFFAIRS

WASHINGTON,   March 7, 1904.

The Superintendent,

Sac and Fox School, Oklahoma.

Sir:-

The Office is in receipt of your letter of 23rd ultimo relative to annuity and lease money due Fannie Keokuk, thirteen year old daughter of Charles Keokuk. You state that this child is delicate and that she is supported and cared for by Mrs. Quigg, her maternal grandmother, who is a white woman; that he father is still living but is totally unfit to care for the child. Because of the delicate health of the girl the agency physician states that it will not be desirable to place her in an Indian school, and you ask to be instructed how you should proceed to procure for her a payment of about $200 out of annuity and lease money to her credit amounting to $1727.04.

Replying thereto I have to suggest that a legal guardian be appointed by the probate court to receive her funds. You are instructed to secure the appointment of a responsible person who will faithfully discharge the duties of guardian, to pay into his hands $200, or such amount as shall be necessary for the child's expenses, from the lease money to her credit in the Sub-Treasury at St. Louis subject to your check, and to take the guardian's receipt for same. If the guardian who shall be appointed is not, in your opinion, a proper person to discharge the duties which are assigned him, you should not pay any money due Fannie Keokuk into his hands.

Very respectfully,

A.C. Tonner
HRH(GO).   Acting Commissioner.

DEPARTMENT OF THE INTERIOR
UNITED STATES INDIAN SERVICE

Oto Indian School, Okla. March 18th, 1904.

W. C. Kohlenberg, Supt.

Sac & Fox, Okla.

Dear Sir:-

There is a boy by the name of Charles Lightfoot on your Annuity Roll, but allotted on this Reservation; I am anxious to have a guardian appointed for him provided there is not already one. Will appreciate any information you can give me in regard to the present status of the boy in reference to a guardian. I have had all Iowas on the Reservation informed of the date of your annuity payment.

Very truly,

H.W. Newman,
Supt.

J.M.N.

Sac and Fox Agency, O. T., March 30/04.

Received of Hon. W. C. Kohlenberg, Supt. & Spl. Disb. Agent, bank certificate of deposit in the sum of $255.55, payable to Milton Bryan as legal guardian for Jesse Chisholm and Nellie Chisholm, minors, to cover the joint share or interest of said minors in and to the northeast quarter (NE1/4) of section twenty-one (21) in township eleven (11) north of range five (5) east of the Indian meridian, Pottawatomie County, Oklahoma Territory.

__Milton Bryan, Legal Guardian__
for
__Jesse Chisholm & Nellie Chisholm__
minors

****

[The above receipt given again]

****

Sac and Fox Agency, O. T., March 30/04.

Received of Hon. W. C. Kohlenberg, Supt. & Spl. Disb. Agent, bank certificate of deposit in the sum of $511.10, payable to Milton Bryan as legal guardian for James Little Bear and Lily Little Bear, minors, to cover the joint share or interest of said minors in and to the northeast quarter (NE1/4) of section twenty-one (21) in township eleven (11) north of range five (5) east of the Indian meridian, Pottawatomie County, Oklahoma Territory.

__Milton Bryan, Legal__
Guardian
__for James Little Bear & Lily Little__
Bear, Minors

****

[The above receipt given again]

****

MILTON BRYAN.   E. C. STANARD

BRYAN & STANARD
LAWYERS
SUITE 3--4 WALLACE BLOCK.

Shawnee, Oklahoma, April 7, 1904.

Hon. W. C. Kohlenberg, Supt.,

    Sac and Fox Agency, Okla.

Dear Sir:

    I send you herewith receipt in duplicate for share of Little Bear and Chisholm minors in consideration meoney[sic] from NE1/4 of 21-11-5, sold to Peyton and Traynor. I have already sent you certificate of guardianship to be attached to receipts.

        Yours very respectfully,

        Milton Bryan

    Received of Horace K. Guffin Adm. estate Ross Guffin deceased, 1st Supt etc, official check #348141 drawn by the said decedent in favor of D.W. Ulam, since deceased, as L.G. Pearl Conger, for $25.00 and endorsed payable to me as subsequent legal guardian of Pearl Conger.

        Lee Patrick
        Legal Guardian

Dated at Sac and Fox Agency O.T.
    June 6th 1904

Certificate of Guardianship attached to the original

[The letter below typed as given]

COTTON BROKERS   TECUMSEH and ASHER

S. S. RAINS & SONS

Dry Goods ... Clothing ... Millinery
HATS AND SHOES

Tecumseh, Okla. July 7th 1904

    Sac & Fox Agency
        Okla

Dear Sir

Yours of the 5th just to hand in reply
I am Not the Guardain of Geo O Morton he had a new
Guardain apointed I think Geo Rose
I sent Minnie Morton $10/$\underline{00}$ and paid Sarah Bear $10/$\underline{00}$
for Minnie Morton I went and saw the Probate Judg and
got the proper athoity

Yours very Truly

S S Rains

DEPARTMENT OF THE INTERIOR

UNITED STATES INDIAN SERVICE

Sac and Fox Agency, Okla.

July 27, 1904.

Mr. L.T. Sammons

Shawnee, Okla.

Dear Sir:-

For statistical and other purposes I have to request that you furnish me with a list of the amounts due the different Indian minors for whom you are legal guardian, and who are under the jurisdiction of this Agency.

Please give me the names and amounts due each minor.

Thanking you in advance for this information which I would like to receive at your earliest opportunity in order that I may complete my reports, etc., I am,

Very respectfully,

W.C. Kohlenberg
Supt & Spl Disb Agent.

8/5/1904

I have never recd any money except Etta Shaw. I have in my hands 432\underline{75}$ due Etta Shaw.   Resp LT Sammons

---

DEPARTMENT OF THE INTERIOR
UNITED STATES INDIAN SERVICE

Sac and Fox Agency, Okla., July 27, 1904.

Mr. Lee Patrick,

    Stroud, Okla.

Dear Sir:-

For statistical and other purposes I have to request that you furnish me with a list of the amounts due the different Indian minors for whom you are legal guardian, and who are under the jurisdiction of this Agency.

Please give me the names and amounts due each minor.

Thanking you in advance for this information which I would like to receive at your earliest opportunity in order that I may complete my reports, etc., I am,

Very respectfully,

W.C. Kohlenberg
Supt & Spl Disb Agent.

Copies to:

Lee Patrick
Milton Bryan,
L.T. Sammons,
Geo. L. Rose,
S.S. Rains,
S. C. Vinson,
H. C. McGaughey,
H. Josey
H. C. Brunt
P. S. Hoffman,
A. D. Wright,
John Foster.

Pearl Conger $1068^{60}

Nothing on other cases

WCK

DEPARTMENT OF THE INTERIOR
UNITED STATES INDIAN SERVICE

Sac and Fox Agency, Okla.

July 27, 1904.

Mr. Geo. L. Rose,

Holdenville I.T.

Dear Sir:-

For statistical and other purposes I have to request that you furnish me with a list of the amounts due the different Indian minors for whom you are legal guardian, and who are under the jurisdiction of this Agency.

Please give me the names and amounts due each minor.

Thanking you in advance for this information which I would like to receive at your earliest opportunity in order that I may complete my reports, etc., I am,

Very respectfully,

W.C. Kohlenberg
Supt & Spl Disb Agent.

Tecumseh, O.T.

Geo Oliver Morton $626^{78}

Respy
Geo L Rose

CHANDLER, O. T.   7--31--1904

Hon. W. C. Kohlenberg, Supt. & Spl. Disb. Agt.,

Sac and Fox Agency, O.T.

Dear Sir:-

Complying with your request of the 27th I give you below list of the minors for whom I am guardian who have funds on hand at the time, together with the amount of same.

Susan Morris -------------$ .63;

Grover Morris -------------$ .63;

Thomas Morris------------$62.12;

Very truly,

A.D. Wright   63.38

No. 6269.

The Union National Bank

Capital $50,000.
SUCCESSOR TO THE

Bank of hoffman, Charles & Conklin
ESTABLISHED 1892

Chandler, Oklahoma,   July 29 1904

OFFICERS AND DIRECTORS

P. S. HOFFMAN,
PRESIDENT
J. B. CHARLES
VICE-PRESIDENT
E. L. CONKLIN
CASHIER
H. C. BRUNT
ASST. CASHIER
R. V. HOFFMAN.

W. C. Kohlenberg, Supt / and Spl. Disb. Agent

Sac and Fox Agency, Oklahoma---

Dear Sir:-   In reply to your request of the 27th for the amounts due Indian
minors for whom I am legal guardian. I am guardian for the following minors
and have on hand at this date, for each, the amount set opposite the name------

George Butler------Seven hundred, forty-one and 25/Dollars ($741.25)

Jane Butler----Nine hundred, forty-six and 25/Dollars, ($946.25)

Yours Respectfully,

H.C. Brunt
Legal Gdn
Geo & Jane Butler

CHANDLER, O. T.   JULY 31, 1904

Hon. W?[sic] C. Kohlenberg, Supt. & Spl. Disb. Agt.,

Sac and Fox Agency, O.T.

Dear Sir:-

Answering your favor of the 27th inst. beg to say that I am guardian for
Fulwood Lincoln and have on hand to ~~his~~ her credit at this time $199.26.

Very truly,

H.C. McGaughey

84

Special Attention to Rentals   *Room 5, over Shawnee Nat'l Bank*

S. C. Vinson,
Real Estate.

Shawnee, Oklahoma,   July 29th   191 4

Mr. W.C. Kohlenberg
             Sac and Fox Agency
                         O.T.
Dear Sir:-

Complying with your request will say that on June 24th-1904 I had cash on hand belonging to Willie and Emma Naw-Aw-She 245\frac{00}{}$ I guess that it belongs to them equally

Very Respectfully

S.C. Vinson

Office of
S. A. CORDELL,
Probate Judge Lincoln County.

Chandler, Okla.,   July 29"   190 4

W.C. Kohlenberg
Supt & Spl. Dis Agt
Sac & Fox Agency Okla.
Dear Sir, I received your letter of the 27" just and in reply will say that to approve of the suggestions made therein, In future when an application is made for appointment of Guardian of Indian Minor, or a report is filed by Guardian of Indian minor, and when petition is filed for Letters of Administration on estate of a deceased Indian I will notify you of the time set for hearing the same so that you may be present and file a protest if you so desire.

Yours truly

S.A. Cordell
Probate Judge

Cushing Okla. Aug. 1, 1904

W. C. Kohlenburg[sic],
     Sac & Fox Agency, Okla.   less

Dear Sir;

     Enclosed find list of indians[sic] for which I am guardian and also the amount of money due them at the present date.

Silas Hawk	$ 807.57$^{less\$}$40
Mary Mansure[sic]	1320.97
Maud Kakaque	892.15
Clara Ellis	185.45
Laura Ellis	543.55
Stella Hawk	767.45
Cora Bass	246.42
Lee Bass	252.37
Walter Kakaque	289.60 Final Settlement
Isadore Neal	470.36
Ben Hull	300.64 } less 26$^{\underline{90}}$
Henry Hull	300.64
Rachel Hall	267.40
Maud Bigwalker	391.16 Final Settlement
Esther Bigwalker	119.46
Harrison Hunter	60.89
Gertrude Hunter	60.89
Daniel S Hunter	60.89
George Peery	709.05
Frank Faulk Springer	$ 16.66
Total	$8315.34

Yours very respectfully,
John Foster

MILTON BRYAN.   E. C. STANARD

BRYAN & STANARD
LAWYERS

SUITE 1 & 2, STEARNS BLOCK.

SHAWNEE, OKLA.

Shawnee, Oklahoma, August 3, 1904.

Hon. W. C. Kohlenberg, Supt.,

Sac and Fox Agency, Okla.

Dear Sir:

In reply to yours of the 26th ultimo, relative to settlement with Lillie Little Bear as legal guardian, I beg to say that the funds are mostly loaned out, and the loans not yet due; but I shall get affairs in shape for a settlement as soon as possible. In the mean time if you will kindly advise me of the ward's immediate necessities I will look after the same.

Very truly yours,

Milton Bryan

MILTON BRYAN.   E. C. STANARD

BRYAN & STANARD
LAWYERS

SUITE 1 & 2, STEARNS BLOCK.

SHAWNEE, OKLA.

Shawnee, Oklahoma, August 3, 1904.

Hon. W. C. Kohlenberg, Supt.,

Sac and Fox Agency, Okla.

Dear Sir:

In response to your request of the 27th ultimo, I beg to report the amounts of funds in my hands as legal guardian for minors under the jurisdiction of your Agency as follows:

Dickson Duncan--$481.67

Allen G. Thurman--$481.67

Bertha Pattequa--$364.00

Addie Pattequa---$364.00

Ida Miller---$000.00

1691.34

Very truly yours,

Milton Bryan

No. 6269.

The Union National Bank

Capital $50,000.
SUCCESSOR TO THE

Bank of hoffman, Charles & Conklin
ESTABLISHED 1892

Chandler, Oklahoma,   8--3--1904

OFFICERS AND DIRECTORS

P. S. HOFFMAN,
PRESIDENT
J. B. CHARLES
VICE-PRESIDENT
E. L. CONKLIN
CASHIER
H. C. BRUNT
ASST. CASHIER
R. V. HOFFMAN.

Hon. W. C. Kohlenberg,

　　　　Supt. & Spl. Disb. Agt.,

　　　　　　Sac and Fox, O.T.

Dear Sir:-

　　　　In reply to your request of the 27th for the amounts due Indian minors for whom I am legal guardian. I am legal guardian for the following named minors and have on hand at this date, for each, the amount seen opposite their names:

　　　　　　Fryor Farnklin[sic] Brown----------$1535.10;

　　　　　　Rachel Smith-----------------------$ 46.07;

　　　　　　Martha Baker-----------------------$ 825.00;

　　　　　　Paul Randall-----------------------$ 82.52.

2488.69

Very truly,

P.S. Hoffman

Chandler, O. T.   8--5--1904

Hon. W. C. Kohlenberg,

      Sac and Fox Agency, O.T.

Dear Sir:-

      Complying with your request of the 27th I desire to say I am guardian of Sadie Ingalls and have in my hands funds to her credit i the sum of $1729.68, at this time.

                Very truly,

                    H. Josey

Refer in reply to the following:
Land.
67866-1904.

Department of the Interior.

OFFICE OF INDIAN AFFAIRS

WASHINGTON,   October 29, 1904

RECEIVED
NOV 1 1904
SAC & FOX AGENCY.
OKLAHOMA.

Ans'd Nov. 1-04

W. C. Kohlenberg, Esq.,
      Superintendent of Indian School,
            Sac and Fox Agency, Oklahoma.

Sir:

      The office is in receipt of a letter from S. C. Vinson, dated Shawnee, Oklahoma, September 28 last asking to be advised if the Department holds money belonging to minors when neither the father nor the mother is living and they have a legal guardian and stating that the Probate Court draws on him for what they need and that you have refused to turn over the lease money to him.

      He encloses a letter from yourself dated September 20 last stating that it is not the custom of your office to turn over to legal guardians money belonging to minors; that when the funds he has are exhausted a check will be given him for expenses incurred in looking after the Nawashe children.

Mr. Vinson's letter and enclosure are enclosed herewith for report of the Nawashe children the lease money due them.   Please return the enclosures with your report.

Very respectfully,

A.C. Tonner

JLD-WDW   Acting Commissioner.

Refer in reply to the following:

Land.
78066-1904.

Department of the Interior.

OFFICE OF INDIAN AFFAIRS

WASHINGTON,   November 8, 1904

RECEIVED
NOV 14 1904
SAC & FOX AGENCY
OKLAHOMA

No Ans

W. C. Kohlenberg, Esq.,
    Superintendent of Indian School,
        Sac and Fox Agency, Oklahoma.

Sir:

The office is in receipt of your letter of the 1st instant, reporting on the complaint of S. C. Vinson of Shawnee, Oklahoma, that you have refused to turn over to him certain lease money belonging to his wards, Willie and Emma Nawshe[sic].

Replying thereto you are advised that the reasons as stated in your letter for withholding said money are satisfactory to this office.   A copy of office letter to Mr. Vinson of this date is enclosed herewith.

Very respectfully,

A.C. Tonner

JLD-WDW   Acting Commissioner.

Refer in reply to the following:
Land.
67866-1904.
78066-1904.

(COPY)
Department of the Interior.

OFFICE OF INDIAN AFFAIRS

WASHINGTON, November 8, 1904.

S. C. Vinson, Esq.,

    Box 536, Shawnee, Oklahoma.

RECEIVED
NOV 14 1904
SAC & FOX AGENCY,
OKLAHOMA.

Sir:

The office acknowledges receipt of your letter of September 28 last, enclosing one from the Superintendent of the Sac and Fox Agency, Oklahoma, and asking to be advised if the Department holds money belonging to minor Indians when neither the father nor the mother are living and they have a legal guardian; and stating that the Probate Court draws on you for what they need and the Agent refuses to turn over to you the lease money. You ask to be advised why the Department holds this money.

Replying thereto you are advised that upon inquiry it appears that your wards, Willie and Emma Nawshe, are in school, - Willie at Carlisle and Emma at Sac and Fox Agency; that on July 29, 1904, you had on hand $245.00 belonging to these children, and the Superintendent of the Sac and Fox Agency has not been advised that you have been to any expense for them since that time. You have been advised, it appears, heretofore that if the occasion should demand it in the future the Superintendent would give you a check on the Assistant Treasurer of St. Louis for the amount needed to pay for necessaries for these children, should they become in need.

All money belonging to Indian minors having guardians is deposited with the Assistant Treasurer at St. Louis, Missouri, and is only paid to the guardians when circumstances demand that minors should be allowed certain money to supply them with the necessities of life or when they are of such age that they should be in possession of a little "pocket" money. All minors' lease money is so held and you are no exception to the rule as other guardians labor under the same restrictions.

Very respectfully,

A. C. Tonner,
Acting Commissioner.

JLD-WDW

JACOB PUCKETT, President.
C. W. CARPENTER, Vice-President.
JOHN FOSTER, Cashier.

DIRECTORS:
JACOB PUCKETT.   L. B. HAY.
C. W. CARPENTER.   J. B. CHARLES.
JOHN FOSTER.   E. L. CONKLIN.
P. S. HOFFMAN.

FIRST NATIONAL BANK

RECEIVED
NOV 23 1904

OF CUSHING.
CAPITAL STOCK, $25,000.00 & FOX AGENCY,
CUSHING, OKLA. NOV 21 1904   OKLAHOMA.

W. C. Kohlenberg,

    Sac & Fox Agency, Okla.

Dear Sir:

    I herewith return all receipts sent me to sign with reference to deposited guardians fund with the U. S. Treasurer. If at any time you think that one of these should be signed for any special benifit[sic] for the indian[sic], if you will make mention of it and I do not have to pay interest on the funds received I will sign same.

    I have taken the matter up with the Probate Judge and he sees no way by which he can allow me to make any report on lands that have been probated through his court for the benefit of an indian without charging me interest on funds received.

        Yours truly,

           John Foster

[The letter below typed as given]

JOHN R. CLARK.

Probate Judge Payne County.

A. L. BROCKMAN, Clerk.

        Stillwater, Oklahoma, 12-27-1904.

W.C. Kohlenberg,

    Sas and Fox Aency,

        Oklahoma.

Dear Sir :-

Inclose please find Letters of Guardianship and receipts duly signed I have used this check in paying up the Court costs, which leaves a balance to the minor of $7.00 for which I will send him a draft. If you wish the minor to have more money you can mail me a check and I will endorse it over to him and mail it to him.

Very truly,

John Foster

Refer in reply to the following:
Land.
78066-1904.

Department of the Interior.

OFFICE OF INDIAN AFFAIRS

WASHINGTON, December 29, 1904

RECEIVED

JAN 2 1905

SAC & FOX AGENCY,
OKLAHOMA.

W. C. Kohlenberg, Esq.,
    Superintendent Indian School,
        Sac and Fox Agency, Oklahoma.

Sir:

There is enclosed herewith a communication from S. C. Vinson, Mr. Vinson transmits with his letter a communication from you and two statements of account. It appears that Mr. Vincent is the guardian of Emma and William Nawashe and that certain accounts of Conkling-Grimm Company for money and supplies furnished these parties have been disapproved by the judge of the probate court. Mr. Vinson for that reason declined to pay the same. It appears that you have presented them to him and requested payment. He is of the opinion that you have made illegal use of the mails in forwarding these accounts in that he claims you have used the Government frank for this purpose.

From the facts before the office, Mr. Vincent's claim does not appear well founded. It is believed perfectly proper and right for you to use the Government frank in the way you evidently have in this case, but this office would be pleased to have a report from you concerning the status of the whole matter of Mr. Vincent's guardianship of the two Indians named.

93

Very respectfully, A.C. Tonner
M.G.-L.M.   Acting Commissioner.

SAMUEL SMITH
PROBATE JUDGE.

W. W. DAUGHERTY
CLERK.

OFFICE OF
Probate Judge, Payne County,

RECEIVED
JAN 13 1906
SAC & FOX AGENCY,
OKLA.

Stillwater, Okla.,   Jan. 12ᵗʰ 1905

W.C. Kohlenberge[sic],
    Sac and Fox Agency,
        Okla.

Dear Sir:-

I beg to advise you that on the 9th inst W.C. Kenworthy of Perkins Okla., filed his petition for Letters of Guardianship of Jack Lincoln and Edward Small.

I have assigned the petitions for hearing on January 25th 1906 at 9 o'clock AM.

Yours very truly
Samuel Smith,
Probate Judge

DEPARTMENT OF THE INTERIOR
UNITED STATES INDIAN SERVICE.

Sac and Fox Agency, Okla.,
January 31 '05.

Payne County Bank of Perkins,
    Perkins, Okla.

Gentlemen:

Enclosed herewith you will find your Certificate of Deposit #107 for $1340.00 payable to John Foster, Guardian of Sam Perry, and dated December 21, '04. You are advised that this certificate is in error. There are other heirs besides John Foster, as guardian. Please send me new certificate of deposit payable for the same amounts, for the same purpose, to the Commissioner of Indian Affairs, in lieu of the one transmitted herewith.

Very respectfully,

W.C. Kohlenberg
Supt. & Spl. Disb. Agent

W
I enclosure

Refer in reply to the following:
Land.
2841-1905.

Department of the Interior.

OFFICE OF INDIAN AFFAIRS

WASHINGTON, February 25, 1905.

RECEIVED

MAR 2 1905

SAC & FOX AGENCY,
OKLAHOMA.

W. C. Kohlenberg, Esq.,
    Superintendent Indian School,
        Sac and Fox Agency, Oklahoma.

Sir:

This Office has carefully considered the statements contained in your letter of January 7 made in reply to the charges of S. C. Vinson, guardian for certain Indian children, and finds no fault with your action in the premises. The Office is also of opinion that there are some grounds for the opinion expressed in your letter that such a man as Vinson should not be permitted to be a guardian for Indian children. It is believed that if you will call to the attention of the court the provisions of Sections 443 to 335, inclusive, of the regulations by which you are to be governed in such matters, ~~that~~ some action will be taken to consider your wishes in regard to the appointment of guardians over minor children.

Very respectfully,

C.F. Larrabee,
Acting Commissioner.

T.B.W.-E.

ROY HOFFMAN   JOHN EMBRY

HOFFMAN & EMBRY

ATTORNEYS AND COUNSELORS AT LAW.

CHANDLER, OKLA.

RECEIVED

MAR 9 1905

SAC & FOX AGENCY,
OKLAHOMA.

3--9--1905

Hon. W. C. Kohlenberg,

      Supt. & Spl. Disb. Agt.,

           Sac and Fox, O.T.

Dear Sir:-

      Enclosed find certified copy of letters of Guardianship, P.S. Hoffman as guardian of Harriet Tohee, John Tohee and Dan Tohee, as per your request of yesterday.

                Very truly,

                   Hoffman & Embry

RECEIVED

Probate Court fees due S.A. Cordell in Case of Indian estates, to wit:

SAC & FOX AGENCY,
OKLAHOMA

Estate of Roger Sullivan P.S. Hoffman Guardian	$6.40
Estate of Paul Randall P.S. Hoffman Guardian	$ 6.60
Estate of Juanitta Davis P.S. Hoffman Guardian	$33.75
Estate of Perry & Jesse Herrin P.S. Hoffman Guardian	$ 3.80
Estate of Farra Roubedoux P.S. Hoffman Guardian	$10.40
Estate of Wm H. Jefferson; Lee Patrick Admin	$11.10
Estate of Vestana Grant P.S. Hoffman Guardian	$ 3.85
Estate of Edna Grass P.S. Hoffman Guardian	$ 3.70

Estate of Harry Hall
John E. Gillmore Adm'n $ 5.20

Estate of Moses Keokuk
Lee Patrick Adm'n bal- $ 3.40

Estate of Mary M Vetter
A.D. Wright Guardian $11.50

Estate of Kirwin Murray
A.D. Wright Guardian $ 4.65

Estate of Henry Miller
Mary Miller Adm'n $14.80

Estate of Jennie Hall
H.C. Brunt Guardian, bal $ 1.00

Estate of Anna Eaves
P.S. Hoffman Guardian $ 4.20

Estate of Edward Small
P.S. Hoffman Guardian $ 4.20

Estate of Jack Small Lincoln
P.S. Hoffman Guardian $ 4.20

Estate of Harriet Tohee, et al
P.S. Hoffman Guardian $ 7.60

Estate of Willie Naw-Aw-She, et al
P.S. Hoffman Guardian $ 5.00

Estate of Mary Small
H. Josey Adm'n $ 5.45

Estate of Mary Harris, et al
P.S. Hoffman Guardian $ 9.50

Estate of Joseph Fox
A.D. Wright Guardian $16.40

Estate of Charles Keokuk
P.S. Hoffman Adm $18.20

Estate of Orilla Davis
Lee Patrick Guardian $ 4.20

Estate of Ida Miller
Milton Bryan Guardian $ 7.00

Estate of John Grant & Theresa Logan
John Arnold Guardian $ 4.20

Estate of Wish-ta-ah [Illegible]
Lee Patrick Guardian   30.60

DIRECTORS:

JACOB PUCKETT, President.   JACOB PUCKETT.   L. B. HAY.
C. W. CARPENTER, Vice-President.   C. W. CARPENTER.   J. B. CHARLES.
JOHN FOSTER, Cashier.   JOHN FOSTER.   E. L. CONKLIN.
                                   P. S. HOFFMAN.

FIRST NATIONAL BANK
OF CUSHING.
CAPITAL STOCK, $25,000.00
CUSHING, OKLA. March 31, 1905

RECEIVED
Apr 1
SAC & FOX AGENCY,
OKLAHOMA.
③

SSS

W. C. Kohlenberg,

Sac & Fox Agency, Okla.

Dear Sir:

Geo P[illegible] and Henry Hull

In looking up the Mary Mansur case ^ I find that these accounts have been paid to one, John Gillmore, administrator appointed by the Probate Court of Lincoln County. I have taken the matter up but have heard nothing concerning the matter. I think that this money that belongs to th[sic] Mary Mansur heirs for which I am guardian and Ben Hull brother of Henry Hull should be returned to me. Of course I do not know what kind of a petition was filed with the court of Lincoln County or upon what authority the administrator was appointed for the Henry Hull estate, as Ben Hull was the sole heir of his estate and I am guardian for said heir. And will further say that this was not done for the purpose of settleing[sic] any debts as al claims against the said deceased were settled by me.

I shall take the matter up again and would like to hear from you in regard to the funds due the heirs for which I am guardian to the said Mary Mansur and Henry Hull. I do not wish to interfere with any thing for which I have no authority but it does seem to me that the guardian for these should be considered in the settlement of this dead.

Yours truly,

John Foster

OFFICE OF

S. A. CORDELL

ATTORNEY AT LAW

SPECIAL ATTENTION GIVEN TO PROBATE MATTERS

RECEIVED
MAR   1905
SAC & FOX AGENCY,
OKLAHOMA.

CHANDLER, OKLA.,   March 31"   190 5

Hon. W. C. Kohlenberg
Sac & Fox Agency Okla
   Dear Sir & friend, I herewith enclose you list of fees due me in Indian cases.
   Please look over it and if any of the parties have funds subject to your check, except in cases where the bill has been sent in to the department, please send me check for same and oblige   Your friend
                                                    S.A. Cordell

---

Department of the Interior.

OFFICE OF INDIAN AFFAIRS

WASHINGTON,

RECEIVED
APR 28 1905
SAC & FOX AGENCY,
OKLAHOMA.

W. C. Kohlenberg, Esq.,
   Superintendent Sac and Fox School,
      Sac and Fox Agency, Oklahoma.

Sir:
         Replying to questions submitted to the Department with reference to the matter of guardians of minor heirs of deceased allottees reporting sales of said minors' interests, in order that the same may be confirmed by the probate courts and regular guardians' deeds ordered and executed, the Acting Secretary of the

Interior Secretary of the Interior the Interior on April 11, 1905, in a communication addressed to the inquirer, stated as follows:

> In answer thereto I will state that it is desirable that these transactions shall be so conducted that they will meet all reasonable objections of conveyancers and abstractors, and where sales of inherited Indian lands are made wherein minor heirs are interested, so far as practicable said sales should be reported by the guardian and an order entered by the probate court directing him to make a deed therefor.
>
> But the Department holds that where the legal guardians of minors join in the conveyances of inherited Indian lands, a separate 'guardian's deed' is not required. The act of May 27, 1902, makes all conveyances of such lands subject to the approval of the Secretary of the Interior, and if it had been intended to make the procedure prescribed by the laws of the various states and territories relating to the sale of real estate of minors apply and control in the sales authorized by said act, some apt expression to convey such meaning would have been used. When a guardian joins the the[sic] other heirs in signing a deed, it is considered sufficient to convey full title of the minors' interest in the land without any approval of the sale by the probate court, or any other deed from the guardian.
>
> The department does not concede the right of the guardian to have control of the funds derived from the sale of a minor's interest in inherited lands, and said funds are deposited in a national bank, subject to the check of the recognized guardians for amounts not exceeding ten dollars to each in any one month when approved by the agent or other officer in charge, and only when so approved, and for sums in excess of ten dollars per month upon the approval of such agent only when specifically authorized by the Commissioner of Indian Affairs.

It will be necessary that a minor's interest in any estate be sold by a guardian duly appointed by the probate court upon the order of such court made upon petition filed by the guardian, as required under the provisions of section 7 of the act of May 27, 1902.

You will please observe the ruling of the Department as hereinabove set forth in all proceedings where minors are interested.

Very respectfully,
C.F. Larrabee
Acting Commissioner.

TBW
C

SAMUEL SMITH
PROBATE JUDGE.

W. W. DAUGHERTY
CLERK.

OFFICE OF
Probate Judge, Payne County,

RECEIVED

APR 25 1905

Stillwater, Okla., ___SAC&FOX24GENCY,1905

W.C. Kohlenburg[sic]
Sac and Fox Agency
Okla -

SAC & FOX AGENCY,
OKLAHOMA.

Dear Sir-

Enclosed find the copies of Guardianship Letters for the parties

asked for

Respcly

W.W. Daugherty
Clerk

REFER IN REPLY TO THE FOLLOWING:

Land.
26250-1905.

RECEIVED
APR 29 1905
SAC & FOX AGENCY,
OKLAHOMA.

DEPARTMENT OF THE INTERIOR
OFFICE OF INDIAN AFFAIRS
WASHINGTON   April 25, 1905.

W. C. Kohlenberg, Esq.,
Superintendent in charge,

Sac and Fox Agency, Oklahoma.

Sir:

This Office is in receipt of your letter of March 14, 1905, inclosing an

order from the Probate Judge at Tecumseh, for Pottawatomie County,

Oklahoma, ordering you to pay to Hiram Holt any funds on deposit to the credit

of certain minor Indians for whom he had been appointed as legal guardian.

You also inclose a letter from the same Judge in which he states that he is

advised that you pay lease money to the minors or to the parents of minors, and

that this is not in accordance with the laws of the Territory, and that he has

concluded to instruct all guardians under his jurisdiction to execute no more

101

leases until an understanding can be had as to the distribution of the lease money.

You say that you never pay lease money to the minors, but have paid small amounts to the minors' parents when it is very evident that the parent is as competent as the legal guardian to attend to the matter. You also state that you have over $13,000.00 on deposit with the Assistant Treasurer at St. Louis, the greater portion of which belongs to minor Indians, and was derived from the lease of Indian allotments; and it is not customary to pay lease money to guardians for the minors except in such small amounts as their wards might require to meet their immediate necessities. You also state that you would not pay any more money to some of the guardians under the jurisdiction of this court than they now have for the reason that you do not consider them proper persons to handle any more funds. You ask to be advised if, under the circumstances, you should pay this money to the guardians as demanded by the said Probate Judge, or if you shall retain the money as heretofore, even if ordered to pay it by the Probate Judge.

You are advised that your letter with the several inclosures was referred to the Department for a ruling as to what instructions should be given you in regard to the questions raised by the Probate Judge. The Office is now in receipt of a letter from the Department, dated April 6, 1905, in which reference is made to a former decision regarding a case where a contention arose between the natural guardian and the legal guardian as to the right to control the leasing of the lands and the possession of the funds of the minor Indians. In that case, the Department ruled that the natural guardian, who was a responsible Indian, should have control of the leasing of the land and the collection of the money, which should be deposited in the Treasury to the credit of the minors, and directed this Office to advise the legal guardian of the decision rendered.

The Department also states that in view of the facts submitted in your letter, you should be directed to decline to comply with the demands of the legal guardian in cases of this character, and to carry out the ruling of the Department to which reference is above made.

You will, therefore, decline to comply with the orders of the Probate Judge to turn over to the legal guardian the money in your hands belonging to minor Indians, except such amounts as may be required during their minority.

Where you find that allotments of minor Indians should be leased, you will direct the natural guardian to execute the lease under your supervision and with your approval, also to collect the lease money, which is to be deposited in the Treasury of the United States to the credit of the minors.   The natural guardian should also collect such annuity money as may become due the minors, and this money should also be deposited to the credit of the minors.   In cases of orphans or where natural guardians are wholly incompetent to attend to such matters, you will report the fact to this Office for further instructions.

Very respectfully,

CF Larrabee
Acting Commissioner.

TBW-WDW

[Copy of original receipt]

No. 29550   U. S. INDIAN SERVICE.
[ORIGINAL.]   Shawnee, Kickapoo, & Pott. Agency, State of Territory of Oklahoma
FRANK A. THACKERY,   MAY 23 1905 , 190

Received of ....
Thirty-seven & 50/100 .... Supt & Spl. Disb. Agt.   U. S. Indian Agent,
.... Dollars ($) on account of semi-
annual payment of rent due .... , 190 , on lease to
.... of .... acres of .... allotment No. ....
located in Sec. ...... , Twp. ...... , R. ......
Witnesses: ....

[Transcription of Receipt given on Page 97]

No. 29550   **U. S. INDIAN SERVICE.**

[ORIGINAL.]   Shawnee, Kickapoo, & Pott. Agency, State of Territory of Oklahoma
.... May 23 1905 .... , 190

Received of .... FRANK A. THACKERY, ... U.S. Indian Agent,

Thirty-seven & 50/100 ....Dollars ($37/⁵⁰) on account of semi-annual payment of rent due.., 190 , on lease to
....of..........acres of..........allotment No.......
located in Sec.............., Twp.........., R.........
                 Sec.............., Twp.........., R.........

Witnesses:⎰ Russell Johnson ....
                ⎱ Thurman Ogee ....

.........L N Ogee.........
Legal Guardian of JohnnyLessor.
Bourassa

[The above Receipt was given in Triplicate]

Refer in reply to the following:

Land.
42357-1905.

Department of the Interior.

OFFICE OF INDIAN AFFAIRS

WASHINGTON, June 8, 1905.

RECEIVED

JUN 12 1905

SAC & FOX AGENCY,
OKLAHOMA.

W. C. Kohlenberg, Esq.,
    Superintendent in charge,
        Sac and Fox Agency, Oklahoma.

Sir:

The Department on May 19, 1905, referred to this Office a letter from C.J. Wrightsman, of Pawnee, Oklahoma, in which he says that in the Territory of Oklahoma, especially in the counties of Lincoln, Payne, Pawnee, Noble and Kay, respectively, where a vast majority of the Indian allottees reside, a condition exists that should have some early action by the Department. He says the probate judges of these several counties and especially in the county of Pawnee, have for the past 12 years permitted guardians of Indian children to handle the rentals, annuities, and proceeds of allotment sales of Indian wards, without accounting for one dollar's interest therefor, and in the majority of instances without providing adequate bonds as such guardians.

He further says he knows of persons appointed, respectively, for a least a dozen or more Indian wards for the sole purpose of using such revenues for their own personal use, and frequently loaning it back to the Indians at the rate of 4% per month. He says he knows of several cases where individuals, without personal assets and with the money of the Indian children held by them as guardians, have started local banks, using this Indian money as a capital stock, without accounting for more than the principal to the estates.

As a matter of protection to the Indians, he suggests that the Attorney General should require the United States District Attorney for Oklahoma to detail a deputy to make a personal investigation of these conditions and if necessary, prosecute applications for removal of all guardians who fail to furnish adequate bonds and to reasonably account for the use of revenues of their wards' estates.

In furnishing to the Department the information called for in regard to this matter, the Office stated that the suggestions of Mr. Wrightsman seemed to meet the requirements of the case and the Office stated that it very much desired that some action be taken whereby the guardians may be required to give ample bonds and also to account for the legal interest on all moneys that have heretofore been placed in their hands.

The matter has been referred to the Department of Justice for such action as may be deemed advisable and the Department, on June 3, 1905, referred to this Office a letter from the Acting Attorney General, dated May 29, 1905, stating that he had written to Horace Speed, United States Attorney at Guthrie, Oklahoma, in regard to the matter. The Acting Attorney General suggests that in order for the United States Attorney to have some definite information on which to base his actions, all agents and superintendents be directed to furnish him with all the specific information obtainable in regard to any guardian who has not given a valid bond or who has not accounted for the legal interest due his ward, or who has in any way made improper use of the funds of his ward.

You are directed to cooperate with the United States Attorney and furnish him all the information you can in regard to any guardian who has failed to fully discharge his duties to his ward. You will also forward to this Office copies of all letters that you write the United States Attorney in regard to this matter, in order that the Office may be fully advised as to the situation and what action has been taken to right the wrongs of which Mr. Wrightsman speaks.

Very respectfully,

C F Larrabee

TBW:LM Acting Commissioner.

5378

THE FIRST NATIONAL BANK

GEO L ROSE Prest   E C NICHOLS vice Prest
H R NICHOLS Cashier

TECUMSEH, OKLA.

June 21, 1905.

Mr. W. C. Kohlenberg,

      Supt. & Spl. Dis. Agt.,

           Sac and Fox Agency, O. T.

Dear Sir:-

Complying with your request in your letter of the 16th inst., I herewith hand you report in the matter of the guardianship of Geo. O. Morton.

I note what you say in your letter about information having been filed in your office, stating that guardians have been appointed for the purpose of getting the revenue belonging to their wards and loaning it back to them at 4% per month, and for the purpose of starting local banks and using the indian[sic] money for capital stocks.

I beg to advise you that I have never yet made an Indian ward of mine a loan at any rate of interest. When they have needed the money and requested I have taken the matter up with the Probate Judge and secured an order and paid them the money and charged it to their account. If they are in school and write me for the money I usually send it if it is a small amount and send it to the Supt. of the school and request him to give it to them when they need it. I am a stock holder and President of two national banks but not one dollar of my wards money have ever been used in purchasing capital stock of the banks.   I have very few Indian wards and every one that I have, have requested my appointment themselves, and time and again other parties have tried to get them to sign a request for the appointment of some other guardian. I have never had but one ward to sign such a request and this ward testified before the Court that the party who wanted to be appointed as guardian had agreed with him that he would see that this ward got all of his money if I was removed, hence he signed the request.   The Court refused to make the appointment and I am still guardian for the ward.

I am aware of the fact that there are a great many "grafters" who try to get hold of the Indian's money for the purpose of speculation and investments.   As stated before, I have never sought a guardianship of these Indian wards and, in fact, do not care for it.   In a great many instances I have refused to accept the guardianship of Indian wards, for the reason that they worry the life out of a man asking for their money every time they come to town.   The Indian wards for whom I am guardian are the best class of Indians and I try to educate them to take care of their money and not spend it foolishly.

As to needing my wards money to carry on by business, will say that I do not need it.   I have ample funds to handle my business and can pay what few wards I have their money, any day, without any trouble.

I appreciate your situation in the matter and do not blame you for asking for these reports and making investigation, but I do not want to be classed with the crown refered[sic] to in your letter.   Rather than be classed with this crown, I prefer to resign and settle up on a moments[sic] notice.

Yours very truly,
Geo. L. Rose
Dict.   Pres.

Sac & Fox – Shawnee
1892-1909   Volume XII

[Copy of Original Letter]

The First National Bank.

OLDEST BANK IN THE COUNTY.

CAPITAL. $25,000.00

STOCKHOLDERS' RESPONSIBILITY. $500,000.00

OUR STOCKHOLDERS

HENRY JOHNSON, Capitalist, Salamanca, N. Y. Has holdings in various banks in the Territories, and also has large investments in Real Estate Mortgages of the Territories

C. M. HAMILTON, Banker, Holdenville, I. T. Has large Real Estate holdings in Indian Territory towns and is also interested in several strong financial institutions.

S. CLAY, Tecumseh, O. T. Formerly in the mercantile business—now retired. Was at one time Government Trader. Has large investments and property holdings in the Territory.

E. C. NICHOLS, Tecumseh, O. T. Formerly senior member of the firm of Nichols & Larsh,—now retired. Has large holdings of various kinds in the Territory.

S. P. LARSH, Tecumseh, O. T. Successor to Nichols & Larsh, hardware dealers. Also has large Real Estate holdings in the county.

H. R. NICHOLS, Cashier.

GEO. L. ROSE, President.

Tecumseh, Okla., MAY 29, *1905.*

MY DEAR SIR:—

This circular letter is to invite you to do your Banking business with the FIRST NATIONAL BANK OF TECUMSEH, O. T.,—the oldest and best bank in the county.

If you are a patron of this bank, it is to thank you for your patronage and to assure you that we appreciate your business and that we stand ready, at all times, to lend any assistance we can to our customers and friends. If you are not our customer and friend we want you to be.

If you have idle money, the amount being great or small, open an account with us and watch it grow. If you put your money in a bank you can save it. If you carry it in your pocket you, usually, spend it.

If you want to borrow money, come and see us. We are always ready to make loans to our customers and friends. We have ample funds to take care of all loans offered where the security is sufficient. We believe we loan money cheaper than any bank in the county, but in return for this we ask for good security.

To our depositors, we offer absolute safety. To our borrowers, we offer every accommodation consistent with good banking. To all of our patrons, we offer our advice and assistance in any deal or transaction. If you wish, we will consult our attorneys about any legal matter for you, free of charge. To every one we offer kindness, courtesy, fair treatment and our best wishes.

We invite your attention to our stockholders, who are men of capital, influence, and integrity. They are not speculators or promoters, but just plain business men.

If you have never done any business with us, come in and get acquainted. Come in and see us—let us be your business friend and you be ours.

We pay interest on time deposits.

Yours very truly,

GEO. L. ROSE, President.

****

(Circular Letter No. 33)

OFFICE OF
GEO. L. ROSE,
FINANCIAL AGENT.

TECUMSEH, O. T., JUNE 1, 1905.

DEAR SIR:-

I want to say to you that I am still making farm loans and doing a general office business, such as I have done here for the last ten years. I want your business in my line. I have the best farm loan agency in Oklahoma and make quicker loans and give better terms than any agency. All business transacted with me and at my office—no delay in getting money—option given to pay all or part of loan at any interest payment **WITHOUT NOTICE**. Can pay at my office—no trouble of sending money away—do your business where there is an agency established and maintained.

Deeds, mortgages, contracts, leases, homestead papers and all kinds of legal instruments drawn. Notary Public in office.

I make a specialty of examining titles, have been in touch with the records since the beginning. I owned the first set of abstract books in this county and sold them on account of so much other business to look after.

Below I give a list of farms which I own and which I decided to sell on account of not having the time to look after them. These are the choice farms which I have purchased during the past ten years—no better farms in the country, and they are well located. Will sell if I get a reasonable cash payment; balance on long time, easy payments and reasonable interest.

I own these lands myself and if you buy from me you will have no commissions to pay.

The W½ of NW¼ of Sec. 9 and Lots 1 and 2 of Sec. 8, all in Twp. 10 N., Range 3 E. – 107½ acres all in North Canadian bottom, 5 miles northwest of Shawnee; black loam land; 100 acres in cultivation; two good wells, and two good box houses and barn One of the best farms in the county. Price $6500.00

The W½ of NW¼ of Sec. 18, Twp. 10 N., R. 3 E., – 80 acres; all prairie; lies 6 miles west and ½ north of Shawnee; all fences; none in cultivation; used for meadow; all could be put in cultivation. One of the best 80 acres of prairie land in the county. Price $2000.00

The E½ of NE¼ of Sec. 13, Twp. 10 N., R. 2 E. – All prairie; lies 6 miles west and ½ north of Shawnee, and joins above described 80 on the west. 50 acres in cultivation; 30 acres in pasture; fairly good house and barn; good well; all fenced; 40 acres bottom. A good farm—none better can be had for the money.
Price $2000.00

The SW¼ of Sec. 22, Twp. 11, R. 3 E. – All prairie; 4 miles north and 2½ miles west of Shawnee; 50 acres in cultivation; 40 acres in pasture and balance meadow land;

40 acres bottom; fairly good house. A fine farm for the money. Price $3750.00. Will divide this farm and sell in 80 acre tracts if desired.

The E½ of NW¼ of Sec. 3, Twp. 11, R. 2 E. – 80 acres; lies 1½ miles north of McLoud; 40 a. bottom land; covered with scattering timber; all fenced; none in cultivation; close to a good town and for sale at a bargain, owing to the distance away. Price $1800.00

The N½ of SE¼ and SE¼ of SE¼ of Sed. 23, Twp. 9, N., R. 3 E. – 120 acres; lies 1 mile south of Tecumseh, on the west line of town; all fenced; poor log houses; two wells; 60 acres in cultivation and balance in pasture; would make a fine fruit and truck farm; children could be sent to school in town from this farm. This farm is considerably broken but it will make a good little home and is for sale at a bargain. Price $1250.00

The NW¼ of Sec, 20, Twp. 8 N., R. 5 E. – 160 acres; lies 1½ miles west and 1½ miles north of Maud, a good town on the M. K. & T. R. R. Most all prairie land; 70 acres in cultivation; 90 acres in pasture; all fenced; a good frame house and a good well of water; improvements above the average. A bargain is offered in this farm. It is so far away to look after. Known as the Lee Duggins farm. Price $2000.00

The SW¼ of Sec. 2, Twp. 8 N., R. 3 E. – 160 acres; lies 4 miles south of Tecumseh on Dance Creek; 90 acres of fine creek bottom; 70 acres of upland; 100 acres in cultivation; balance timber; all fenced; one good house and barn; two good tenant houses. A beautiful creek bottom farm. Price $2750.00

The S½ of NE¼ of Sec. 11. Twp 9, N. R. 3 E. – 80 acres, ½ mile N. of Tecumseh, in city school district; nearly all prairie and meadow; all fenced; 25 acres in cultivation; would make a beautiful home.
Price $4000.00.

The SE¼ and E½ of SW¼ of Sec. 2, Twp. 9, N., R. 3 E. – 240 acres; lies 1 mile north of Tecumseh, in Tecumseh school district; 160 acres prairie; 80 acres timber; 65 acres in cultivation; 100 acres meadow; all fenced and cross fenced; fair house and barn; good well; one of the most beautiful upland farms in the county and lies between Tecumseh and Shawnee, in full view of both towns. Price $12000.00. Will divide this farm into 40 acre tracts if desired.

The W½ of SE¼ of Sec. 3, Twp. 14 N., R. 14 E. – 80 acres in the Creek Nation; 12 miles northeast of Okmulgee, one of the best towns in the Indian Territory; nearly all in cultiuation[sic]; good box house; all fenced; part prairie creek bottom and part prairie upland. A beautiful tract of land. Price $2000.

The E½ of NE¼ and NW¼ of NE¼ of Sec. 16, Twp. 11 N., Range 11 E. – 120 acres in Creek Nation; 70 acres in cultivation; 60 acres bottom; box house; box barn; creek with running water; lies 5 miles northwest of Weleetka, a good town with two railroads, electric lights, waterworks, etc. Price $2400.00

The W½ of SE¼ and SE¼ of SE¼ of Sec. 4, Twp. 8, N., Range 8 E. – 120 acres in Creek Nation, 5 miles northeast of Wewoka, capital of the Seminole Nation; 45 acres in cultivation; all fenced; all timber land; good log houses and barns. Price $2000.00

The SE¼ of SE¼ of Sec. 1 and W½ of NE¼ of NE¼ of Sec. 12, Twp. 6 N., Range 9 E., and N½ of SW¼ of SW¼ Sec. 6, Twp. 6 N., R. 10 E. – 80 acres in Creek Nation, 9 miles southeast of Holdenville, one of the best towns in the Creek Nation; nearly all in cultivation; all fences; two log houses; barn, etc.; all creek bottom—an excellent farm. Price $2000.00

The S½ of NE¼ and W½ of SE¼ and SE¼ of SE¼ of Sec. 17, Twp. 7 N. Range 10 E. – 200 acres in Creek Nation, 6 miles east of Holdenville; nearly all prairie creek bottom; box house; 40 acres in cultivation. The best farm anywhere in that section of the country. Price $4000.00

The SW¼ of Sec. 30, Twp. 8, R. 2 E. – 160 acres, 2½ miles west of Burnett and 1 mile south; all timbered land and unimproved; all upland; 120 acres could be put in cultivation; known as the James Travis farm. This farm had some little improvements on it but they are now in bad repair and not worth mentioning. It is a good farm. Price $1200.00.

If you want any further information regarding these tracts of lands or the terns of sale, etc., write me or call at my office.

Should this circular letter not interest you, kindly lay it aside and when some friend of yours is talking to you about a loan or about buying some land, hand it to him and it might be the means of helping him to get a good home.   Yours very truly,

GEO. L. ROSE.

Should you bet a letter from some friend asking about the country, mail him this.

[Copy of Original]

Gro. L. Rose. President.   E. C. Nichols, Vice President.   H. R. Nichols, Cashier

OFFICIAL STATEMENT (Condensed)

First National Bank,

TECUMSEH, OKLA.   (OLDEST BANK IN THE COUNTY)

To the Comptroller of the Currency at the close of business May 29th, 1905.

RESOURCES.			LIABILITIES.	
Loans	$ 47,793 16		Capital	$ 25,000 00
Overdrafts	488 05		Surplus and Profits	6,567 61
U. S. Bonds	12,500 00		Circulation	12,500 00
Premium on Bonds	625 00		**DEPOSITS**	**90,756 03**
Stocks, securities etc. (Warrants)	1,122 66			
Bank Building and Fixtures	8,549 51			
Other Real Estate	2,263 00			
Five per cent fund	625 00			
CASH	**60,657 25**			
	$134,823 64			$134,823 64

DIRECTORS:
E. C. Nichols, S. P. Larsh, C. M. Hamilton, H. R. Nichols, Geo. L. Rose.

The above statement is correct.
H. R. NICHOLS,
Cashier

CALLING YOUR ATTENTION to the above statement which shows the largest Cash Reserve, in proportion to deposits, of any bank in the County, I solicit your banking business and guarantee to you absolute safety and every accommodation consistent with safe banking. Our cash is protected by the best Burglary Insurance. Our real estate is protected by Fire and Tornado Insurance. Our assets are gilt-edged in every respect. Our profits may not be as great as some, but we pride ourselves on doing a conservative and safe banking business.

Respectfully,   H. R. NICHOLS,
Cashier.

112

RECEIVED
JUL 24 1905
SAC & FOX AGENCY,
OKLAHOMA.

DENNIS,

JOHN A. HANSEN

REAL ESTATE.
FARM AND CHATTEL LOANS.
BONDED ABSTRACTERS.
THE MOST COMPLETE SET OF
ABSTRACT BOOKS IN NOBLE COUNTY.

PERRY. OKLA.

July 20, 1905

Mr. Joe Springer,

Perkins, Okla.

Dear Sir:

I am in receipt of your postal of the 18th inst. in regard to Chas Lightfoot, and in reply I beg to say, that it will be almost impossible for me to come over there and see the boy, as I am tied down pretty close to business here. I received a letter from the Agent at the Sac and Fox Agency, and I replied stating that if he sent the vouchers to me for signature, I would sign them up, and gladly turn the money over to you to assist in the care of the boy. Since writing him, however, I have had no reply, and would suggest that you go over to the Agency and call his attention to the fact that I am willing to have the money used for the care of the boy, and request him to send the receipts for signature.

Yours very truly,

John A Hansen

Department of Justice.

———

Office of the United States Attorney.
District of Oklahoma.
Guthrie.

RECEIVED
AUG 1 1905
SAC & FOX AGENCY,
OKLAHOMA.

July 31st, 1905.

The Clerk in Charge,

Sac & Fox Agency,

Sac & Fox, Okla.

113

Dear Sir:-

I was sent here by the Department of Justice to investigate charges of breach of trust by guardians of infant Indians.

I would be obliged to you for an itemized statement of the dates and amounts of payments made to such guardians in the last five years.

I shall go to Stroud in a few days.

Respectfully,

Jno. S. Mosby

JACOB PUCKETT, President.
C. W. CARPENTER, Vice-President.
JOHN FOSTER, Cashier.

DIRECTORS:

JACOB PUCKETT.   L. B. HAY.
C. W. CARPENTER.   J. B. CHARLES.
JOHN FOSTER.   E. L. CONKLIN.
P. S. HOFFMAN.

FIRST NATIONAL BANK
OF CUSHING.
CAPITAL STOCK, $25,000.00

CUSHING, OKLA. August 2, 1905

RECEIVED

W. C. Kohlenberg,

Sac & Fox Agency, Okla.

AUG 4 1905

SAC & FOX AGENCY,
OKLAHOMA.

Dear Sir:

Yours of the 1st inst. received and will say that I have no letter such as you refer to and do not remember of receiving one. Will say there has been no change in the guardian accounts since the first of the year which I suppose you have a record of. If you still need this report you can send me blanks and I will take off the amounts due each indian[sic] and return them to you.

Yours respectfully,

John Foster

Cashier

A. D. Wright,

Drugs, Paints, Oils, Glass, Wall Paper, Books, Stationery,
Toilet Articles, Etc.

RECEIVED

AUG 2 1905

SAC & FOX AGENCY,
OKLAHOMA.

Chandler, Okla.,   Aug 2   190 5

Mr. W. C. Kolenberg[sic]
 Sac & Fox Agt
Dear Sir- Yours in regard to report on Wards received
I made you a full report on all of them a short time ago did you not get it? did
not keep a copy of same and will take a little time to make another but will do so
if you did not get the other & Wish
Yours very truly
AD Wright

George O. Morton.   Geo. L. Rose, legal grdn.

Copy of Guardian's Reports.

REPORT. Dated Aug. 2, 1905.

Dr.	From sale of land		308.33
	" " " "		335.00
	Rebate on bond		2.25
	Cash from Ross Guffin, Agent.		100.00
	Ditto		10.00
			755.58

Cr.	L.A. Hardin, atty., allowed by W.L. McFall	8.35	
	Premium on bond	9.00	
	Publication fees	9.80	
	Geo. O. Morton, clothing	10.00	
	" " " expense money	5.05	
	Notary public fees	.75	
	S.E. Simpson, order of court	15.00	
	Comm. 5% on $755.58	37.75	
	Time in court making deeds, leases, reports, etc 15.00		110.70
	Balance		644.88

115

Vouchers attached:

S.E. Simpson, services rendered 15.00
H.R. Nichols, three notary acknowled-
  gements to leases .75
Geo. O. Morton 5.05
Ditto 10.00
Publication of notice grdnship matters 2.90
Oct. 15'03 "Stroud Messenger" pub.notice 4.00
Premium on $1800 bond with American
  Bonding Co., A.B. Conner, Agt. 9.00
L.A.Hardin 1/3 attorney fees in con-
  nection with Morton heirs land sale,
  purchased by C.M. Cade 8.35

JACOB PUCKETT, President.
C. W. CARPENTER, Vice-President.
JOHN FOSTER, Cashier.

DIRECTORS:
JACOB PUCKETT.   L. B. HAY.
C. W. CARPENTER.   J. B. CHARLES.
JOHN FOSTER.   E. L. CONKLIN.
P. S. HOFFMAN.

FIRST NATIONAL BANK
OF CUSHING.
CAPITAL STOCK, $25,000.00

CUSHING, OKLA. August 7, *190*

W. C. Kohlenberg,

Sac & Fox Agency, Okla.

Dear Sir:

It is impossible for me to make a complete report as this sheet requires, for the following reasons;

First, my bonds are filed with the Probate Court and as I have a bond made for each indian[sic] I do not know just who the bondsmen are on each one.

Second, A part of the money for which I have been signing deeds as guardian has never been paid over to me and some of the costs for the sale of land is still unsettled.

Will say that they money that is listed on the sheet enclosed is all deposited in the First National Bank of Cushing, Okla. I have not made any loans but have been figureing[sic] with the officials of the Bank as to just what interest they will allow me on the annual deposits for each minors[sic] account where the account is One Hundred dollars or more and will remain for one year. As a number of the minors for which I am guardian have been selling their land and I notice petitions are still out for the sale of some and I think it has been the ruling of yours that the expense for the sale of this land shall be paid out of the minors funds now in possession of the guardian.

If you wish a full and complete report as to the names of the bondsmen you will have to send this sheet to the Probate Judge.

Yours respectfully,

John Foster

****

P. S. Hoffman, Guardian.

RECEIVED
JUL 10 1906
SAC & FOX AGENCY
OKLAHOMA

Ward.	Amt. to cred. and where deposited.	To whom loaned.	On what security is the money loaned?	Rate of income.	Amount of Bond and Names of Guardian's Bondsmen.
Fryor Franklin Brown	$22.70 Union Natl. Bank	$1332.00 J.A. & Mary E. Hoffman	Real Estate	6%	$3000.00-- $500.00 H.C. McGaughey, Fred Neal
Rachel Smith	$46.07 Union Natl. Bank				
Martha Baker	$39.65 Union Natl. Bank	$208.00 Louis C. & Ida Meyers	Real Estate	6%	$600.00 A.D. Wright Charles Sparks, Chas. A. Filtsch
Paul Randall	$ 9.20 Union Natl Bank	$368 Jno. O. Arnold			
Stephen Harrison					$1000.00 J.B.Charles, E.L.Conklin
					$1000.00--$500.00 H.B.Gilstrap, Charles Sparks, Chas. A. Filtsch

Remarks.

(The Hoffmans to whom money is loaned is no relation to Guardian

Guardian discharged.

****

117

L. T. Sammons, Guardian.

Ward.	Amt. to cred. and where deposited.	To whom loaned.	On what security is the money loaned?	Rate of income.	Amount of Bond and Names of Guardian's Bondsmen.
Etta Shaw	384\frac{45}{}$ Maud estate[sic] Bank Maud, O.T.	No one	———	——	1000$\frac{00}{}$ Home. alot

Remarks.

under J.W. Sammons

****

Geo. L. Rose, Guardian.

Ward.	Amt. to cred. and where deposited.	To whom loaned.	On what security is the money loaned?	Rate of income.	Amount of Bond and Names of Guardian's Bondsmen.
George Oliver Morton	605\frac{98}{}$ 1$\frac{st}{}$ Nat'l Bk Tecumseh I.T.			4%	1800\frac{00}{}$ American Bonding Co

Remarks.

****

Lee Patrick, Guardian.

Ward.	Amt. to cred. and where deposited.	To whom loaned.	On what security is the money loaned?	Rate of income.	Amount of Bond and Names of Guardian's Bondsmen.
William Jefferson Pearl Conger Fanny Keokuk	962\frac{80}{}$ in Stroud St Bank In debt to me	Will send you copy of my report.			$2500.

Remarks.

Order of Court to loan $1200 but funds on last sale not rec$\frac{d}{}$ so order cannot be executed.

****

S. S. Rains, Guardian.

Ward.	Amt. to cred. and where deposited.	To whom loaned.	On what security is the money loaned?	Rate of income.	Amount of Bond and Names of Guardian's Bondsmen.
Mamie Morton	S S Rains Full amt $492^{43} Paid out 13410 total $358.33				Sam Clay

Remarks.

I think the Bond was made five thousand or more

I have kept the money after so long a time I used it my self and will pay same interest the other Guardians pay

I paid the girl and some other money the court ordered paid

This July 1st 1905 S S Rains Guardian for Mamie Morton

****

H. C. Brunt, Guardian.

Ward.	Amt. to cred. and where deposited.	To whom loaned.	On what security is the money loaned?	Rate of income.	Amount of Bond and Names of Guardian's Bondsmen.
George Butler Jane Butler	$240.10 Union Natl. Bank Chandler, O.T.	$1500.00 J. Fair & F.V. Fair	Real estate and personal	10% per annum	$1000.00 P.S. Hoffman $3600.00 A.D. Wright, Charles Sparks, Chas. A. Filtsch (Additional Bond)

Remarks.

Money turned over to George Butler upon his marriage and Guardian discharged

****

H. C. McGaughey, Guardian.

Ward.	Amt. to cred. and where deposited.	To whom loaned.	On what security is the money loaned?	Rate of income.	Amount of Bond and Names of Guardian's Bondsmen.
Fulwood Lincoln	$73.71 Union Natl. Bank				$1000.00 P.S. Hoffman

Remarks.

****

A.D. Wright

Ward.	Amt. to cred. and where deposited.	To whom loaned.	On what security is the money loaned?	Rate of income.	Amount of Bond and Names of Guardian's Bondsmen.
Harvey Madison	$236.40 $ 22.63 Int. Union Natl. Bank	$1200 Lewis E. and Ida M. Martin	Real estate	8%	$500.00 HC McGaughey Wm. Mullins
Thomas Morris	$450.36 $ 18.91 Int. Union Natl. Bank	$ 300.00 John P. Miller	Real Estate	10%	$1000.00 Geo.W.Bateman and Ed G. Keegan
Grover Morris	$279.92 $ 15.18 Int. Union Natl. Bank				"
Susan Morris	$540.57 $ 19.53 Int. Union Natl. Bank				"
Edward L. Morris	$612.70 $ 16.80 Int Union Natl. Bank				$500.00 Fred Neal, H.C. McGaughey
Mary Vetter					$500.00 P.S.Hoffman "
Fred Vetter					"

Remarks.

I have received interest on average daily balance from time of opening the account to Aug. 1, 05, $22L63[sic]

I have received interest on average daily balance from time of opening the account to Aug. 1, 05, $18.91

I have received interest on average daily balance from time of opening the account to Aug. 1, 05, $15.18

I have received interest on average daily balance from time of opening the account to Aug. 1, 05, $19.53

I have received interest on average daily balance from time of opening the account to Aug. 1, 05, $16.80

No money ever received by me.

No money ever received by me.

No money ever received by me.

****

John Foster, L. G.

Ward.	Amt. to cred. and where deposited.	To whom loaned.	On what security is the money loaned?	Rate of income.	Amount of Bond and Names of Guardian's Bondsmen.
Silas Hawk	$1197.38				
Mary Mansur	Dead				
Maud Kakaque	885.87				
Clara Ellis {of age	193.57				
Laura Ellis	551.67				
Stella Hawk	742.45				
Cora Bass	202.27				
Lee Bass	210.37				
Ione C. Bass.	210.42				
Isadore Neal	295.19				
Ben Hull	392.26				
Henry Hull	Dead				
Rachel Hall	489.15				
Esther Bigwalker	112.11				
Harrison Hunter	13.99				
Gertrude Hunter	13.24				
Daniel S. Hunter	13.03				
Frank Falk Springer	2.57				
Chas. Mohee	21.25				

Remarks.

Department of Justice.

———

Office of the United States Attorney.
District of Oklahoma.
Guthrie.

August 7th, 1905.

The Superintendent,

  Sac & Fox Agency,

    Sac & Fox, Okla.

Dear Sir:-

  I write a line to inform you that in company with Mr. Allen, a Special Agent of the Interior Department, I shall visit your Agency in the course of a week when I hope you will have ready the itemized statement I requested.

  I also wrote to the Probate Judge at Chandler requesting him to furnish certain data in regard to Indian guardians.   There have been complaints at Washington of gross mismanagement of their trust funds.

      Respectfully,

      Jno. S. Mosby

———

J.B. CHARLES, PRESIDENT P.S. HOFFMAN, VICE PRESIDENT H. JOSEY, CASHIER LEE PATRICK, ASST. CASHIER.

STROUD STATE BANK

DIRECTORS
J. B. CHARLES. H. JOSEY.
P. S. HOFFMAN. E. L. CONKLIN.
LEE PATRICK.

Stroud Okla. 8 7 5.

Hon. W. C. Kohlenberg,

  Supt. Etc.

    Sac and Fox, O. T.

Dear sir:-

Your letters relative to the Bayles $205 and the Guardianship matters are received, will be at the Agency in ad day or two and fix up both matters with you.

Very truly

Lee Patrick

Depa rtment of Justice.

——

Office of the United States Attorney.
District of Oklahoma.
Guthrie.

August 10th, 1905.

Superintendent of Indian Schools,

    Sac & Fox Agency,

        Sac & Fox, Okla.

Dear Sir:-

I beg to enclose you herewith a list of questions which you will please present in writing by letter in your own name to each and all of the guardians of Indian allottees under your jurisdiction.

Just as soon as the questions are answered, you will forward the same from time to time to me at Guthrie. I trust you will expedite this matter at once.

Enc.   Very respectfully,

Jno. S. Mosby

BANK OF COMMERCE

CHAS E DENNIS Pres't   Da F C SEIDS V Pres'   JOHN A HANSEN Cash

RECEIVED
SEP 8 1905
SAC & FOX AGENCY,
OKLAHOMA.

Perry, Okla. Sept. 7, 1905

Mr. W. C. Kohlenberg, Supt.,

Sac and Fox Agency, Okla.

Dear Sir:

I am in receipt of your favor of Aug. 25 enclosing check for $13.33 on Chas Lightfoot account, and I signed up the receipts and sent them to you in the envelope you enclosed.

I received several letters from a party down there stating that Charles was having trouble with his eyes and wanting me to send the amount of this check to him to assist in his care. Will you kingly advise me whether or not this is the case?

The certificate from the Probate Court of Noble County as to my appointment as Guardian will be forwarded to-morrow.

Yours very truly,

John A Hansen
Guardian

DEPARTMENT OF THE INTERIOR

UNITED STATES INDIAN SERVICE

RECEIVED
SEP 19 1905
SAC & FOX AGENCY,
OKLAHOMA.

Kaw Training School,
Washunga, Okla.,
September 18, 1905.

Supt. W. C. Kohlenberg,
Sac & Fox Agency,
Okla.

Dear Mr. Kohlenberg:

I expect to arrive at Chuckaho on the train leaving Kaw at 10 o'clock Wednesday morning. Mrs. Allen and my little daughter will be with me and I will be greatly obliged if you will have us met at the station.

I shall want to get at the records of the Probate Judge relating to guardianship of Indian minors. At Pawnee and Ponca Agencies, the Probate Judges of the Counties concerned allowed me to take the records to the Agency where the work that I have to do may be performed more expeditiously and more satisfactorily. Do you suppose that the Judge at Chandler would be equally accommodating?

Yours truly,

Edgar A Allen
JRS.   Special Indian Agent.

If you can provide us a name at the school and opportunity to board with the school [illegible] I will be under further obligations to you
Ed A

RECEIVED

OCT 9 1905

SAC & FOX AGENCY,
OKLAHOMA.

Fred A. Wagoner,
Probate Judge.

Chandler, Okla. Oct 7/05

Hon W C Kohlenburg[sic]
Sac & Fox Agency O.T.

Dear Sir

Find enclosed 6 certificates of guardianship in the case of Fannie Keokuk which I am requested by Mr. Lee Patrick to mail direct to you.

Yours truly
Fred A Wagoner

R E C E I V E D

NOV 1 1905

SAC & FOX AGENCY,
OKLAHOMA.

DEPARTMENT OF THE INTERIOR
UNITED STATES INDIAN SERVICE

Whiteagle, O. T., Oct. 31, 1905.

Supt. W. C. Kohlenberg,

Sac & Fox Agency, O. T.

Dear Mr. Kohlenberg:

Complaint has reached me that Milton Bryan has not yet made final settlement with Lillie LittleBear though she has been married for nearly two years. Will you please ascertain the facts in the case and let me know. I would like if possible an affidavit from her stating the date of her marriage, the amounts that was due her from her guardian at the time of her marriage, the circumstances connected with any demand made for settlement by her, any arrangement made between the guardian and the Probate Judge, if any has been made, for paying her in installments, the amount now due her, and any other facts of interest that she may have in relation to the matter. I will be greatly obliged if you will attend to the matter as soon as possible and sent your reply to Room #4   Masonic Building, Oklahoma City.

With best wishes,

Sincerely yours,

Edgar A Allen
Special Indian Agent.

Notice of Hearing Petition for Letters of Guardianship.

NOTICE.

Territory of Oklahoma, County of Lincoln, ss.

IN THE PROBATE COURT OF SAID COUNTY.

Notice is hereby given that on the 24 day of November 190 5 that Robert Keokuk, filed in the Probate Court of Lincoln County, Oklahoma Territory, a petition praying for Letters of Guardianship to be issued to F. G. Dennis upon the person and estate of

Robert Keokuk

Sac & Fox – Shawnee
1892-1909   Volume XII

---

minor child___of___Charles Keokuk____deceased.

And pursuant to an order of said court the _11_ day of _December_ 190_5_ at the hour of _10_ o'clock _a_ M., of said day at the Probate Court room in Chandler in said County and Territory, has been appointed as the time and place for hearing said petition, when and where any person interested may appear and show cause, if any they can, why such appointment should not be made.

Witness my hand and seal of said Court, at my office in said Lincoln County, Oklahoma Territory, this _24_ day of _November_ 190_5_

_____Fred A Wagoner_____
Probate Judge.

Special Attention to Rentals   *Room 5, over Shawnee National Bank*

S. C. Vinson
Real Estate Broker

RECEIVED
JUN 1 1906
SAC & FOX AGENCY,
OKLAHOMA.

Shawnee, Okla. January 25, 1906

Miss Emma Naw-ah-she,

Carlyle,

Pa.

Dear Emma:-

I had your money ready when I received your letter stating you hate that you ever seen me as your guardian. The court would only let me send $5.00.

I know of nothing new, we are haveing[sic] lovely weather at the present. Must close for the present, mind your teacher and learn fast.

Respectfully,

S.C. Vinson

127

A. D. Wright,

Drugs, Paints, Oils, Glass, Wall Paper, Books, Stationery,
Toilet Articles, Etc.

Chandler, Okla.,   2--1--_1906   *190*

Hon. W. C. Kohlenberg,

Sac and Fox Agency, O.T.

Dear Sir:-In accordance with your letter of January 31st I have signed the enclosed check making the funds payable to yourself for the treatment of Mary Vetter's eyes. Of course, as explained to you before, I know nothing about these funds and must decline to be responsible or accountable in any way for funds that do not come into my hands. I am doing his as an accommodation to you and at your request and will expect you to hold me harmless from any liability.

Very truly,

A D Wright

W. N. Maben,

Probate Judge

Pottawatomie County,
Tecumseh,   Oklahoma.

J. E. Simpson,
Probate Clerk.

Tecumseh, Okla.

Feb. 2" 1906.

Hon W. C. Kolenberg[sic],

Supt. and Spl. Disb. Agt.

Sac and Fox Okla.

Dear Sir:-

Refering[sic] to your letter of Jany 31" relative to the appointment of a new guardian for the estate of Mamie Morton, a minor, I beg to advise, that on the application of the minor who alleges to be past the age of 14 years, H. C. Beard, of Shawnee was duly appointed as guardian instead of Mr Rains, and the said Beard is at this time the duly appointed, qualified and acting guardian of this minor'[sic] estate. Any information I can furnish you in these matters, just call on me and I will gladly do so.

Very Respectfully,

__J.E. Simpson__
Clerk Probate Court.

ROBERT A. LOWRY   CHESTER H. LOWRY

Lowry & Lowry
Attorneys at Law,
POWELL BLOCK.
STENOGRAPHER AND NOTARY IN OFFICE.
Stillwater, Okla.

February 12, 1906.

W. C. Kohlenburg[sic],

Disbursing Agent,

Sac & Fox Agency, Okla.

Dear Sir:--

John B. McClelland, of the Sac & Fox Tribe, has been by the Probate Court of this County, appointed guardian of the estate of Sam Moore. Moore is the Indian, who, it is alleged, killed his wife and uncle, at the Sac & Fox Agency, and has been since about the 1st of September, 1905, in the jail in this county, and is under two indictments for murder. Our firm has been employed by the guardian to assist C. L. Burdick, of this city, in Moore's defense. We have no doubt but what this Indian is insane and has been for a year or two last past. We are confirmed in this by the jailer who has had him in charge for the past six months, and by a number of witnesses who testified in the Probate Court upon the application for a guardian, as well as by several physicians who have examined him. If a jury believe him to be sane and find him guilty, the probabilities are that he will suffer the death penalty. If he were insane at the time of the commission of the act, he should have the same rights that the law gives to a white man. The probate Judge upon examination in open court finds that he is insane and wholly incompetent to transact any business. It is for this reason that McClelland has been appointed guardian of Moore's estate. McClelland informs us that it is his understanding that there is now, or will be within a short time, in your hands the sum of $1500.00, the proceeds from the sale of certain inherited Indian land, which will be payable to Sam Moore, Albert Moore and Ruth Moore, $500.00 each. We also understand from Mr. Burdick that Sam Moore has an allottment[sic] of 160 acres, to which he will receive patent about July 1st, 80 acres of which will be subject to alienation. There will necessarily be some expense in preparing Moore's case for trial. Witnesses who know his mental and physical condition, and have known it for the last two years, must be hunted up and arrangements made for their attendance. Also, it will be necessary that we have the services of one or more expert physicians. We do not expect to be paid more than a minimum reasonable fee, which must be passes upon and allowed by the Probate Court of this county. This Indian has the means to pay a reasonable attorney fee, and it is certainly important that his rights be protected by competent counsel, and of course, if we act for him we shall expect to be paid as such. Please give us information in relation to any inherited lands due, or to become due, this defendant. Also, please give us the numbers of his alottment[sic].

Yours respectfully,

Lowry & Lowry

Fred A. Wagoner,
Probate Judge.

RECEIVED

MAR 2 1906

SAC & FOX AGENCY,
OKLAHOMA.

Chandler, Okla. 3/1/06.

Mr. W. C. Kollenberg[sic],

Sac and Fox Agency, Okla.

Dear Sir:-

Enclosed please find Certified copy of Letters of Guardianship in the Robert Keokuk matter as per letter of F. G. Dennis. Also find enclosed Four Certificates showing appointment of Guardian in the matter of Stephen Harrison, insane, Elmer Manatowa, John and Harry Crane and Thressa Logan, and Orlando Johnson.

Yours Truly,

Lula Divine
Probate Clerk.

No. 6269.

The Union National Bank

Capital $50,000.
SUCCESSOR TO THE

Bank of hoffman, Charles & Conklin
ESTABLISHED 1892

OFFICERS AND DIRECTORS
R E C E I V E D
PRESIDENT
MAR 5 1906
E. L. CONKLIN
SAC & FOX AGENCY,
H. C. BRUCE
OKLAHOMA.
R. V. HOFFMAN.

Chandler, Oklahoma,   March 2, 1906

Hon. W. C. Kohlenberg, Supt. & Spl. Disb. Agt.,

Sac and Fox Agency, O. T.

Sir:-

Replying to your last letter referring to payment for medical treatment of my ward's (Harriet Tohee) eyes.

As stated before I have never received any funds as guardian of this ward. There ought to be some funds belonging to her as proceeds arising from the sale of her interests in a tract of inherited land, but none have ever come into my hands nor have I been advised as to what disposition was made of same. As I have never had any report of same and have never been given control or custody thereof, and am unable to render the court any accounting as my obligation and the law requires, and as I have been unable to discover where this money is, or how much thee is of it, or what is being done with it, it seems to me it would be an act of presumption and perhaps of personal liability on my part to attempt to pledge it.

As to checking upon it, Sec. 601 of Art. 46 Wilsons Rev. & An. Statutes of Oklahoma deals with what is commonly termed "kiting checks" and declares a felony, punishable in the Territorial prison "the use of a matured check or other order for the payment of money ...... by any person who knows that the drawer thereof is not entitled to draw for the sum specified therein."

I am also advised that our statutes prohibit, under penalties any guardian or other person, concealing or failing to disclose any money goods, or effects, belonging to any ward or his estate.

Now, no funds belonging to this ward, ever having come into my custody, or under my control, to draw an order on someone to pay would violate the letter, if not the spirit, of our criminal statutes. And failing to report funds, if there are any, and where they are and what use is being made of them, is also a violation of my express duty under our laws.

I wish to do everything for the best interests of this ward. I think immediate medical treatment should be given this child. I wish to co-operate with you and the department in every way I can for the good care and control of the wards whose guardian I have been appointed. But I have responsibilities and duties to our courts as well which cannot be ignored.

I suppose under your statement there must be some funds somewhere which have been kept from me and which belong to this ward. This being the case I have to request that you at once give me full information, if any such you have, concerning same, that it may be reported to the court and may be available for the wants and necessities of my ward; and, while we are upon the subject if you know of any other funds belonging to the Indian wards, fow[sic] whom I am guardian, I believe it is my duty under our laws, to ask you at once to furnish me with similar information regarding same.

I am guardian for the following Indian wards:

Junitta Davis,	Fryor Franklin Brown,
Paul Randall,	Farra Roubidoux,
Harriet Tohee	John Tohee
Dan Tohee	Charlie Smithxxxxxxxxx
Rachel Smith	Martha Baker

Now, this is in no sense intended as a criticism of yourself or the department or its policy. I wish to do my full duty in the matter and discharge my trust with the approbation of the Indian department as well as to our courts and under our laws. If you will write me that there is $100.00 or approximately near that sum available and which you will see is paid me to reimburse me for the outlay I will advance my personal check immediately for the $100.00 to pay the doctor's bill and I will send my check in the next mail after I receive your statement to that effect, so that no delay will be occasioned.

Very truly,

P.S. Hoffman

N° 6306   **R E C E I V E D**

FIRST NATIONAL BANK ~~1906~~

H.M. JOHNSON, PRESIDENT.
F. G. DENNIS, VICE PRESIDENT.
F.D. BEARLEY, CASHIER.

CAPITAL $ 25,000.00
SURPLUS & PROFITS $6,805.00   SAC & FOX AGENCY,
STROUD, O.T.   OKLAHOMA.

3/10-06

Mr. W. C. Kohlenberg
        Sac & Fox

Dear Sir

I herewith hand you a letter from Probate Judge which will explain itself. Please send me ck for 5^{\underline{00}}$ to cover this matter.

Yours Truly
FG Dennis
Gdn

REFER IN REPLY TO THE FOLLOWING:

DEPARTMENT OF THE INTERIOR,

Land.
22, 058-1906.

OFFICE OF INDIAN AFFAIRS,

WASHINGTON.

March 14, 1906.

The Superintendent

in charge of Sac and Fox Agency,

Oklahoma.

Sir:

The Office acknowledges the receipt of your letter of February 24, last, reporting on the actions of S.C. Vinson, of Shawnee, Oklahoma, who is guardian for William and Emma Nawashe, minors, 15 and 12 years old, respectively. These children are the heirs of their mother, Susan Nawashe, who was allotted Lots 1 and 2 and south half of northeast quarter, section 4, township 10, range 4.

Mr. Vinson's actions as guardian of these children formed the subject of your letters of November 1, 1904 and January 7, 1905. These letters with that of February 24, 1906, were forwarded to the Department on the 6th instant for consideration and action

In view of the facts reported the First Assistant Secretary on the 9th instant advised this Office to instruct you to take immediate steps to present this matter to the Probate Court with a view to the removal of Vinson as guardian, and the appointment of yourself in his place. In the meantime all moneys accruing to these heirs should be held by you pending final disposition of the matter.

Very respectfully,

CF Larrabee
(J.L.D.) P.   Acting Commissioner.

Fred A. Wagoner,
Probate Judge.

Chandler, Okla.   3-14-06

Hon W.C. Kohlenberg
            Agency O.T.
Dear Sir
        Find enclosed 2 notices in each of the following Guardian cases.

Fulwood Lincoln - Lucy Mary & Fred Vetter
and Junitta Davis.   Please acknowledge receipt in each case on one of the notices and return the same to me. If you can I would like to have you here on the date for the hearing of these reports.

Yours truly
Fred A Wagoner

NOTICE OF SETTLEMENT OF ACCOUNT.

TERRITORY OF OKLAHOMA,⎫
⎬ SS.   IN PROBATE COURT.
COUNTY OF LINCOLN,⎭

NOTICE.

In the Matter of the Estate of Lucy Vetter, Mary Vetter & Fred Vetter ~~deceased~~ Minors

Notice is hereby given, that ____A. D. Wright____

the duly appointed and qualified _Guardian of Lucy Vetter, Mary Vetter and_

Fred Vetter ____ Minors ____ ~~deceased~~,

ha **s** ____rendered and presented for settlement, and filed in said Court, __his annual__

account and report of ___his___ administration as such _____Guardian_____

and that__Monday__ ~~day~~, the ____26"____day of____March___A.D. 190_6

being a day of a Regular Term of said Court, to-wit: of the___March___term, A.D. 190_6

at_10_o'clock in the__fore___noon of said day, at the probate court room in the____City

of__Chandler_____in the said County of Lincoln has been duly appointed by the said

Court, for the settlement of said account, at which time and place any person interested in

said estate may appear and file his exceptions in writing to the account and contest the

same.

IN TESTIMONY WHEREOF, I have hereunto set my hand and

affixed the seal of said Court this__14"__day of__March__190_6

[SEAL]   _____Fred A Wagoner_____
Probate Judge.

NOTICE OF SETTLEMENT OF ACCOUNT.

TERRITORY OF OKLAHOMA,⎫
⎬ SS.   IN PROBATE COURT.
COUNTY OF LINCOLN,⎭

NOTICE.

In the Matter of the Estate of _____Fulwood Lincoln_____ ~~deceased~~

Notice is hereby given, that_____H. C. McGaughey_____

the duly appointed and qualified __Guardian__ of the estate of _____

_____Fulwood Lincoln_____ Minor __deceased,

ha s ____rendered and presented for settlement, and filed in said Court, __his annual____

account and report of___his____administration as such _____Guardian_____

and that___Monday_____day, the _____26"_____day of_____March___A.D. 190_6

being a day of a Regular Term of said Court, to-wit: of the__March___term, A.D. 190_6

at_10_o'clock in the_fore___noon of said day, at the probate court room in the____City

of__Chandler_____in the said County of Lincoln has been duly appointed by the said

Court, for the settlement of said account, at which time and place any person interested in

said estate may appear and file his exceptions in writing to the account and contest the

same.

IN TESTIMONY WHEREOF, I have hereunto set my hand and

affixed the seal of said Court this__14"__day of__March___190_6

[SEAL]   _____Fred A Wagoner_____
                                              Probate Judge.

NOTICE OF SETTLEMENT OF ACCOUNT.

TERRITORY OF OKLAHOMA,⎫
                       ⎬ SS.   IN PROBATE COURT.
COUNTY OF LINCOLN,   ⎭

NOTICE.

In the Matter of the Estate of _____Junitta Davis, Minor_____ ~~deceased~~

Notice is hereby given, that_____P.S. Hoffman_____

the duly appointed and qualified _Guardian__ of__Junitta Davis_____

_____ Minor __deceased,

ha s ____rendered and presented for settlement, and filed in said Court, __his annual____

account and report of___his____administration as such _____guardian_____

and that___Monday_____day, the _____26"_____day of_____March___A.D. 190_6

being a day of a Regular Term of said Court, to-wit: of the__March___term, A.D. 190_6

at_10_o'clock in the__fore___noon of said day, at the probate court room in the____City of   Chandler _____ in the said County of Lincoln has been duly appointed by the said Court, for the settlement of said account, at which time and place any person interested in said estate may appear and file his exceptions in writing to the account and contest the same.

IN TESTIMONY WHEREOF, I have hereunto set my hand and affixed the seal of said Court this__14"__ day of __March__ 190_6_

[SEAL]   _____Fred A Wagoner_____

                                                                   Probate Judge.

[Copy of Original]

Record _____ Page _____

No.

IN PROBATE COURT,

TERRITORY OF OKLAHOMA,
LINCOLN COUNTY.

In the Matter of the Estate of

                                        Deceased

Notice of Settlement of Account.

Attorney _ for _____

RECEIVED

MAR 15 1906

SAC & FOX AGENCY,
OKLAHOMA.

Supt. & Spl. Disb. Agt.

Territory of Oklahoma, Lincoln County, ss.

I, _____ of lawful age, being duly sworn on oath say:

That I am a resident of said Lincoln County, and not interested in the estate of _____ deceased, and that on the _____ day of _____

A. D 190___ at the request of the Judge of said Probate Court, I posted correct and true copies of the foregoing notice in three of the most public places in Lincoln County as follows, to-wit:

One at _____ one at _____

One at _____

and one at _____ in said Lincoln County.

Subscribed and sworn to before me, the _____ day of _____ 190___

Judge of the Probate Court.

137

𝔉𝔯𝔢𝔡 𝔄. 𝔚𝔞𝔤𝔬𝔫𝔢𝔯,
ℜ𝔯𝔬𝔟𝔞𝔱𝔢 𝔍𝔲𝔡𝔤𝔢.

𝔈𝔥𝔞𝔫𝔡𝔩𝔢𝔯, 𝔒𝔨𝔩𝔞. 3/17/06.

Robert Keokuk, et al, minor,
Moses Keokuk, Guard.

Dear Sir:-

I desire to call your attention to the fact that there is now due and owing to this office in the above entitled matter the sum of 3\frac{30}{}$ ⌢⎯⎯⎯⎯ being the amount of costs due to the first day of January, 1906, and as I desire and am required to make settlement with the county commissioners for all business done in this office for the year, 1905, I would take it as a great favor if you will remit the above amount by draft, check or money order o or before the first day of April, 1906, so I can make settlement with the commissioners on the first day of April of this year for all business done for the year 1905.

I will take it as a great favor if you can and will comply with this request.

Hoping to hear from you soon, I remain,

Yours truly,

Fred A. Wagoner
Probate Judge.

NOTICE OF SETTLEMENT OF ACCOUNT.

TERRITORY OF OKLAHOMA,⎫
                        ⎬ SS.   IN PROBATE COURT.
COUNTY OF LINCOLN,   ⎭

NOTICE.

In the Matter of the Estate of John & Harry Crane and Theresa Logan ____ deceased Minor

Notice is hereby given, that_____ John O. Arnold _____

the duly appointed and qualified Guardian of John & Harry Crane _____

___ and Theresa Logan _____ Minor _____ deceased,

ha s ____ rendered and presented for settlement, and filed in said Court, __ his annual ___

account and report of ___ his ___ administration as such _____ Guardian _____

and that___ Friday ___ day, the ____ 13th ____ day of_____ April ____ A.D. 190 6

being a day of a Regular Term of said Court, to-wit: of the ___ March ___ term, A.D. 190 6 at 11 o'clock in the fore noon of said day, at the probate court room in the City

of Chandler in the said County of Lincoln has been duly appointed by the said

Court, for the settlement of said account, at which time and place any person interested in

said estate may appear and file his exceptions in writing to the account and contest the

same.

IN TESTIMONY WHEREOF, I have hereunto set my hand and

affixed the seal of said Court this 28" day of March 190 6

(Seal)

[SEAL]   Fred A Wagoner
                                         Probate Judge.

[Copy of Original]

IN PROBATE COURT,

TERRITORY OF OKLAHOMA,
LINCOLN COUNTY.

In the Matter of the Estate of

Deceased

Notice of Settlement of Account.

Attorney for

RECEIVED
MAR 29 1906
SAC & FOX AGENCY.

Supt. & Spl. Disb. Agt

REFER IN REPLY TO THE FOLLOWING:

RECEIVED

MAR 26 1906

Land.

DEPARTMENT OF THE INTERIOR,

SAC & FOX AGENCY,

25, 120-1906.

OFFICE OF INDIAN AFFAIRS,

OKLAHOMA.

WASHINGTON.

March 22, 1906.

The Superintendent

in charge of Sac and Fox Agency,

Sac and Fox Agency, Oklahoma.

Sir:

Referring to Office letter of August 22, 1905, requiring natural guardians to furnish certificates of guardianship when leasing their children's lands, you are advised that the draft of a Bill has been prepared for the approval of Congress, which provides that lands of minor Indians may be leased under such rules and regulations as the Secretary may prescribe, and any leases of such lands made in conformity with the rules by an Indian Agent or Superintendent, a parent, or other person designated by the Secretary for that purpose, shall have the same force and effect as if executed by a legal guardian.

On the 20th instant the First Assistant Secretary, in accordance with Office recommendation, granted authority for Agents and Superintendents in charge of such lands, pending action by Congress in this matter, to sign leases for such minor Indians, for terms not exceeding one year.

You will please acknowledge receipt on the enclosed card.

Very respectfully,

C.F. Larrabee,

(J.L.D.) P.

Acting Commissioner.

𝔉𝔯𝔢𝔡 𝔄. 𝔚𝔞𝔤𝔬𝔫𝔢𝔯,
𝔓𝔯𝔬𝔟𝔞𝔱𝔢 𝔍𝔲𝔡𝔤𝔢.

RECEIVED

APR 3 1906

**SAC & FOX AGENCY,
OKLAHOMA.**

ℭ𝔥𝔞𝔫𝔡𝔩𝔢𝔯, 𝔒𝔨𝔩𝔞.   4/2/06.

Mr. W. C. Kohlenberg,

Sac & Fox Agency

Dear Sir:-

Enclosed please find certified copy of letters of Guardianship in the estate of Robert Keokuk, minor, wherein F. G. Dennis is Guardian.

On the 1st day of March, 1906, I sent to F. G. Dennis a certified copy of the above named letters for you.

Hoping this will reach you safely,

I remain,

Yours truly,

Lula Divine
Probate Clerk

𝔉𝔯𝔢𝔡 𝔄. 𝔚𝔞𝔤𝔬𝔫𝔢𝔯,
𝔓𝔯𝔬𝔟𝔞𝔱𝔢 𝔍𝔲𝔡𝔤𝔢.

RECEIVED

APR 4 1906

**SAC & FOX AGENCY,
OKLAHOMA.**

ℭ𝔥𝔞𝔫𝔡𝔩𝔢𝔯, 𝔒𝔨𝔩𝔞.   4/4/06.

E. L. Conklin,

Sac & Fox Agency,

Dear Sir,-

Yours of the 27" inst. is at hand and contents noted. Enclosed please find two certificates one for E.L. Conklin Guardian of Harry Benson and P.S. Hoffman as Guardian of Paul Randall. Also find enclosed five blank certificates for your own use.

Yours truly

Fred A. Wagoner
Probate Judge
per Lula Divine,
Clerk

Sac & Fox – Shawnee
1892-1909 Volume XII

MAJOR W. A. MERCER, 11TH CAVALRY · SUPERINTENDENT

JOHN R. WISE · ASSISTANT SUPERINTENDENT

W. G. THOMPSON · SUPERINTENDENT OF INDUSTRIES

DEPARTMENT OF THE INTERIOR
UNITED STATES INDIAN SERVICE
INDIAN INDUSTRIAL SCHOOL
CARLISLE, PENNA.

April 6, 1906.

Mr. W. C. Kohlenberg,

Supt. Indian School,

Sac and Fox Agency, Okla.

Dear Sir:

Referring to your letter of the 27th ultimo inclosing petitions to the probate judge by Emma and William Newashe, students at this school, to have their present guardian, S. C. Vinson, removed and yourself appointed instead, the matter has been taken up with the children and after having been explained to them they readily consented to sign the petitions which are returned to your herewith.

Very respectfully,

WA Mercer
Major 11th Cavalry,

Superintendent.

JRW-S

ℱred A. Wagoner,
Probate Judge.

RECEIVED

APR 7 1906

SAC & FOX AGENCY,
OKLAHOMA.
Chandler, Okla. 4/6/06.

W. C. Kohlenberg, Esq.
Sac & Fox Agency, Okla.

Dear Sir:-

Enclosed please find certificate of Guardianship in the estate of Gertie King, a minor child of Michael King, deceased, and Jefferson R. McDaniel which is sent you by the request of Mr. McDaniel over the phone.

Yours truly,   Fred A Wagoner
Probate Judge
per Lula Divine, Clerk

142

The Payne County Bank

A General Banking Business Transacted

C. P. ROCK, PRESIDENT
J. A. HERT, VICE-PRESIDENT
C. W. KENWORTHY, CASHIER

R E C E I V E D

APR 11 1906

SAC & FOX AGENCY,
OKLAHOMA.

Perkins, Okla.   Apr. 10   190 6

W. C. Kohlenberg, Agt.

Sac and Fox Agcy O.T.

Dear Sir:-   I enclose you Letters of Guardianship, Jack Lincoln. When I signed the [illegible] lease I was not aware that Jack Lincoln was one of the heirs, as his name was not in the lease and had not heard his name mentioned in regard to it.

Yours truly
C.W. Kenworthy

Fred A. Wagoner,
Probate Judge.

R E C E I V E D

APR 11 1906

SAC & FOX AGENCY,
OKLAHOMA.

Chandler, Okla.   4/10/06.

Mr. W. C. Kohlenberg,
Sac & Fox Agency, Okla.

Dear Sir:-

Enclosed please find certificate showing Walter Battice to be the legal guardian of Stephen Harrison, Insane, per request of yourself.

Yours truly,

Fred A Wagoner
Probate Judge
per Lula.

[The letter below typed as given]

Special Attention to Rentals   *Room 5, over Shawnee National Bank*

S. C. Vinson
Real Estate Broker

RECEIVED

Shawnee, Okla. April 24,   1906

Miss Emma Nawashe,

Carlyle,

Pa.

Dear Emma:-

I received yours and Willies letters some time ago , and hope you will not get mad at me for not writing sooner , but I did not have time to look after what you wanted, In the next few dayes I will send a check there for you and Willie. I am glad to see that both of you are improveing so nicely in your writing. Improve your time . I saw Aunt Jane , and she said your uncle died some time ago. Dont fail to let Willie know you have heard from me. I will send the check as soon as the Court allows it. Am glad to hear from you often . Respectfully,   S.C. Vinson

****

[The letter below typed as given]

Special Attention to Rentals   *Room 5, over Shawnee National Bank*

S. C. Vinson
Real Estate Broker

RECEIVED

Shawnee, Okla. May 15th   1906

Miss Emma Nawawshe,

Carlyle,

Pa.

Dear Emma:-

I wrote you and Willie   a few dayes ago and told you that the Court has refused to appoint Kohlenburg[sic] as your guardian,   I sent you a check for $ 10.00 at the same time. I must know at once what you are going to do about signing the request I sent to have me retained . If you dont let me hear from you at once I will stop the payment on the checks I sent you. Advise me at once.

See Willie and let me know   S.C. Vinson
See Wille and let me know

REFER IN REPLY TO THE FOLLOWING: **R E C E I V E D**

Land.   **DEPARTMENT OF THE INTERIOR,** MAY 26 1905

Auth. 99, 411.   **OFFICE OF INDIAN AFFAIRS,**   SAC & FOX AGENCY,

WASHINGTON.   OKLAHOMA.

Ack.s 5/26/06 card

May 22, 1906.

The Superintendent

     in charge of Sac and Fox Agency,

          Oklahoma.

Sir:

     Referring to Office letter of March 22, last, advising you of Departmental letter of March 20, granting temporary authority for you to sign, as guardian, leases of allotted lands of minor Indians under your charge who have no guardians, you are advised that in accordance with Office recommendation the Secretary on the 19th instant granted authority for you to pay the money received upon such approved leases to the parents of the minors.

     Please acknowledge the receipt of this letter on the enclosed card.

          Very respectfully,

             C.F. Larrabee,

(J.L.D.) P.   Acting Commissioner.

SAMUEL SMITH, Probate Judge

O. C. LOWRY, Clerk

- OFFICE OF -

PROBATE JUDGE

RECEIVED
MAY 30 1906
SAC & FOX AGENCY,
OKLAHOMA.

PAYNE COUNTY

Stillwater, Oklahoma, May 30, 1906

W.C. Kohlenberg,
Sac and Fox Agency, Okla.

Dear Sir:-

On the 26th inst. John Foster filed his petition asking that he be appointed guardian for one Ben Hull, minor.   The application has been assigned for hearing on June 13th 1906 at 10 o'clock A.M. I am,

Yours very truly,

Samuel Smith
Probate Judge

****

SAMUEL SMITH, Probate Judge

O. C. LOWRY, Clerk

- OFFICE OF -

PROBATE JUDGE

RECEIVED
MAY 30 1906
SAC & FOX AGENCY,
OKLAHOMA.

PAYNE COUNTY

Stillwater, Oklahoma, June 4th, 1906

W. C. Kohlenberg,

Supt & Spl. Dis. Agt.

Sac and Fox Agency, Okla.

Dear Sir:-

In reply to yours of the 1st inst, relative to the application of John Foster for the appointment of himself as guardian for one Ben Hull, a minor Indian, beg to advise you that the records of this office show the following facts, to-wit: On the 17th day of August 1901 Mr. Foster filed his petition asking for the appointment of him-self as the Guardian of both Henry and Ben Hull, and attached to his application there is a letter signed by Lee Patrick as U. S. Indian Agent directing the Probate court to make said appointment and also stating that as indian[sic] agent his consent was all that was

146

necessary, and the Probate Judge acting under this direction and instruction, issued the order making the appointment as prayed for without giving of notice either personal or by posting, as by law required. Under the laws of this territory such an appointment is absolutely null and void and as a sale of lands has been had by virtue of the letters of guardianship issued at that time, they are now endeavoring to secure valid letters with the expectation of having another sale of said lands. I am

Yours very truly,

Samuel Smith
Probate Judge.

[The letter below typed as given]

Special Attention to Rentals

Room 5, over Shawnee National Bank

S. C. Vinson

RECEIVED
JUN 18 1906
SAC & FOX AGENCY,
OKLAHOMA.

Real Estate Broker

Shawnee, Okla.   June 6   1906

Mr William Naw-aw-she,
Carlyle,
Pa.

Dear Sir:-

  I was called away from home, and when I got back found your letter, with the request from you to the Probate Judge. Now that you have ask for me to be your guardian I expect to do the best I can for you. I will take it up with the Judge and [illegible] if I can get the $10^{00} you [illegible].

The Court would not appoint Kohlenberg as he did not like the way he acted in basing your land. He was getting $150^{00} for one track and you was only to get $120.^{00} I refused to base it through him and got you $150^{00}. If you can find his old letter I wish you would send it to me. Emma is not old enough to [illegible...] so the Court appointed me. I hope you are learning fast and when you come out of school, I want to see you make something of yourself.

  I want you to write the Probate Judge at Tecumseh and ask him to send me and order for $10^{00} for you tell him what you want with it. Write him a short nice letter and he will send me the order. Kolenburg has $1500^{00} of your and Emma money and if I had it I would put it out on interest for you, but or it is he is not doing any thing with it for you.

Will close for this time

Respectfully   S.C. Vinson

****

MAJOR W. A. MERCER. 11TH CAVALRY   JOHN R. WISE   W.G. THOMPSON
      SUPERINTENDENT   ASSISTANT SUPERINTENDENT   SUPERINTENDENT OF INDUSTRIES

DEPARTMENT OF THE INTERIOR
UNITED STATES INDIAN SERVICE
INDIAN INDUSTRIAL SCHOOL
CARLISLE. PA.

June 6, 1906.

RECEIVED

JUN 9 1906

SAC & FOX AGENCY.
OKLAHOMA.

Mr. W. C. Kohlenberg,

Supt. & Special Disbursing Agent,

Sac and Fox Agency, Okla.

Dear Sir:

Referring to my recent letter relative to the guardianship of Wm. and Emma Newashe, I inclose herewith three letters written by S. C. Vinson to Emma Newashe. These letters have just been brought to the office by William who says he received them from Emma who is at West Chester, Pa., under our outing, with a letter saying that she had not signed the letter which Mr. Vinson sent for her signature. As previously stated, we wrote to Emma about the matter but as yet have not received a reply.

Very respectfully,

W.A. Mercer
Major 11th Cavalry,

Superintendent.

AES

3 inclosures.

UNDER NEW MANAGEMENT.

RECEIVED
JUN 9 1906
& FOX AGENCY,
OKLAHOMA.

RATES $2.00, 2.50 PER DAY

The Elks

R. G. GREEN, Prop.

SAMPLE ROOMS

The most elegantly furnished
hotel in Oklahoma Territory.

GUTHRIE, O.T.,

June 7" 1906.

W. Kohlenberg, Esq.
    Sac & Fox Agency, Okla.

Sir:

In the examination of guardian's accounts in the Probate Court of Payne County it is learned that the matter as to what amount would be a reasonable charge for attorneys services, in connection with the sale of land belonging to minor heirs, under your Agency, was submitted to three leading attorneys of Stillwater. It seems that John Foster, guardian, demurred to attorney's fee charged by Roy Hoffman, as being excessive. The matter was referred to the Probate Judge for settlement & he in turn took the affidavits of these three attorneys as to what they considered a reasonable charge.

The amounts named by them were in excess of what Foster considered reasonable & he refused to pay the fees charged by Hoffman or those suggested by the aforesaid attorneys. This all happened in December, 1903, & it is reported that a record of this case was made in the Probate Court at the time. The present Probate Judge made a lengthy search for such record but was unable to find it. Hoffman & Foster finally compromised the matter of attorney's fees, Foster agreeing to pay $50\$^{00}$ fee in each land sale where there was but one minor heir, and $25\$^{00}$ fee in against each minor heir where there were two or more.

I am advised that you have knowledge of this incident. Can you throw any light on this matter? If you can, please advise the Colonel at Pawhuska, as we will return there in a few days.

149

Yours truly,

W. M. Plake

MAJOR W. A. MERCER, 11TH CAVALRY   JOHN R. WISE   W.G. THOMPSON
Superintendent   Assistant Superintendent   Superintendent of Industries

DEPARTMENT OF THE INTERIOR
UNITED STATES INDIAN SERVICE
INDIAN INDUSTRIAL SCHOOL
CARLISLE, PA.

June 13, 1906.

Mr. W. C. Kohlenberg,

    Supt. & Special Disbursing Agent,

        Sac and Fox Agency, Okla.

RECEIVED

JUN 18 1906

SAC & FOX AGENCY,
OKLAHOMA.

In connection with our correspondence with you regarding the guardianship of Emma and William Newashe I inclose herewith a letter dated the 6th instant from S. C. Vinson to William Newashe, which the latter brought to us recently. I thought it well that you should have the information therein contained in order that you may take such steps and make such representations to the court as you may see fit. You will note that he charges that you are getting $150 rent for the boy's land and he is being paid but $120. He states that he refused to lease the land through you and got $150. The boy would like to have a statement in reference to this matter.

Mr. Vinson also says that you have $1500 of the money of these children and William is very anxious to know whether this is correct and if so where the money is now deposited and what use is being made of it. Of course the same should be invested in some way so as to bring in a return if practicable.

Very respectfully,

W.A. Mercer
Major 11th Cavalry,
Superintendent.

JRW-S

1 incl.

SAMUEL SMITH, Probate Judge

O. C. LOWRY, Clerk

- OFFICE OF -

PROBATE JUDGE

PAYNE COUNTY

Stillwater, Oklahoma, June 15th 1906.

W. C. Kohlenberg,
    Supt. & Spl. Dis. Agent,
        Sac and Fox Agency, Okla.

Dear Sir:-

In re Guardianship of Silas Hawk, Stella Hawk, Laura Ellis and Maud Ka-ka-que, Indian minors;

On the 14th inst. the guardian's annual reports for the above named minors, were assigned for hearing on the 5th day of July 1906, at 10 o'clock A.M.

These reports were assigned for hearing for the purpose of requiring the guardian to report a reasonable rate of interest for wards' money in his possession.

Yours very truly,
Samuel Smith
Probate Judge.

A. D. Wright,

*Drugs, Paints, Oils, Glass, Wall Paper, Books, Stationery,
Toilet Articles, Etc.*

RECEIVED
JUN 27 1906
SAC & FOX AGENCY,
OKLAHOMA.

Chandler, Okla., June 26 *190*6

Hon. W. C. Kohlenberg,
    Supt. & Spl. Disb. Agent,
        Sac and Fox, O.T.

Dear Sir:-

I acknowledge receipt of your favors of June 23rd and 30th respectively regarding my wards Grover Morris and Harvey Madison. The latter date is doubtless an error of your stenographer. I have complied with your suggestion, turning down the claim of Madison except for $2.00 which I gave him for expense money, and I gave Grover Morris the $15.00.

Very truly,

A.D. Wright

Department of Justice.

—

Office of the United States Attorney.
District of Oklahoma.
Guthrie.

June 30, 1906.

W. C. Kohlenberg,

Supt. & Spl. Disb. Agent,

Sac & Fox, Oklahoma.

Sir:-

Your letter of recent date regarding the taking up of the Indian Guardianship matters has been referred to me by Mr. Scothorn

In the next few months I will be with you and we will take the matter up at that time.

Very respectfully,

Cassius R Peck
Assistant U.S. Attorney.

W. N. Maben,

Probate Judge

Pottawatomie County,

Tecumseh,   Oklahoma.

J. E. Simpson,
Probate Clerk
R E C E I V E D
JUL 5 1906
SAC & FOX AGENCY,
OKLAHOMA.

Tecumseh O.T.
July 3" 1906

Hon W.C. Kohlenberg

Sac & Fox Agency O.T.

Dear Sir:-

The appointment of [illegible] as guardian of the Nawashe minors has been made and your bond fixed at 500\frac{00}{}$

When you file the bond and same is approved letters of guardianship will be duly issued.

Sac & Fox – Shawnee
1892-1909   Volume XII

Yours truly
W.N. Maben
Probate Judge
****
[The above letter given again.]

[The letter below typed as given]

R E C E I V E D

JUL 14 1906

SAC & FOX AGENCY,
OKLAHOMA.
Otoe, Ok. Ty.
July 13/1906

Sac & Fox Agent.

Dear Sir,

Well I like to know about what you have done, Mr. Jensen the gardian I got him to seen for some money for my little girl but I never here from him yet. I know the girl need some of that money while she out of school, she need some cloths and something else the $ is the reason I have to write to you. Now please seen some to her to me I am the mother and I will get what she want because I have turn the guardianship papers to the Agent here because she need it. Now another thing, I seen my application for somethings I need by the Agent here, to seen it down there an I never here from you for long time. Their Indians here get theres back from Department inside 10 or 15 days. Now please when you get this letter, ans. soon and send the girl some money Please. That is all, Your Friend

Birdie Deroin   about $25.^{00}

W. N. Maben,

Probate Judge
Pottawatomie County,
Tecumseh,   Oklahoma.

J. E. Simpson,
Probate Clerk.

Tecumseh O T
July 13-1906

Hon W.C. Kohlenberg
Sac & Fox Agency O.T.

153

Dear Sir:-

Enclosed I return the application for the sale of my wards interest in certain lands which I trust is properly signed. If you need any certified copies of my app
ointment let me know and I will furnish you with such.

Yours truly

J.E. Simpson

John A. Bland
President

Cash Capital $ 1,500,000

Geo. R. Callis,
Secretary-Treasurer

T. M. UPSHAW,
GENERAL AGENT.

H. H. HOWARD,
ATTORNEY,

The United States Fidelity and Guaranty Company
Baltimore, Md.

Oklahoma City, Okla.   July 14, 1906.

Mr. M. W. Lynch,

Stroud, Okla.

Dear Sir,-

I have your favor of the 13th relative to rate on a bond for a minor indian[sic].

I herewith enclose an application which please have the guardian to fill out and return to me. The rate on this character of a bond is $5.00 per annum per thousand.

Yours very truly,

Enc.

T.M. Upshaw
General Agent

John R. Bland
President

Cash Capital $ 1,700,000

Geo. R. Callis.
Secretary-Treasurer

The United States Fidelity and Guaranty Company

RECEIVED
JUL 26 1906
SAC & FOX AGENCY,
OKLAHOMA.

Baltimore, Md.

T. M. UPSHAW,
GENERAL AGENT.

H. H. HOWARD,
ATTORNEY.

Oklahoma City, Okla.   July 21, 1906.

Mr. W. C. Kohlenberg,

     Sac and Fox Agency, Okla.

Dear Sir,-

     In compliance with your request of the 19th, I herewith enclose blank applications for guardian bonds.

     Thanking you for any business you may offer us, I remain,

     Yours very truly,

Enc.

     T.M. Upshaw
     General Agent

DEPARTMENT OF THE INTERIOR
UNITED STATES INDIAN SERVICE.

RECEIVED
JUL 26 1906
SAC & FOX AGENCY,
OKLAHOMA.

Sac and Fox School, Iowa.

Toledo, July 24, 1906.

Mr. W. C. Kohlenberg,

     Supt. & Spl. Disb. Agent,

     Sac and Fox Agency, Okla.

Sir:-

     I have the honor to herewith transmit, Petitions for the continuation of the trust period by the U. S. over certain allotted lands in Okla. for an additional ten years, signed by Allen G. Thurman, William,   Nancy, and Seba Davenport, (by his lagal[sic] guardian, S. C. Huber), but return thos prepared for Emma Hunter without signature, because of her refusal to sign the same. I visited her on two several

155

occasions at her home at the Indian Camp, and exhausted my persuasive powers in a vain attempt to induce her to place her signature to the said petitions, because I believed it to be for her best interests so to do, but a few guttural sounds uttered by an old retrogressive Indian, appeared to be more potent in controlling her action, than all of my arguments and eloquence combined.

Up to date, I have been unable to find any trace of To-Ne-Go-Ha, but will make further search and inquiry, and if unable to find her, will return the receipts to you. One of our people suggests the thought, that she is related to the Iowas, rather than the Sacs and Foxes, and is probably at the Great Nemaha Agency, Nebr.

Very respectfully,

W^m G Malin
Supt. & Spl. Disb. Agent.

No ....

COUNTY COURT.

County of Cleveland, Territory of Oklahoma.

In the Matter of the Guardianship of

John A. Myers

Minors.

Letters of Guardianship to Minors.

Frank A. Thackery

Guardian.

Filed _____ ~~July 30~~ _____ 190 _____

Probate Judge.

Record at page 474 of Record No 2
of Petitions - Bonds - [Illegible] and
Letters of Guardians

****

Letters of Guardianship of Minor.

TERRITORY OF OKLAHOMA. ⎫
⎬ ss.
CLEVELAND COUNTY. ⎭

The Territory of Oklahoma to all whom it may concern, and especially to _____

_____ Frank A. Thackery _____ Greeting: –

KNOW YE, THAT WHEREAS, Application has been made to the Probate Court of said County for the appointment of a guardian to

_____ John A. Myers _____ aged ___ 11 months _____ years,

_____ aged ___ —— _____ years,

_____ aged ___ —— _____ years,

_____ aged _____ years,

_____ aged _____ years,

_____ aged _____ years,

minor heirs of _____ Henry A. Myers _____ deceased, and it appearing to the

Court that it is necessary to appoint a guardian to said _____ ~~Frank A. Thackery~~ _____

___ John A. Myers _____

_____

_____

_____

_____

and the said _____ Frank A. Thackery _____

having been approved for said trust by the Court, and having given bond as required by law, which has been approved, filed and recorded in said Court:

NOW, THEREFORE, Trusting in your care and fidelity, we have appointed, and do by these presents appoint you, the said ____ Frank A. Thackery _____ as such guardian, hereby authorizing and empowering you to take and to have the custody ~~of said minor , and the care of education, and the~~ care and management of _his_ estate until _he_ arrive _s_ at the age of __21__ years or until you shall be discharged according to law.

And requiring you to make a true inventory of all the estate, real and personal, of the said ward ____ that shall come to your possession or knowledge, and to return the same into the Probate Court within three months from the date of these Letters, or at any other time the Court shall direct, to dispose of and manage all such estate according to law, and for the best interest of the ward ___, and faithfully to discharge your trust in relation thereto, and also when required, in relation to the care, custody and education of the ward___, to render an account on oath of the property, real and personal, of the said ward__ in your hands, and all proceeds and interests derived therefrom, and of the management and disposition of the same, within one year after your appointment, and annually thereafter, and at such other times as the proper court shall direct, and at the expiration of your trust to settle your account with the Probate Court, or with the ward__, if _he_ shall be of full age, or ___his___ legal representatives. And to pay over and deliver all the property, real and personal, remaining in your hands or due from you on such settlement to the person lawfully entitled thereto.

IN TESTIMONY WHEREOF, we have caused the seral of our said Probate Court to be hereunto affixed.

WITNESS, _____ N.E. Sharp _____

Judge of our said Court, at _____ Norman _____ in said County, this __30___day of _____ July _____ A.D., 190_6_.

_____ N.E. Sharp _____
Probate Judge.

Department of Justice.

Office of the United States Attorney.
District of Oklahoma.
Guthrie.

August 3, 1906.

W. C. Kohlenberg,

Supt. & Spl. Disb. Agent,

Sac & Fox Agency, Oklahoma.

Sir:-

I am advised that some of the guardians of the Sac & Fox and Iowa Indian minors contemplate filing their final accounts in Payne and Lincoln Counties, asking their discharge as guardians. In such event we shall ask your appointment as guardian of such minors. Gen. Section 1542, 1423, 1346 and 1345, of the statutes of Oklahoma, 1893, when combined and construed together, seem to provide the only rule for notices in the hearing of the final accounts of guardians. It is my opinion that these sections require that, upon filing the final accounts, the court should make an order fixing a date of hearing not later than four nor more than ten weeks from the date of such orders; that notices should be given to the minors and all persons interested, either by publication for four successive weeks in a news paper or by notice served personally at least ten days before the date of hearing. Of course, should the minor and persons interested sign a written assent that the accounts should be heard on some certain date the notices would not be necessary.

To publish these notices in the news paper for four weeks would cost too much; and I thought that you would be able to cause some one to serve these notices personally at a very light expense.

Where the children are away at school the notices could be sent to the principal of the school and served by him and he could make his return by affidavit written on the notices.

Where the Indians are in Payne or Lincoln County I think a man could find them without much difficulty, make service and attach his affidavit to the notice showing such service.

I make these suggestions to you with a view of getting your idea as to the best and cheapest way to close up these guardianship matters. Please write me fully. I wish you would send me a full list of the minors, with the names of their guardians.

Very respectfully,

John Embry
U.S. Attorney.

****

Department of Justice.

Office of the United States Attorney.
District of Oklahoma.
Guthrie.

RECEIVED
AUG 6 1906,
SAC & FOX AGENCY,
OKLAHOMA.

August 4, 1906.

W. C. Kohlenberg,

Supt. & Spl. Disb. Agent,

Sac & Fox Agency, Oklahoma.

Dear Sir:-

Inclosed herewith you will find notice of settlement of Wright and McGaughey guardians of minor Indians belonging to your Agency. I received these notices this morning. I wrote you yesterday explaining service of the notices. In each of these cases I desire you to make out your petition for the appointment of your-self as guardian and send the petitions along with the notices so the minors of 14 years or over may sign a nomination. You can get blanks at Chandler at the Probate Judges[sic] office for making out these petitions. The blanks indicate what they sould[sic] and you will have no difficulty in making out the petitions. Where the minor is a much as 14 years old you will write on the back of the petition these words, "I hereby nominate W.C. Kohlenberg as my guardian" and have the Indian ward sign this. Minors over 14 years of age have a right to nominate their own guardians and this written on the back of the petition and signed by the minor would satisfy that provision of law.

I will assign an assistant U.S. Attorney to aid you just as soon as I can. I find an accumulation of work in the office and I will give you the help of one man just as soon as I can get to it, possibly, some time next week.

Very respectfully,

John Embry
Inclosure: U.S. Attorney.

IN PROBATE COURT

COUNTY OF POTTAWATOMIE.

In the matter of the Guarnianship of the Person
and Estate of

Mah-mah-to-me-ah

an Incompetent person

Minors.

LETTERS OF GUARDIANSHIP OF MINORS.

Filed . . . . 190 . . .

Judge of the Probate Court

****

161

[Copy of Original]

Letters of Guardianship of Minors.

Territory of Oklahoma, Pottawatomie County. S. S.

THE TERRITORY OF OKLAHOMA, To all whom it may concern, and especially to ....

...........................Frank A. Thackery........................ GREETING:

KNOW YE, THAT WHEREAS, Application has been made to the Probate Court of said County for the appointment of a Guardian to

Mah-Mah-to-me-ah ...... aged ..... Incompetent .... years,

.... aged... years,

.... aged... years,

.... aged... years,

.... aged... years,

.... aged... years,

minor heirs of.. deceased, and it appearing to the Court that it is necessary

to appoint a guardian to said Mah-Mah-to-me-ah. Incompetent ....

....

....

....

....

....

and the said ...... Frank A. Thackery ....

having been approved for said trust by the Court and having given bond as required by law, which has been approved, filed and recorded in said Court:

NOW, THEREFORE, Trusting in your care and fidelity, we have appointed, and do by these presents appoint you, the said

...... Frank A. Thackery ...., as such guardian, hereby authorizing and empowering you to take and to have the custody of said minor incompetent and the care of his education and the care and management of his estate until .... arrive at the age of........ ....or until you shall be discharged according to law.

And requiring you to make a true inventory of all the estate, real and personal, of the said ward....that shall come to your possession or knowledge, and to return the same into the Probate Court within three months from the date of these letters, or at any other time the Court shall direct, to dispose of and manage all such estate according to law, and for the best interest of the ward...., and faithfully to discharge your trust in relation thereto, and also when required, in relation to the care, custody and education of ward...., to render an account on oath of the property, real and personal, of the said ward.... in your hands, and all proceeds and interest derived therefrom, and of the management and disposition of the same, within one year after your appointment, and annually thereafter, and at such other times as the proper Court shall direct, and at the expiration of your trust to settle your account with the Probate Court, or with the ward...., if............ shall be of full age, or ....legal representatives. And to pay over and deliver all the property, real and personal, remaining in your hands or due from you on such settlement to the person lawfully entitled thereto.

IN TESTIMONY WHEREOF, We have caused the seal of our said Probate Court to be hereto affixed.

WITNESS W. H. Mabee .... , Judge of our said Court, at Tecumseh, in said County,

this 14th day of ...... August ....189 6.

W. H. Mabee Probate Judge
W. H. Mabee Probate Judge

Filed Aug 14 6.

[The letter below typed as given]

Fred A. Wagoner,
Probate Judge.

RECEIVED
AUG 15 1906
SAC & FOX AGENCY,
OKLAHOMA.

Chandler, Oklahoma.   Aug 14th 1906.

Hon W C Kohlenberg.
        Cac[sic] and Fox Agency.
Dear Sir.

Your letter of recent date found on my desk upon my return from Illinois, and in answer will say: That I am sending you under seperate cover 20 blank petition for the appointment of guardian.

You ask that I send my bill for these petition, we make no charges fo for the petitions, but they are charged as costs in each case.

I find that in several of these Indian cases that the guardian has no not handled any money and that there are some court costs which has not b been paid. I think Judge Cordell has costs in several cases of that character, and I have a few.

I wish you would take that matter up with the department so that these old matters can all be closed up at the time we make the change of guardians.

It is also necessary that all of the old guardians make and file with me their re[ort, before they are discharged.

Please excuse the delay in sending you the blank petitions.

Yours truly.

Fred A Wagoner

IN PROBATE COURT

COUNTY OF POTTAWATOMIE.

In the matter of the Guarnianship of the Person
and Estate of

Gertrude,[sic] Elephant, and
Henry Elephant.

Minors.

LETTERS OF GUARDIANSHIP OF MINORS.

Filed ... August 14". 1906 .. .. 190 ....

Judge of the Probate Court.

-- COPY --

Exhibit "D"

Letters of Guardianship of Minors.

Territory of Oklahoma, Pottawatomie County, S.S.)--- COPY ---

THE TERRITORY OF OKLAHOMA, To all whom it may concern, and especially to _____

_____ Frank A. Thackery, _____ GREETING:

KNOW YE, THAT WHEREAS, Application has been made to the Probate Court of said County for the appointment of

a Guardian to _____ Gertrude Elephant, _____ aged __16-__ _____ years,

and _____ Henry Elephant, _____ aged __18-__ _____ years,

_____ aged _____ years,

_____ aged _____ years,

_____ aged _____ years,

minor heirs of _____ Elephant _____ deceased, and it appearing to the Court that it is necessary

to appoint a guardian to said _____ minor heirs, _____

_____

_____

_____

_____

and the said _____ Frank A. Thackery, _____

having been approved for said trust by the Court and having given bond as required by law, which has been approved,

filed and recorded in said Court:

NOW, THEREFORE, Trusting in your care and fidelity, we have appointed, and do by these presents appoint you,

the said _____ Frank A. Thackery, _____ as such guardian, hereby authorizing and empowering you to

take and to have the custody of said minor___ and the care of _them_[sic] education and the care and management of

their estate until _they_ arrive at the age of _Majority_ or until you shall be discharged according to law.

And requiring you to make a true inventory of all the estate, real and personal, of the said ward____ that shall come
to your possession or knowledge, and to return the same into the Probate Court within three months from the date of
these letters, or at any other time the Court shall direct, to dispose of and manage all such estate according to law, and
for the best interest of the ward____, and faithfully to discharge your trust in relation thereto, and also when required,
in relation to the care, custody and education of ward____ to render an account on oath of the property, real and
personal, of the said ward____ in your hands, and all proceeds and interest derived therefrom, and of the management
and disposition of the same, within one year after your appointment, and annually thereafter, and at such other times as
the proper Court shall direct, and at the expiration of your trust to settle your account with the Probate Court, or with
the ward___, if _they_ shall be of full age, or _their_ legal representatives. And to pay over and deliver all the
property, real and personal, remaining in your hands or due from you on such settlement to the person lawfully entitled
thereto.

IN TESTIMONY WHEREOF, We have caused the seal of our said Probate Court to be hereto affixed.

WITNESS, _____ W. N. Maben, _____ Judge of our said Court, at Tecumseh, in said County,

this __14"__ day of __August____ 190 6

Seal.
_____ W. N. Maben, _____ Probate Judge

Filed _August 14"_ 190 6
_____ W. N. Maben, _____ Probate Judge

Territory of Oklahoma, Pottawatomie County, S.S.

I, J. E. Simpson, Clerk of the Probate Court within and for said County and Territory aforesaid, do hereby certify that the instrument hereto attached is a full, true and correct copy of Letters of guardianship issued to Frank A. Thackery, as guardian of Gertrude and Henry, ~~is the duly appointed, qualified and acting Guardian of the estate of~~

Elephant minors.

as the same now appears of record in my office.

Witness my hand and official seal of said Court this 28" day of May 1907. A.D. 190

J. E. Simpson
Clerk of the Probate Court.

IN PROBATE COURT

COUNTY OF POTTAWATOMIE.

In the matter of the Guardianship of the Person and Estate of

Pe-can,

Minor.

LETTERS OF GUARDIANSHIP OF MINORS.

Filed September 25" 1906. 190

W. N. Maben,
Judge of the Probate Court.

--- COPY ---

Exhibit "C"

Letters of Guardianship of Minors.

Territory of Oklahoma, Pottawatomie County, S.S. --- COPY ---

THE TERRITORY OF OKLAHOMA, To all whom it may concern, and especially to _____

_____ Frank A. Thackery, _____ GREETING:

KNOW YE, THAT WHEREAS, Application has been made to the Probate Court of said County for the appointment of

a Guardian to _____ Pe-can, _____ aged _____ years,

_____ aged _____ years,

_____ aged _____ years,

_____ aged _____ years,

_____ aged _____ years,

minor heirs of _____ deceased, and it appearing to the Court that it is necessary

to appoint a guardian to said _____ Pe-can   a minor _____

_____

_____

_____

_____

and the said _____ Frank A. Thackery, _____

having been approved for said trust by the Court and having given bond as required by law, which has been approved,

filed and recorded in said Court:

NOW, THEREFORE, Trusting in your care and fidelity, we have appointed, and do by these presents appoint you,

the said _____ Frank A. Thackery, _____ as such guardian, hereby authorizing and empowering you to

take and to have the custody of said minor ___ and the care of his ___ education and the care and management of

his ___ estate until he ___ arrive at the age of majority ___ or until you shall be discharged according to law.

And requiring you to make a true inventory of all the estate, real and personal, of the said ward ____ that shall come to your possession or knowledge, and to return the same into the Probate Court within three months from the date of these letters, or at any other time the Court shall direct, to dispose of and manage all such estate according to law, and for the best interest of the ward ____, and faithfully to discharge your trust in relation thereto, and also when required, in relation to the care, custody and education of ward _____ to render an account on oath of the property, real and personal, of the said ward ____ in your hands, and all proceeds and interest derived therefrom, and of the management and disposition of the same, within one year after your appointment, and annually thereafter, and at such other times as the proper Court shall direct, and at the expiration of your trust to settle your account with the Probate Court, or with the ward ___, if he ___ shall be of full age, or his ___ legal representatives. And to pay over and deliver all the property, real and personal, remaining in your hands or due from you on such settlement to the person lawfully entitled thereto.

IN TESTIMONY WHEREOF, We have caused the seal of our said Probate Court to be hereto affixed.

WITNESS, _____ W. N. Maben, _____ Judge of our said Court, at Tecumseh, in said County,

this 25" day of September 1906. 190

_____ W.N. Maben, _____ Probate Judge

September 25" 1906
Filed _____ 190

_____ W. N. Maben, _____ Probate Judge

(seal).

Territory of Oklahoma, Pottawatomie County, S.S. --- COPY ---

I, J. E. Simpson, Clerk of the Probate Court within and for said County and Territory aforesaid, do hereby certify

that ___ the instrument hereto attached is a full, true and correct copy of Letters of guardianship issued to Frank A. Thackery, as guardian ~~is the duly appointed, qualified and acting Guardian of the estate of~~ _____

__of Pe-can, __a minor_____

as the same now appears of record in my office.

Witness my hand and official seal of said Court this_S_28"__day of___May___1907.____ A.D. 190___

Tecumseh Oklahoma.

(seal).

_____J. E. Simpson_____
Clerk of the Probate Court.

SAMUEL SMITH, Probate Judge   O. C. LOWRY, Clerk

- OFFICE OF -

PROBATE JUDGE

RECEIVED
AUG 18 1906
SAC & FOX AGENCY,
OKLAHOMA.

PAYNE COUNTY

Stillwater, Oklahoma, Aug. 17, 1906.

W. C. Kohlenberg,

Supt. & Spl. Dis. Ag't.

Sac & Fox agency[sic], Okla.

Dear Sir:-

I have recently noticed in two or three of the Territorial papers statements to the effect that the department had requested the resignation[sic] of all guardians of indian[sic] minors, and that they were settling the accounts just as rapidly as possible.

Will you kindly advise me as to whether or not such a ruling has been made and oblige.

Yours very truly,

Samuel Smith
Probate Judge.

THE COLUMBIA BANK AND TRUST CO.

C.R.BROOKS, President.
C.J.PRATT, Vice President.
S.F.SWINFORD, Vice President.
W.E.HODGES, Secy & Treas.
A.J.M^cMAHAN, Asst. Secy.

CAPITAL $200,000.00

OKLAHOMA CITY, OKLA.

RECEIVED
AUG 20 1906
SAC & FOX AGENCY,
OKLAHOMA.

Aug. 18th, 1906

Supt. & Den 'l[sic] Dis. Agent,

Sac and Fox Agency,

Sac & Fox, Okla.

Dear Sir:-

Your letter of the 17th inst., relative to Guardianship bond at hand. Yes, the Territory accepts our bonds as it has authorized us to make bond of this class and all others, as you will see by the Certificate of the Territorial Treasurer enclosed. I also enclose to you a blank application to be made by Guardians, but I would suggest that you had probably better correspond with the District Attorneys office relative to this matter, as that office had the ⬛ter[sic] up with us, and partially arranged with this Company to make guardianship bonds for all the agents in the Territory, but recently notified us that they had made other arrangements, and I feel sure that this applies to all the agents, yourself included. I suppose they succeeded in getting some individual to make the bonds at less rate than we could afford to make them. However we will make your bonds for you if you desire.

Respectfully,

C.R. Brooks
President.

****

Territory of Oklahoma, :
           : ss.   C E R T I F I C A T E .
County of Logan. :

I, C. W. Rambo, Territorial Treasurer of the Territory of Oklahoma, do hereby certify that the COLUMBIA BANK AND TRUST COMPANY, a corporation of Oklahoma City, Oklahoma Territory, has fully complied with the laws of this Territory relative to the organization of savings and trust companies in this Territory, and pursuant to the requirements thereof has duly deposited with me, as Treasurer of the Territory of Oklahoma, securities and money in the aggregate sum of Fifty Thousand ($50,000.00) Dollars, and

That the said The Columbia Bank and Trust Company is now authorized, under the laws of this Territory and permitted to qualify as guardian, executor, administrator, assignee, receiver and trustee either by deed, will or judicial appointment, without giving bond as such, or to become sole guarantor or surety in or upon any bond required to be given under the laws of this Territory, and to insure the fidelity of persons holding places of public or private trust.

IN WITNESS WHEREOF, I have hereunto set my hand at Guthrie, Oklahoma, this the __8th__ day of November, 1905.

___C. W. RAMBO._____
Territorial Treasurer of the Territory
of Oklahoma.

I, C. W. Rambo, Treasurer of Oklahoma Territory, do hereby certify that the above is a true and perfect copy of the certificate issued by me as such Treasurer, to the Columbia Bank and Trust Company of Oklahoma City, Oklahoma, on the 8th day of November, 1905.

Dated this___22___day of November, 1905.

___C.W. Rambo_____

TRIPLICATE

CASH.

Voucher No. _____1_____

FOR

TRAVELING EXPENSES

_____Second_____ Quarter, 190 7

_____W. C. Kohlenberg,_____

$ 1.75 _____

Paid in _____ or by Check No. 481440

Dated October 5, 1906;

DRAWN ON

Assistant Treasurer, U. S., St. Louis, Mo.

IN FAVOR OF

_____W. C. Kohlenberg,_____

State whether paid in cash or by check; if by check, give the number and date of the check and the name of the bank or institution upon which and in whose favor it is drawn.

(VOUCHER FOR ..... Traveling Expenses .....)

The United States.

To   W. C. Kohlenberg,   Dr.

DATE 1906.		Sub-voucher.	DOLLARS.	Cts.
Aug. 23	R. R. fare on train from Stroud, O.T. to			
	Chandler, O. T.			50
Aug. 23	Dinner at Chandler, O. T.			25
Aug. 23	R. R. fare from Chandler O. T. to Stroud, O. T.			50
Aug. 23	Supper			50
			$ 1	75

NOTE 1:- Above expense incurred in making a trip to
Chandler, O. T., with the Asst. U. S. Attorney
in looking after guardianship matters.

NOTE 2:- No vouchers are attached for the reason that
that I had no blanks with me at the time.

RECEIVED at .. Sac and Fox Agency, Oklahoma, ... October 5, ..., 190 6

of .... W. C. Kohlenberg, ... Supt. & Spl. Disb. Agt. .... , U. S. Indian Agent,

...... One and 75/100 ($1.75) .... dollars in full of the above account.

...... W.C. Kohlenberg ....

I solemnly swear that the foregoing account is correct and just; * that the different charges in detail have been taken from and verified by my memorandum; that the amount charged was actually paid; that no part of the journey charged for has been made under any free pass on any railway, steamboat, or other public conveyance; that the number of days for which the same is charged was necessarily consumed in unavoidable delays incident to travel, and the performance of the duty ordered or services rendered; that the journey was performed by the shortest usually traveled routes under orders *(copy annexed)* or for the purpose

of .... See note 1 above ....

.............................; and that I have this ... 23rd ... day of ..... August ...., 190 6

actually paid the amount thereof, viz: ... One and 75/100 ($1.75) ....

dollars, and have taken claimant's receipt therefor in triplicate.

...... W.C. Kohlenberg ....

U. S. Indian Agent.

Sworn to and subscribed before me this ..... 28" ... day of .... August ...., 190 6

...... Harry L. Elmslee ....

My Commission expires 10-11-08   ...... Notary Public ....

WM. P. HARPER, JUDGE
E. M. HUSBY, CLERK
INEZ MINSHALL, STENOGRAPHER

G. W. GARRISON, SHERIFF
W. F. JONES, BAILIFF

Probate Court
OKLAHOMA COUNTY, OKLAHOMA

OKLAHOMA CITY, August 24, 1906

Hon. Frank A. Thackery,

Indian Agent,

Shawnee, Oklahoma.

Dear Sir.-   Nothing was done in the Indian guardianship matters on the 20th inst. and I have this morning made orders re-setting them for hearing on the 4th of September at nine o'clock A.M.

Would be glad if you would come up at that time so am not to incur further expense in giving new notices.

Yours truly,

Wm P Harper

The State National Bank

WILLARD JOHNSTON, PRES'T
GEO E M°KINNIS, VICE PRES'T
C M CADE, CASHIER
C R JOHNSON, ASS'T CASH'R

CAPITAL STOCK $100 000

SHAWNEE, OKLA.

Aug. 25th, 1906.

Hon. Frank A. Thackery, Agent,

Shawnee, O. T.

Dear Sir,--

My Attorney advises me that it is necessary for me to collect all the money due me as guardian for all lands sold by me for Edward and Bertha Fox, Mary Lewis, John Lewis, Hattie or Che-wa-nee Lewis, and Leo Starr before I can make my final report, and get released.

I will ask that you kindly make a settlement with me as guardian in these cases so I can make a final settlemtn[sic] and get a discharge.

Yours very truly,

Willard Johnston

Legal Guardian

For Edward Fox
Mary Lewis
John   "
Hattie   "
Leo Starr

Department of Justice.

Office of the United States Attorney.
District of Oklahoma.
Guthrie.

August 29, 1906.

Frank A. Thackery,

Supt. & Spl. Disb. Agent,

Shawnee, Oklahoma.

Dear Sir:-

I return herewith Mr. Johnston's letter. You will not pay Mr. Johnston any more money. We are asking him to account for what he has received and will make him no further payments. I think your reply to him was along the right line.

Very respectfully,

John Embry

Inclosure: U.S. Attorney

C O P Y .

Finance   DEPARTMENT OF THE INTERIOR,

71371/1906

71759/06   Office of Indian Affairs,

Auth./ 101154

3 Encls.   Washington.   August 30, 1906.

Superintendent,

    Sac and Fox School, Oklahoma.

  Sir:

     Authority has been granted for you to settle an indebtedness amounting to $27.31, incurred during the first quarter, 1907[sic], for traveling and incidental expenses on official business, and for telephoning; as requested and for the reasons stated in your letters of the 13th and 15th instant, and evidenced by the vouchers herewith returned for completion and file with your accounts.

     Very respectfully,

     Signed   F. E. Leupp,

CFCK.   Commissioner.

DEPARTMENT OF THE INTERIOR

UNITED STATES INDIAN SERVICE

RECEIVED
SEP 19 1906
SAC & FOX AGENCY,
OKLAHOMA.

    Sac and Fox Agency, Oklahoma,

     Sept. 3, 1906.

Hon. G.L. Williams, Supt.,

    Hoyt, Kansas.

Dear sir:

     Inclosed please find a number of notices of final settlement of Lee Patrick, legal guardian of Wishteyah Lemont, one of your Indians.   Mr. Patrick was appointed at the request and on the petition of Wishteyah in order that he might dispose of his inherited land under the jurisdiction of this agency, quickly, and he has never been discharged. Nor, have the costs been paid. Will you kindly have copies served on wishteyah[sic], and his next of kin, (his heirs in case of his death) and make your return on the copy containing the affidavit. When notices have been served please return the copy containing affidavit so it may be filed with the court. Also ask Wishteyah about the court costs, which should be paid, or the guardian can be held for them.

Very respectfully,

W.C. Kohlenberg

W CK   Supt. & Spl. Disb. Agt.

Please send me the amount of court costs due-
Respt
[illegible] 17/06   G.L. Williams

Department of Justice.

Office of the United States Attorney.
District of Oklahoma.
Guthrie.

September 4, 1906.

Frank A. Thackery

    Supt. & Spl. Disb. Agent,

        Shawnee, Oklahoma.

Sir:-

Inclosed I hand you application for citation in the matter of the guardianship of Chuck-e-shin-ah-wa and also in the case of the guardianship of Wah-pe-puck-e. If Mr. Johnston has not filed his report I wish you would sign these applications and have them filed by the Probate Court and ask him to issue a citation requiring Johnston to appear on the 24th day of September and show cause why he should not file his report and why he should not be removed.

I will prepare the citations in the other cases as rapidly as I can. On account of some Supreme Court work I have been unable to prepare any except the two submitted.

I had a talk with Mr. Johnston on the train and he promised that he would file his reports but he has changed his mind so many times about it

176

that I have no confidence in him. If his reports have been filed we do not want the citations filed but will take the matter up with the Court and show why he should be charged interest and with other money that he has failed to account for.

I presume Mr. Outcelt has arranged to continue the hearing of Rose's reports until week after next.

I would be very glad to know as to how you got along with the guardianship cases at Sacred Heart, and also whether Riley and Bryon have filed their reports yet.

It is altogether probable that I will be down the last of the week, at any rate I will be there about the middle of next week.

Very respectfully

Inclosure.   J.W. Scothom

Asst. U.S. Attorney.

TRIPLICATE

CASH.

Voucher No. ____16____

FOR

TRAVELING EXPENSES

____First____ Quarter, 190 7

W. C. KOHLENBERG
...... *Supt. & Spl. Dis. Agt.* ....

$17\46

Paid in .... or by Check No. 481367
Dated Sept. 5ᵗʰ 1906
DRAWN ON

Assistant Treasurer U. S.,
St. Louis, Missouri

IN FAVOR OF

W. C. KOHLENBERG

State whether paid in cash or by check; if by check, give the
number and date of the check and the name of the bank or
institution upon which and in whose favor it is drawn.

****

The United States.

To   W. C. Kohlenberg, ... , Dr.

DATE		Sub-voucher.	DOLLARS.	Cts.
1906				
Aug. 9	R. R. Fare, Davenport to Cushing, O. T.	1		60
10	Hotel,- meals and lodging	2	3	50
10	Feeding Team, dinner and supper			60
11	Hire of team	3	2	00
11	Supper Aug. 10, lodging and breakfast Aug. 11		1	00
11	Telephone to Agency from Cushing,			25
12	Meals and lodging	4	2	00
12	Bus from hotel to depot			25
12	R. R. fare, Cushing to Tyron, O.T.,	5		50
12	Hire of team $1.50, dinner 25¢	6	1	75
12	R. R. fare from Tyron to Fallis, O.T.	7		41
12	Bus fare from depot to hotel			25
13	Meals and lodging	8	1	25

13	Hire of team	9	1 $\underline{00}$
13	Telephone from Fallis O.T. to Agency,		25
13	R. R. Fare from Fallis to Luther O.T.	10	23
13	Supper		50
13	R. R. fare, from Luther to Stroud, O. T.,	11	1 10
	Carried Forward		$ 17 46
	Seventeen and 46/100 ($17.46) Dollars		

****

(VOUCHER FOR ......Traveling expense......)

𝔗𝔥𝔢 𝔘𝔫𝔦𝔱𝔢𝔡 𝔖𝔱𝔞𝔱𝔢𝔰.

𝒯ₒ W. C. Kohlenberg, Supt. & Spl. Disb. Agent , 𝒟𝓇.

DATE		Sub-voucher.	DOLLARS.	Cts.
1906				
August	To Amount brought forward		$ 17	46
	Looking after leases; location of Public			
	Highways; serving notice of final settlement of			
	guardians on minors and their next of kin prepa-			
	ratory to turning such guardianships over to			
	Superintendent.			

RECEIVED at ___Sac and Fox Agency, Oklahoma,_____September 5th_____, 190_6

of_____W. C. Kohlenberg,_____Supt. & Spl. Disb. Agt._____, U. S. Indian Agent,

_____Seventeen and 46/100 ($17.46)_____dollars in full of the above account.

___W.C. Kohlenberg_____

I solemnly swear that the foregoing account is correct and just; * that the different charges in detail have been taken from and verified by my memorandum; that the amount charged was actually paid; that no part of the journey charged for has been made under any free pass on any railway, steamboat, or other public conveyance; that the number of days for which the same is charged was necessarily consumed in unavoidable delays incident to travel, and the performance of the duty ordered or services rendered; that the journey was performed by the shortest usually traveled routes under orders *(copy annexed)* or for the purpose

of_____See note above_____

_____; and that I have this____5th____ day of___September_____, 190_6

actually paid the amount thereof, viz:____Seventeen and 46/100 ($17.46)_____

dollars, and have taken claimant's receipt therefor in triplicate.

___W.C. Kohlenberg_____
Supt. & Spl. Disb. Agt U. S. Indian Agent.

Sworn to and subscribed before me this_____14th____ day of_____August_____, 190 6

____Harry L. Elmslee_____

My Commission expires 10-11-08.   ____Notary Public_____

REFER IN REPLY TO THE FOLLOWING:

RECEIVED

Land.   **DEPARTMENT OF THE INTERIOR,** SEP 24 1906
77468-1906.   **OFFICE OF INDIAN AFFAIRS,**   SAC & FOX AGENCY,
                              WASHINGTON.   OKLAHOMA.

September 20, 1906.

The Superintendent,

    In charge of Sac and Fox Agency,

        Oklahoma.

Sir:

    The Department on September 5, 1906, referred to this Office a letter dated August 29, 1906, from the Acting Attorney General, enclosing a copy of a letter of August 27, 1906, from Mr. John Embry, United States Attorney at Guthrie, saying that Assistant United States Attorney Outcelt had taken up the matter of Indian guardianships in Lincoln County, Oklahoma, and that a number of cases had been set for hearing about September 24, 1906. The Acting Attorney

General suggested that the Superintendent in charge of the Agency be directed to be present.

You are therefore requested to attend the hearing in these cases and aid the Assistant United States Attorney in the examination of the accounts of the legal guardians of Indians under your charge, in order to secure the resignation of said guardians and the appointment of yourself in their stead.

Very respectfully,

CF Larrabee

TBW.Ph.   Acting Commissioner.

DEPARTMENT OF THE INTERIOR,

Finance
78719/1906   Office of Indian Affairs,
Auth. 101492
1 enc.   Washington.   September 22, 1906

The Superintendent,

     Sac and Fox School,

         Oklahoma.

Sir:

Authority has been granted for you to settle an indebtedness amounting to $24.32, incurred during the current quarter for traveling expenses on official business; as requested and for the reasons stated in your letter of the 7th instant and evidenced by the voucher herewith returned for file with your accounts.

Very respectfully,

(Signed)   Frank M. Conser,

DTG.   Chief Clerk.

Department of Justice.

————

Office of the United States Attorney.
District of Oklahoma.
Guthrie.

September 22, 1906.

W.C. Kohlenberg, Esq.,

    Supt. & Spl. Disb. Agent,

        Sac & Fox Agency, Oklahoma.

Sir:-

I have the honor to acknowledge receipt of yours of the 17th instant, giving me the address of Mr. Wm. E. Johnson; and of your letter of the same date transmitting statements of the accounts of the following named legal guardians appointed by the Probate Court of Pottawatomie County, Oklahoma:

> Henry Jones, guardian of Ellen Easley Jones,
> Geo. L. Rose, guardian of George O. Morton,
> Milton Bryan, guardian of Dickson Duncan, and
> Allen G. Thurman,
> Milton Bryan, guardian of Bertha and Addie Pattequa,
> Milton Bryan, guardian of Ida Miller,
> Hiram Holt, guardian of Mary Thorp, Adeline Thorp,
> Edward Thorp, James Thorp
> L.T. Sammons, guardian of Etta Shaw,
> S.S. Rains, guardian of Mamie Morton,
> Geo. L. Rose, guardian of Clifford Morton,

These statements will be referred to Mr. John W. Scothorn[sic], Assistant U.S. Attorney, for his information in the adjustment of these accounts.

Very respectfully,

John Embry

U.S. Attorney.

TRIPLICATE

CASH.

Voucher No. ____27____

FOR

TRAVELING EXPENSES

____First____Quarter, 190 7

W. C. KOHLENBERG

$ 24\32

Paid in _____ or by Check No. 481398

dated Sept 27, 1906

DRAWN ON

Assistant Treasurer U. S.,
St. Louis, Missouri

IN FAVOR OF

W. C. KOHLENBERG

State whether paid in cash or by check; if by check, give the
number and date of the check and the name of the bank or
institution upon which and in whose favor it is drawn.

****

(VOUCHER FOR ___Traveling Expense___ *)*

The United States,

To ___W. C. Kohlenberg,_____, **Dr.**

DATE 1906.		Sub-voucher.	DOLLARS.	Cts.
August 28	Transportation, Davenport to Stillwater, O.T.	1	2	42
August 28,	Telephone from Stillwater to Perkins, O.T.			15
August 30,	Meals and lodging.	2	7	00
August 30,	Bus fare from hotel to depot			25
August 30,	R.R. transportation Stillwater to Perkins, O.T.	3	1	22
August 30,	Livery hire.	4	1	75
August 30,	Dinner for self and stenographer	5	1	00
August 30,	R. R. transportation from Perkins to Shawnee, O.T.	6	4	00
August 31,	Meals and lodging	7	3	00
August 31,	Interurban care-fare from Shawnee to Tecumseh and return for self and stenographer @ .30¢ each			60
August 31,	Telephone to Agency from Davenport, O.T.			15
August 31,	Dinner for self and stenographer, @ .50¢ each	8	1	00
August 31,	R.R. transportation from Shawnee to Davenport	9	1	78
			$ 24	32

Note:- Visiting Stillwater, County seat, Payne Co., to examine guardianship accounts; Visiting Perkins to serve notice in guardianship matters, and visiting Shawnee and Tecumseh to examine guardianship accounts.

RECEIVED at ___Sac and Fox Agency,_____ September 25th _____, 190 6

of _____W. C. Kohlenberg,_____ Supt. & Spl. Disb. Agt._____, U. S. Indian Agent,

____Twenty four and 32/100 ($24.32)_____ dollars in full of the above account.

___W.C. Kohlenberg_____

I solemnly swear that the foregoing account is correct and just; * that the different charges in detail have been taken from and verified by my memorandum; that the amount charged was actually paid; that no part of the journey charged for has been made under any free pass on any railway, steamboat, or other public conveyance; that the number of days for which the same is charged was necessarily consumed in unavoidable delays incident to travel, and the performance of the duty ordered or services rendered; that the journey was performed by the shortest usually traveled routes under orders *(copy annexed)* or for the purpose of

_____See note above_____

_____; and that I have this 25th day of ____September_____, 190 6

actually paid the amount thereof, viz: ___Twenty four and 32/100 ($24.32)_____

dollars, and have taken claimant's receipt therefor in triplicate.

W.C. Kohlenberg
Supt. & Spl. Disb. Agt. ~~U. S. Indian Agent.~~

Sworn to and subscribed before me this_____7"_____day of_____September_____, 190 6

Harry L. Elmslee
My Commission expires 10-11-08.   Notary Public

TRIPLICATE
CASH.

Voucher No._____31_____

FOR

TRAVELING EXPENSES

_____1st_____Quarter, 190 7

$ 7\\ ^{45}

Paid in_____or by Check No.__46238_

DRAWN ON

Asst. Treas. St. Louis, Mo

IN FAVOR OF

Peter P. Ratzlaff

State whether paid in cash or by check; if by check, give the number and date of the check and the name of the bank or institution upon which and in whose favor it is drawn.

****

VOUCHER FOR TRAVELING EXPENSES
(OTHER THAN DISBURSING OFFICERS.)

The United States,

To .... Peter P. Ratzlaff .... , Dr.

DATE			Sub-voucher.	DOLLARS.	Cts.
1906		Traveling expenses incurred by Peter P. Ratzlaff, Add'l Farmer, serving notices on Indians to appear at Probate court on Indian guardianship matters.			
July 17	To	Dinner for self	1		25
		Feed for team	2		40
18		Supper lodging and breakfast,	3	1	50
		Feed and care for team over night.	4	1	
		Dinner for self	5		50
		Feed for team	6		40
		Supper for self	7		40
19		R. R. fare from Shawnee to McLoud and return	8		75
		Dinner for self	9		50
		Livery rig from McLoud, Okla., to home of Quen-ne-pe-thot distance 3 miles and return,	10	1	50
		Buss[sic] fare from Hotel to R. I. depot	10		25

Total - - - - - - $ 7 45

I solemnly swear that the foregoing account is correct and just; * that the different charges in detail have been taken from and verified by my memorandum; that the amount charged was actually paid; that no part of the journey charged for has been made under any free pass on any railway, steamboat, or other public conveyance; that the number of days for which the same is charged was necessarily consumed in unavoidable delays incident to travel, and the performance of the duty ordered or services rendered; that the journey was performed by the shortest usually traveled routes under orders *(copy annexed)* or for the purpose of ... Serving notices on Indians to appear at Court on Indian Guardianship matters

...... Peter P. Ratzlaff ......

Sworn to and subscribed before me this ... 29th ... day of ... September ... , 190 6.

...... Walter F. Dickens ......

My Commission expires January 1, 1908   ...... Notary Public ......
My certificate on file in the Indian Office.

RECEIVED at ... Shawnee, Oklahoma, ... September 29, 1906. ... , 190 ..

of ... Frank A. Thackery, ... Supt. & Special Disb. Agent, ... , U. S. Indian Agent,

... Seven and 45/100 ... dollars in full of the above account.

...... Peter P. Ratzlaff ......

I certify, on honor, that the above account is correct and just, and that I have this ... 29th ... day of ... September ... , 190 6 , actually paid the amount thereof, viz: ... Seven & 45/100- dollars, and have taken claimant's receipt therefor in triplicate.

186

Dated at _____ Shawnee, Oklahoma. _____ ⎫   _____ Frank A. Thackery _____

_____ September 29, 1906. _____, 190 ⎰   __ Supt. & Spl. Disbursing Agent

---

TRIPLICATE

CASH.

Voucher No. _____ 33 _____

FOR

TRAVELING EXPENSES

_____ 1st _____ Quarter, 190 7

$ 6\$^{55}$ _____

Paid in _____ or by Check No. 46238

DRAWN ON

_____ Asst. Treas. St. Louis, Mo _____

IN FAVOR OF

_____ Peter P. Ratzlaff _____

State whether paid in cash or by check; if by check, give the number and date of the check and the name of the bank or institution upon which and in whose favor it is drawn.

****

VOUCHER FOR TRAVELING EXPENSES
(OTHER THAN DISBURSING OFFICERS.)

The United States,

𝕿𝖔 .... Peter P. Ratzlaff ...., *Dr.*

DATE 1906	Traveling expenses incurred by Peter P. Ratzlaff, Add'l Farmer, Serving notice on Mex. Kickapoo Indians to appear at Court on Indian Guardianship	Sub-voucher.	DOLLARS.	Cts.
Aug. 10	To Supper, lodging and breakfast	1	1	50
	Feed and care for team over night	2		80
	Dinner for self	3		50
	Feed for team	4		40
11	Supper, lodging and breakfast,	5	1	50
	Feed and care for team over night	6	1	
	Dinner for self	7		35
	Feed for team	8		50
	Total - - - - - - - -$		6	55

I solemnly swear that the foregoing account is correct and just; * that the different charges in detail have been taken from and verified by my memorandum; that the amount charged was actually paid; that no part of the journey charged for has been made under any free pass on any railway, steamboat, or other public conveyance; that the number of days for which the same is charged was necessarily consumed in unavoidable delays incident to travel, and the performance of the duty ordered or services rendered; that the journey was performed by the shortest usually traveled routes under orders *(copy annexed)* or for the purpose of ....Serving notice on Indians to appear at Court on Indian guardianship matters

.... Peter P. Ratzlaff ....

Sworn to and subscribed before me this ..... 29th .... day of ..... September ...., 190 6 .

.... Walter F. Dickens ....

My Commission expires January 1, 1908
My certificate on file in the Indian Office.   .... Notary Public. ....

RECEIVED at ... Shawnee, Oklahoma, September 29, 1906. ...., 190 ...
of.......... Frank A. Thackery, Supt. & Spl Disbursing Agent. ...., U. S. Indian Agent,

..... Six & 55/100 - - - - - - - - - - - - - - - - - - dollars in full of the above account.

.... Peter P. Ratzlaff ....

I certify, on honor, that the above account is correct and just, and that I have this.......... 29th .... day of ..... September ....., 190 6 , actually paid the amount thereof, viz: ..... Six & 55/100- - - - - - -
- dollars, and have taken claimant's receipt therefor in triplicate.

Dated at .... Shawnee, Oklahoma. .... ⎫   .... Frank A. Thackery ....
.... September 29, 1906. ...... , 190 ⎭   .. Supt. & Spl. Disbursing Agent.

TRIPLICATE

CASH.

Voucher No. ..... 44 ....

FOR

TRAVELING EXPENSES

.... 1st .... Quarter, 190 7

$ 3^{00} ....

Paid in .... or by Check No. 416215

DRAWN ON

.... Asst. Treas. St. Louis, Mo. ......

IN FAVOR OF

.... Frank A. Thackery ....

State whether paid in cash or by check; if by check, give the number and date of the check and the name of the bank or institution upon which and in whose favor it is drawn.

****

(VOUCHER FOR ___Traveling expenses___ *)*

The United States,

𝒯𝑜 _____ Frank A. Thackery _____, *Dr.*

DATE		Sub-voucher.	DOLLARS.	Cts.
1906.	Traveling Expenses incurred by the Superintendent and Special Disbursing Agent, Assisting the Asst. U. S. Atty. in Indian Guardianship matters.			
Aug 28	To Dinner for self,			50
	Feed for team.			50
29	Supper for self.			50
	Feed for taem[sic].			50
30	Dinner for self.			50
	Feed for team.			50
	Total - - - - -$ 3			00

RECEIVED at ___ Shawnee, Oklahoma, September 29th, 1906 ___, 190 ___

of ___ Frank A. Thackery, ___ Supt. & Spl. Disbursing Agent. ___, U. S. Indian Agent,

___ Three & no/100 - - - - - - - - - - - - - - - - - - - dollars in full of the above account.

___ Frank A. Thackery ___

I solemnly swear that the foregoing account is correct and just; * that the different charges in detail have been taken from and verified by my memorandum; that the amount charged was actually paid; that no part of the journey charged for has been made under any free pass on any railway, steamboat, or other public conveyance; that the number of days for which the same is charged was necessarily consumed in unavoidable delays incident to travel, and the performance of the duty ordered or services rendered; that the journey was performed by the shortest usually traveled routes under orders *(copy annexed)* or for the purpose of ___.

___ assisting Asst. U. S. Atty as above stated ___; that where sub-vouchers were not furnished it was impossible to obtain them; and that I have this ___ 29th ___ day of ___ September ___, 190 6

actually paid the amount thereof, viz: ___ Three & no/100 -

dollars, and have taken claimant's receipt therefor in triplicate.

Frank A. Thackery
U. S. Indian Agent.
Supt. & Spl. Disbursing Agent.
Sworn to and subscribed before me this ___29th___ day of _____September_____, 190 6

Walter F. Dickens
My Commission expires January 1, 1908   Notary Public.
My certificate on file in the Indian Office.

TRIPLICATE
CASH.

Voucher No. ___27___

FOR

TRAVELING EXPENSES
(OTHER THAN DISBURSING OFFICERS.)

_____1st_____Quarter, 190_7_

_____Indian Gdnship matters_____

$ 14\\^{90}

Paid in _____or by Check No. 416238

DRAWN ON

Asst. Treas. St. Louis, Mo

IN FAVOR OF

Peter P. Ratzlaff

State whether paid in cash or by check; if by check, give the number and date of the check and the name of the bank or institution upon which and in whose favor it is drawn.

****

VOUCHER FOR TRAVELING EXPENSES
(OTHER THAN DISBURSING OFFICERS.)

𝕿𝖍𝖊 𝖀𝖓𝖎𝖙𝖊𝖉 𝕾𝖙𝖆𝖙𝖊𝖘,

To ....Peter P. Ratzlaff............................ , *Dr.*

DATE 1906	Traveling expenses incurred by Peter P. Ratzlaff, Add'l Farmer, taking Indians to Oklahoma City Oklahoma, in Indian Guardianship matters.	Sub-voucher.	DOLLARS.	Cts.
Sept 3	To Dinner for self	1		50
	Feed for team	2		45
	R. R. fare from Harrah to Oklahoma City & ret.	3	1	15
	Buss[sic] fare from R. I. depot to Lee hotel			50
4	Board and lodging from supper on the 3rd to dinner on Sept 4th, dated inclusive	4	2	50
	Buss fare from Lee hotel to R. I depot			50
	Five tickets for 5 Indians from Harrah to Oklahoma City and return	5	5	75
	Feed for tea, from night Sept. 3rd to noon Sept. 4th, inclusive,	6	1	25
5	Supper, lodging and breakfast	7	1	50
	Feed and for team overnight	8		80
	Total - - - - - - - - - - - - - - - -		$ 14	90

I solemnly swear that the foregoing account is correct and just; * that the different charges in detail have been taken from and verified by my memorandum; that the amount charged was actually paid; that no part of the journey charged for has been made under any free pass on any railway, steamboat, or other public conveyance; that the number of days for which the same is charged was necessarily consumed in unavoidable delays incident to travel, and the performance of the duty ordered or services rendered; that the journey was performed by the shortest usually traveled routes under orders *(copy annexed)* or for the purpose of........ Taking Indians to Oklahoma City Court on Indian Guardianship matters ....

...........Peter P. Ratzlaff...........

Sworn to and subscribed before me this .... 29th .... day of ...... September .... , 190 6.

...........Walter F. Dickens..........

My Commission expires January 1, 1908   ....Notary Public.............
My certificate on file in the Indian Office.

RECEIVED at ...... Shawnee, Oklahoma, September 29, 1906. .... , 190 ...
of........... Frank A. Thackery, Supt. & Spl. Disbursing Agent. ...., U. S. Indian Agent,

...... Fourteen & 90/100 - - - - - - - - - - - - - - - - - - dollars in full of the above account.

...........Peter P. Ratzlaff...........

I certify, on honor, that the above account is correct and just, and that I have this......... 29th ....day of....... September ......, 190 6 , actually paid the amount thereof, viz:...... Fourteen & 90/100 - - - -
- dollars, and have taken claimant's receipt therefor in triplicate.

Dated at _____ Shawnee, Oklahoma. _____ ⎫   _____ Frank A. Thackery _____
_____ September 29, 1906. _____, 190 __ ⎭   _ Supt. & Spl. Disbursing Agent.

TRIPLICATE

CASH.

Voucher No. _____ 42 _____

FOR

TRAVELING EXPENSES

_____ 1st _____ Quarter, 190 7

$ 9^{10} _____

Paid in _____ or by Check No. 416215

DRAWN ON

_____ Asst. Treas. St. Louis. Mo. _____

IN FAVOR OF

Frank A. Thackery

State whether paid in cash or by check; if by check, give the
number and date of the check and the name of the bank or
institution upon which and in whose favor it is drawn.

****

(VOUCHER FOR ..... Traveling expenses ..... *)*

The United States,

To .... Frank A. Thackery .... , *Dr.*

DATE	Traveling Expenses incurred by the	Sub-voucher.	DOLLARS.	Cts.
1906	Superintendent and Special Disbursing Agent, on trip to Oklahoma City attending Court on Indian Guardianship matters.			
Sept. 3	To R. R. fare from Shawnee to Oklahoma City Oklahoma,	1	1	05
4	Board and lodging from supper on Sept 3 to dinner on September 4, inclusive.	2	2	50
	Dinner for 5 witnesses to 50¢ each	3	4	50
	R. R. fare from Oklahoma City to Shawnee	4	1	05
	Total - - - - - - - - - - - - - - - - - - -		$ 9	10

(The witnesses were not subpoenaed in the above case, therefore the Court would not pay expenses, fees, etc.)

RECEIVED at .... Shawnee, Oklahoma, September 29th, 1906 .... , 190 ...

of .... Frank A. Thackery, ... Supt. & Spl. Disbursing Agent. .... , U. S. Indian Agent,

.... Nine & 10/100 - - - - - - - - - - - - - - - - - - - dollars in full of the above account.

.... Frank A. Thackery ....

I solemnly swear that the foregoing account is correct and just; * that the different charges in detail have been taken from and verified by my memorandum; that the amount charged was actually paid; that no part of the journey charged for has been made under any free pass on any railway, steamboat, or other public conveyance; that the number of days for which the same is charged was necessarily consumed in unavoidable delays incident to travel, and the performance of the duty ordered or services rendered; that the journey was performed by the shortest usually traveled routes under orders *(copy annexed)* or for the purpose of .....

. Attending Probate Court on Indian Guardianships .... ; that where sub-vouchers were not furnished it was impossible to obtain them; and that I have this .... 29th .... day of .... September .... , 190 6 actually paid the amount thereof, viz: .. Nine & 10/100 - dollars, and have taken claimant's receipt therefor in triplicate.

Sac & Fox – Shawnee
1892-1909   Volume XII

<table>
<tr><td></td><td>.....Frank A. Thackery.............</td></tr>
</table>

.....Frank A. Thackery.............
U. S. Indian Agent.
Supt. & Spl. Disbursing Agent.

Sworn to and subscribed before me this____29th____day of_____September_____, 190 6

.....Walter F. Dickens..........

My Commission expires January 1, 1908
My certificate on file in the Indian Office.

.....Notary Public..........

[Copy of Original]

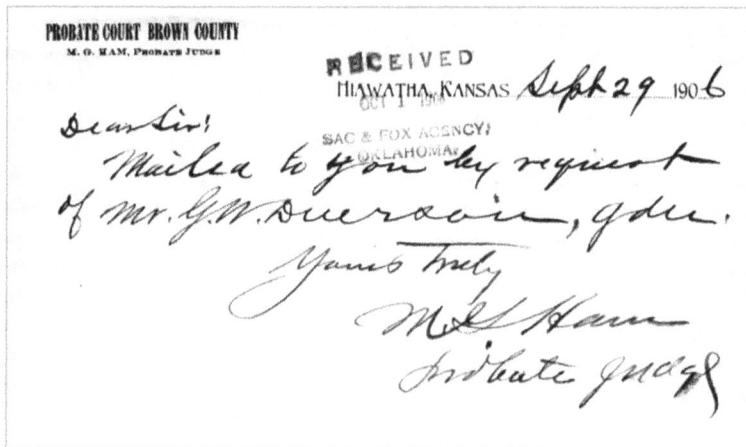

[Transcription of above postcard]

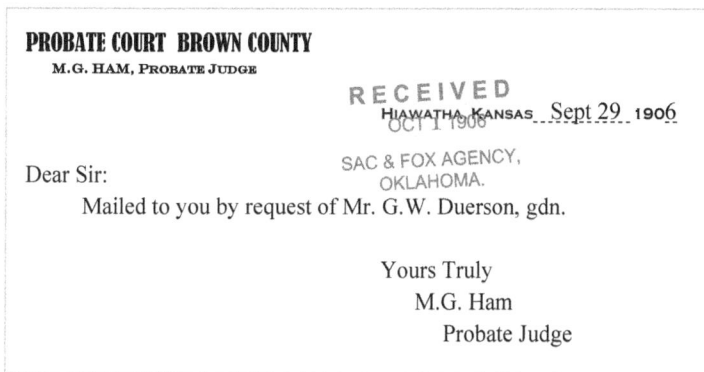

PROBATE COURT BROWN COUNTY
M.G. HAM, PROBATE JUDGE

RECEIVED
HIAWATHA, KANSAS...Sept 29 1906

SAC & FOX AGENCY,
OKLAHOMA.

Dear Sir:
Mailed to you by request of Mr. G.W. Duerson, gdn.

Yours Truly
M.G. Ham
Probate Judge

TRIPLICATE
CASH.

Voucher No. _____40_____

FOR

TRAVELING EXPENSES

_____1st_____Quarter, 190 7

$ 10^{27} _____

Paid in _____ or by Check No. 416215

DRAWN ON

_____Asst. Treas. St. Louis. Mo._____

IN FAVOR OF

_____Frank A. Thackery_____

State whether paid in cash or by check; if by check, give the number and date of the check and the name of the bank or institution upon which and in whose favor it is drawn.

****

Sac & Fox – Shawnee
1892-1909   Volume XII

(VOUCHER FOR ....Traveling expenses.....)

The United States,

To ....Frank A. Thackery............, *Dr.*

DATE	Traveling inpenses[sic] incurred by the	Sub-voucher.	DOLLARS.	Cts.
1906	Superintendent and Special Disbursing Agent, attending at Chandler, Oklahoma, in the matter of his appointment as legal guardian of minor Indians.			
Sept. 13	To Ry., fare from Shawnee, Okla. To Okla. Cy.	1	1	05
14	Lodging and beakfast[sic],	2	1	50
	Buss[sic] fare from Lee Hotel to St. L. & S. F. R.	3		50
	Ry. fare from Okla. Cy. to Chandler, Okla.	3	1	46
	Buss fare from St. Cloud, Hotel to Frisco depot			25
	Ry. fare from Chandler to Okla. cy[sic]. O. T.	4	1	46
	Buss fare from Frisco Depot to Lee hotel			50
15	Buss fare from Lee hotel to Rock Island depot			50
	Supper lodging and breakfast Okla. Cy.	5	2	
	Ry. fare from Oklahoma Cy. to Shawnee, Okla.	6	1	05
	Total,- - - - - -		$ 10	27

RECEIVED at .....Shawnee, Oklahoma, September 29th, 1906....., 190..

of.....Frank A. Thackery, Supt. & Spl. Disbursing Agent....., U. S. Indian Agent,

.....Ten & 27/100 - - - - - - dollars in full of the above account.

.....Frank A. Thackery.....

I solemnly swear that the foregoing account is correct and just; * that the different charges in detail have been taken from and verified by my memorandum; that the amount charged was actually paid; that no part of the journey charged for has been made under any free pass on any railway, steamboat, or other public conveyance; that the number of days for which the same is charged was necessarily consumed in unavoidable delays incident to travel, and the performance of the duty ordered or services rendered; that the journey was performed by the shortest usually traveled routes under orders *(copy annexed)* or for the purpose of_____.
Attending Court at Chandler, Okla. on gdnship matter; that where sub-vouchers were not furnished it was impossible to obtain them; and that I have this 29th day of September, 190 6 actually paid the amount thereof, viz: Ten & 27/100 - - - - - - - - - - dollars, and have taken claimant's receipt therefor in triplicate.

197

Frank A. Thackery
U. S. Indian Agent.
Supt. & Spl. Disbursing Agent.

Sworn to and subscribed before me this _____ 29th _____ day of _____ September _____ , 190 6

Walter F. Dickens

Commission expires January 1, 1908

Notary Public.

ertificate[sic] on file in the Indian Office.

TRIPLICATE

CASH.

Voucher No. _____ 39 _____

FOR

TRAVELING EXPENSES

_____ 1st _____ Quarter, 190 7

$ 9¹²

Paid in _____ or by Check No. 416215

DRAWN ON

Asst. Treas. St. Louis, Mo.

IN FAVOR OF

Frank A. Thackery

State whether paid in cash or by check; if by check, give the
number and date of the check and the name of the bank or
institution upon which and in whose favor it is drawn.

****

(VOUCHER FOR ..... Traveling expenses ..... *)*

The United States,

To .... Frank A. Thackery ...., *Dr.*

DATE		Sub-voucher.	DOLLARS.	Cts.
1906	Traveling expense incurred by Frank A. Thackery Supt & Spl. Disbursing Agent, in the matter of his appointment as legal guardian of certain minor and adult Indians under the jurisdiction of this Agency,			
Sept. 10	To R. R. fare from Shawnee, to Okla., City, O.T.	1	1	50
	Supper lodging and breakfast,	2	1	50
	R.R. fare from Okla. Cy, to Chandler, Okla.	3	1	46
	Dinner for self	4		50
	R. R. fare from Chandler, to Okla. Cy., Okla.	5	1	46
	Supper for self,	6		70
	Lodging and breakfast	7	1	
	Dinner for self at Oklahoma City,			50
	R. R. fare from Okla. Cy. to Shawnee, Okla.	8	1	05
	Total.- - - - - - $		9	12

RECEIVED at .... Shawnee, Oklahoma, September 29th, 1906 ...., 190 ...

of .... Frank A. Thackery, Supt. & Spl. Disbursing Agent. ...., U. S. Indian Agent,

.... Nine & 12/100 - - - - - - - - - - - - - - - - - dollars in full of the above account.

.... Frank A. Thackery ....

I solemnly swear that the foregoing account is correct and just; * that the different charges in detail have been taken from and verified by my memorandum; that the amount charged was actually paid; that no part of the journey charged for has been made under any free pass on any railway, steamboat, or other public conveyance; that the number of days for which the same is charged was necessarily consumed in unavoidable delays incident to travel, and the performance of the duty ordered or services rendered; that the journey was performed by the shortest usually traveled routes under orders *(copy annexed)* or for the purpose of ......

.... Attending Court in guardianship matters ....; that where sub-vouchers were not furnished it was impossible to obtain them; and that I have this .... 29th .... day of ...... September ...., 190 6

actually paid the amount thereof, viz: Nine & 12/100 - dollars, and have taken claimant's receipt therefor in triplicate.

Frank A. Thackery
Supt. & Spl. Disbursing Agent.

Sworn to and subscribed before me this ____ 29th ____ day of _____ September _____ , 190 6

Walter F. Dickens

My commission expires January 1, 1908
Certificate on file in the Indian Office.

Notary Public.

TRIPLICATE

CASH.

Voucher No. ____ 30 _____

FOR

TRAVELING EXPENSES
(OTHER THAN DISBURSING OFFICERS.)

_____ 1st _____ Quarter, 190 7

$ 41⁰⁰

Paid in _____ or by Check No. 416238

DRAWN ON

Asst. Treas. St. Louis, Mo

IN FAVOR OF

Peter P. Ratzlaff

State whether paid in cash or by check; if by check, give the
number and date of the check and the name of the bank or
institution upon which and in whose favor it is drawn.

VOUCHER FOR TRAVELING EXPENSES
(OTHER THAN DISBURSING OFFICERS.)

The United States,

To .... Peter P. Ratzlaff .... , Dr.

DATE		Sub-voucher.	DOLLARS.	Cts.
1906	Traveling expenses incurred by Peter P. Ratzlaff, Add'l Farmer, on trip to Chandler, Okla., with Indian witnesses in the matter of the appointment of Frank A. Thackery, S.S. D. A. Guardian of minor and incompetent Indians.			
Sept. 13	To Supper lodging and breakfast for self	1	1	50
	Feed for team over night	2	1	
14	Supper, lodging and breakfast, for self	3	1	50
	Seven tickets for self and six Indians from Harrah, Oklahoma City and return at $1.15 ea	4	8	05
	Breakfast for six Indians	5	1	75
	Buss[sic] fare from Lee hotel to Frisco depot			50
	Breakfast for self,	6		75
	R. R. fare from Oklahoma City to Chandler and return for self and six Indians at $2.65 ea.	7	18	55
	Buss fare from Frisco depot to St. Cloud hotel			50
	Dinner for self,	8		50
	Buss fare from St. Cloud hotel to Frisco depot			50
	Supper for self	9		75
	Supper for six Indians at 25¢ each,	10	1	50
15	Breakfast for self			50
	Dinner for self	11		65
	Board and care for team from noon Sept 13 to			
	Total - - - - - - - - - - -		$ 41	00

I solemnly swear that the foregoing account is correct and just; * that the different charges in detail have been taken from and verified by my memorandum; that the amount charged was actually paid; that no part of the journey charged for has been made under any free pass on any railway, steamboat, or other public conveyance; that the number of days for which the same is charged was necessarily consumed in unavoidable delays incident to travel, and the performance of the duty ordered or services rendered; that the journey was performed by the shortest usually traveled routes under orders *(copy annexed)* or for the purpose of ..... Taking Indians to Chandler Court on Indian Guardianship matters .....

.... Peter P. Ratzlaff ....

Sworn to and subscribed before me this ..... 29th ..... day of ..... September ..... , 190 6.

.... Walter F. Dickens ....

My Commission expires January 1, 1908 .... Notary Public. ....
My certificate on file in the Indian Office.

RECEIVED at ___ Shawnee, Oklahoma, September 29, 1906, _____ , 190__,
of _____ Frank A. Thackery, Supt. & Spl. Disbursing Agent, _____ , U. S. Indian Agent,
_____ Forty one & no/100 - - - - - - - - - - - - - - - - - - - dollars in full of the above account.

___ Peter P. Ratzlaff _____

I certify, on honor, that the above account is correct and just, and that I have this _____ 29th _____ day
of _____ September _____ , 190 6 , actually paid the amount thereof, viz: ___ Forty one & no/100 - - - -
- dollars, and have taken claimant's receipt therefor in triplicate.

Dated at _____ Shawnee, Oklahoma. _____ ⎫
_____ September 29, 1906, _____ , 190 __ ⎬   _____ Frank A. Thackery _____
                                            ⎭   __ Supt. & Spl. Disbursing Agent.

TRIPLICATE
CASH.

Voucher No. _____ 43 _____

FOR

TRAVELING EXPENSES

_____ 1st _____ Quarter, 190 7

- -

$ 4⁹⁰

Paid in _____ or by Check No. 416215

DRAWN ON

_____ Asst. Treas. St. Louis, Mo. _____

IN FAVOR OF

_____ Frank A. Thackery _____

State whether paid in cash or by check; if by check, give the number and date of the check and the name of the bank or institution upon which and in whose favor it is drawn.

****

(*VOUCHER FOR* ___Traveling expenses___ *)*

The United States,

$\mathscr{To}$ ___Frank A. Thackery___, $\mathscr{Dr.}$

DATE	Traveling expenses incurred by the	Sub-voucher.	DOLLARS.	Cts.
1906	Superintendent and Special Disbursing Agent, on a trip to Oklahoma City, Oklahoma, on matters pertaining to Indian Guardianships.			
Sept. 17	To R. R. fare from Shawnee to Oklahoma City, Oklahoma, and return.	1	1	90
	Buss[sic] fare from Rock Island depot to Stewart hotel,			50
18	Supper, lodging and breakfast at 50¢ ea.	2	1	50
	Dinner for self.			50
	Buss fare from Stewart hotel to R. I. depot.			50
	Total- - - - - - - -$		4	90

RECEIVED at ___Shawnee, Oklahoma, September 29th, 1906___, 190___

of ___Frank A. Thackery, Supt. & Spl. Disbursing Agent.___, U. S. Indian Agent,

___Four & 90/100 - - - - - - - - - - - - - - - - - -___ dollars in full of the above account.

___Frank A. Thackery___

I solemnly swear that the foregoing account is correct and just; * that the different charges in detail have been taken from and verified by my memorandum; that the amount charged was actually paid; that no part of the journey charged for has been made under any free pass on any railway, steamboat, or other public conveyance; that the number of days for which the same is charged was necessarily consumed in unavoidable delays incident to travel, and the performance of the duty ordered or services rendered; that the journey was performed by the shortest usually traveled routes under orders *(copy annexed)* or for the purpose of ___ .

___ attending Probate Court on Indian Gdnship matters. ___ ; that where sub-vouchers were not furnished it was impossible to obtain them; and that I have this ___ 29th ___ day of ___ September ___ , 190 6 actually paid the amount thereof, viz: ___ Four & 90/100- dollars, and have taken claimant's receipt therefor in triplicate.

___ Frank A. Thackery ___
Supt. & Spl. Disbursing Agent.

Sworn to and subscribed before me this ___ 29th ___ day of ___ September ___ , 190 6

___ Walter F. Dickens ___

My Commission expires January 1, 1908   ___ Notary Public. ___
My certificate on file in the Indian Office.

DEPARTMENT OF THE INTERIOR,

Finance

Office of Indian Affairs,

76132/1906

Washington.

Auth. 101687

3 Enclosures.   October 1, 1906.

The Superintendent,

Sac and Fox School, Oklahoma.

Sir:-

Authority has been granted for you to settle an indebtedness amounting to $21.58, incurred during the first quarter, 1907, for traveling and incidental expenses on official business, as requested and for the reasons stated in your letter of August 29, 1906, and as evidenced by the vouchers herewith returned for completion and file with your accounts.

Very respectfully,

(Signed) C. F. Larrabee,

WAP(0)   Acting Commissioner.

204

DEPARTMENT OF THE INTERIOR,
INDIAN INDUSTRIAL SCHOOL,
OFFICE OF SUPERINTENDENT.
CARLISLE, PA.

RECEIVED
OCT 5 1906
SAC & FOX AGENCY,
OKLAHOMA.

Oct. 2, 1906.

Mr. W. C. Kohlenberg, Supt.,

Sac and Fox Agency, Okla.

Sir:

There is inclosed herewith copy of notice relating to the discharge of Lee Patrick as the guardian of Orilla Davis, bearing affidavit of Joseph S. Barber that a copy of same has been delivered to Orlando Johnson.

Very respectfully,

WA Mercer
Major 11th Cavalry,
Superintendent.

AES
Incl.

****
[Copy of Original]

State of ~~Pennsylvania~~ New Jersey, :ss
County of _Mercer_)

I, _Joseph S. Barber_ do solemnly swear that I delivered a true and correct copy of the within notice to Orlando Johnson on the _1st_ day of ~~September~~ October, A. D., 1906.

Joseph S. Barber

Subscribed and sworn to before me this _1st_ day of October, 1906.

Chas J. Steel
~~Notary Public.~~ Justice of the Peace

My Comission expires Jan 1st 1907

IN PROBATE COURT

TERRITORY OF OKLAHOMA,
LINCOLN COUNTY.

In the Matter of the Estate of

Orilla Davis Minor child

of Jeff Davis

deceased

Notice of Settlement

of Final Account

205

Sac & Fox – Shawnee
1892-1909   Volume XII

[Transcription of Notice of Settlement on Page 205]

New Jersey   )
State of ~~Pennsylvania~~,   :
County of___Mercer___)

    I, _____Joseph S. Barber___ do solemnly swear that I delivered a true
and correct copy of the within notice to Orlando Johnson on the _1ˢᵗ_ day of
~~September~~, A. D., 1906.
 October

                           ___Joseph S. Barber___

                           October
Subscribed and sworn to before me this_1ˢᵗ_day of ~~September~~, 1906.

                      ___Chas. J. Steel___
My Comission[sic] expires Jan 1ˢᵗ 1907   ~~Notary Public.~~ Justice of the Peace

No._____

IN PROBATE COURT

TERRITORY OF OKLAHOMA }
LINCOLN COUNTY.

In the Matter of the Estate of

Orilla Davis Minor child of Jeff Davis

----
                       deceased

Notice of Settlement

of _____Final_____Account

****

Notice of Settlement of Account.

NOTICE.

Territory of Oklahoma, County of Lincoln, ss.

IN PROBATE COURT.

In the Matter of the Estate of __Orilla Davis, Minor__ _____ deceased.

Notice is hereby given, that_____ __Lee Patrick_____ the duly appointed and

qualified_____ __guardian_____ of the estate of ____Orilla Davis, Minor child of___

_____ __Jeff Davis____ _____

deceased, has____ rendered and presented for settlement, and filed in said Court,_____

____his final_____ account and report of___his___administration as such __guardian__

__and resigning as such guardian_____

and that_____ __Wednesday_____, the ___3rd____day of____October_____A.D. 190_6

being a day of a Regular Term of said Court, to-wit: of the___ __September____term, A.D.

190_6_ at___10___o'clock in the___ __fore___noon of said day, at the probate court room in

the City of Chandler in the said County of Lincoln has been duly appointed by the said

Court, for the _____ __final_____settlement of said account, at which time and place any

person interested in said estate may appear and file his exceptions in writing to the

account and contest the same.

IN TESTIMONY WHEREOF, I have hereunto set my hand and

affixed the seal of said Court this_ __28__ day of__ __August___190_6

[SEAL]   _____Fred A Wagoner_____
                                          Probate Judge.

Finance

63038/1906

Auth. 101755

2 Enclosures.

DEPARTMENT OF THE INTERIOR,

Office of Indian Affairs,

Washington.

October 5, 1906.

Sac & Fox – Shawnee
1892-1909   Volume XII

The Superintendent,

Sac and Fox School,

Oklahoma.

Sir:

Authority has been granted for you to settle an indebtedness amounting to $9.75, incurred during the 1st quarter, 1907, for traveling and incidental expenses on official business and for telephoning, as requested and for the reasons stated in your letter of the 20th ultimo, and as evidenced by the vouchers herewith returned for completion and file with your accounts.

Very respectfully,

(Signed)   C. F. Larrabee,

WAP(0)   Acting Commissioner.

Finance   DEPARTMENT OF THE INTERIOR,
84442/1906
Authy 101815   Office of Indian Affairs,
1 Inclos   Washington.   October 6, 1906.

The Superintendent,

Sac and Fox School, Okla.

Sir:

Authority has been granted for you to expand the sum of $9.80 in the settlement of an indebtedness incurred during the first quarter, 1907. for traveling expenses on official business, as requested and for the reasons stated in your letter of the 24th ultimo and as evidenced by the voucher returned herewith for completion and file with your account.

Very respectfully,

(Signed)   C. F. Larrabee,

Acting Commissioner,

WAP(W)

REFER IN REPLY TO THE FOLLOWING:

RECEIVED
OCT 11 1906
SAC & FOX AGENCY,
OKLAHOMA.

73097-1906.   **DEPARTMENT OF THE INTERIOR,**

OFFICE OF INDIAN AFFAIRS,

WASHINGTON.

October 6, 1906

Superintendent in Charge, Sac & Fox Agency,

San[sic] and Fox Agency,

Oklahoma.

Sir:

This Office in in receipt of your letter of August 20, 1906, saying that the matter of the dismissal of the legal guardian of the Sac & Fox and Iowa Indians had been taken up with a view to having yourself appointed instead, and that there would be several thousand dollars turned over to you. You request to be informed if you should deposit this money in the same banks in which the inherited land funds are deposited, and whether you should use the same form of bond as these banks are using for such funds.

In answer I have to say that as you will be required by the Court to give bonds for the safe-keeping of these funds, it is a personal matter with you, and you should select the bank that you consider the most reliable. The form for bond used by the banks could not well be used by you. It is presumed that the bonding company from which you will secure the bonds will have a form of their own.

Very respectfully,

C.F. Larrabee,

Acting Commissioner.

T.B.W;E.

TRIPLICATE

CASH.

Voucher No. ____7____.

FOR

TRAVELING EXPENSES

_____Second_____Quarter, 190 7

_____W. C. Kohlenberg,_____

$ 3.50 _____

Paid in _____ or by Check No. 481456 .
Dated October 8, 1906;

DRAWN ON

Assistant Treasurer, U. S.,
_____St. Louis, Mo._____

IN FAVOR OF

_____W. C. Kohlenberg,_____

State whether paid in cash or by check; if by check, give the
number and date of the check and the name of the bank or
institution upon which and in whose favor it is drawn.

****

Sac & Fox – Shawnee
1892-1909   Volume XII

(VOUCHER FOR ....Traveling Expenses....)

The United States,

        ℔ ....W. C. Kohlenberg,........................, *Dr.*

DATE		Sub-voucher.	DOLLARS.	Cts.
1906.				
Sept. 17,	Telephone to Agency, from Chandler, O. T.			25
Sept. 18,	Meals and lodging	1	2	00
Sept. 18.	Feeding and stabling team	2	-- 1	25
			$ 3	50

Note 1:- Filing return of guardianship notices
      and peitions[sic] for appointment of self as guardian

Not 2:- Delay over night was due to stormy weather.

RECEIVED at ..Sac and Fox Agency, Oklahoma,.................. October 8,........, 190 6

of............ W. C. Kohlenberg,............ Supt. & Spl. Disb. Agt.........., ~~U. S. Indian Agent,~~

....Three and 50/100 ($3.50).................... dollars in full of the above account.

..........W.C. Kohlenberg..............

I solemnly swear that the foregoing account is correct and just; * that the different charges in detail have been taken from and verified by my memorandum; that the amount charged was actually paid; that no part of the journey charged for has been made under any free pass on any railway, steamboat, or other public conveyance; that the number of days for which the same is charged was necessarily consumed in unavoidable delays incident to travel, and the performance of the duty ordered or services rendered; that the journey was performed by the shortest usually traveled routes under orders *(copy annexed)* or for the purpose

of .... See note 1, above ....
..................................; and that I have this ___8th___ day of ____October____, 190 6

actually paid the amount thereof, viz: ....Three and 50/100 ($3.50)..........................

dollars, and have taken claimant's receipt therefor in triplicate.

....W.C. Kohlenberg..............
Supt. & Spl.Disb.Agt. ~~U. S. Indian Agent~~

Sworn to and subscribed before me this _____20th___ day of _____September_____, 190 6

..........Harry L. Elmslee..........
My Commission expires 10-11-08   ....Notary Public..........

211

TRIPLICATE

CASH.

Voucher No. __8__

FOR

TRAVELING EXPENSES

__Second__ Quarter, 190 7

__W. C. Kohlenberg,__

$ 6.25

Paid in _____ or by Check No. 481457
Dated October 8, 1906;

DRAWN ON

Assistant Treasurer, U. S.,
St. Louis, Mo.

IN FAVOR OF

__W. C. Kohlenberg,__

State whether paid in cash or by check; if by check, give the
number and date of the check and the name of the bank or
institution upon which and in whose favor it is drawn.

****

(VOUCHER FOR ..... Traveling Expenses .....)

𝕿𝖍𝖊 𝖀𝖓𝖎𝖙𝖊𝖉 𝕾𝖙𝖆𝖙𝖊𝖘,

𝓣𝓸   W. C. Kohlenberg, ..., 𝒟ʀ.

DATE 1906		Sub-voucher.	DOLLARS.	Cts.
Sept. 13,	Supper.			50
Sept. 13,	Hire of team and driver for 12-1/2 hours	1	4	00
Sept. 14,	Meals and lodging	2	1	00
Sept. 14,	Phone to Agency, from Shawnee, Okla			25
Sept. 14,	Dinner.			50
			$ 6	25

Note:- Serving guardianship notices near Shawnee, Oklahoma.
Other expenses on this same trip were paid by U. S. Marshall since I
was in attendance before the U. S. Grand Jury as a witness, Sept. 11
and 12th.

See copy of authority attached to Voucher

No 7- Second Quarter 1907

RECEIVED at .. Sac and Fox Agency, Oklahoma, ... October 8. ...., 190 6

of .... W. C. Kohlenberg, ... Supt. & Spl.Disb.Agt. ...., U. S. Indian Agent,

..... Six and 25/100 ($6.25) .... dollars in full of the above account.

.... W.C. Kohlenberg ....

I solemnly swear that the foregoing account is correct and just; * that the different charges in detail have been taken from
and verified by my memorandum; that the amount charged was actually paid; that no part of the journey charged for has been
made under any free pass on any railway, steamboat, or other public conveyance; that the number of days for which the same is
charged was necessarily consumed in unavoidable delays incident to travel, and the performance of the duty ordered or services
rendered; that the journey was performed by the shortest usually traveled routes under orders *(copy annexed)* or for the purpose

of .... See Note above ....

....; and that I have this .. 8th .. day of .... October ...., 190 6

actually paid the amount thereof, viz: .. Six and 25/100 ($6.25) ....
dollars, and have taken claimant's receipt therefor in triplicate.

.... W.C. Kohlenberg ....
Supt. & Spl.Disb.Agt. U. S. Indian Agent.

Sworn to and subscribed before me this ..... 20th .... day of .... September ...., 190 6

.... Harry L. Elmslee ....
My Commission expires 10-11-08   Notary Public

Department of Justice.

RECEIVED
OCT 15 1906
SAC & FOX AGENCY,
OKLAHOMA.

Office of the United States Attorney
District of Oklahoma.
Guthrie.

October 12, 1906.

W. C. Kohlenberg, Esq.,

Supt. & Spl. Disb. Agent,

Sac & Fox Agency, Oklahoma.

Dear Sir:-

Mr. Outcelt informed me over the phone that you had finished up the first part of the guardianship cases at Chandler, and that the remaining case would be heard on a later date. In all cases where the settlements are not satisfactory, appeals must be taken within 10 days from the date of judgment or decree in the case. Such appeals are taken by filing a notice of appeal and a bond with the Probate Court rendering the judgment. Mr. Outcelt has not yet reported the facts in any of the cases settled, nor advised me of the character of the judgments rendered. If the settlements, in these cases, are not satisfactory to you, or any judgment is unsatisfactory, and you think an appeal should be taken, you will please advise me at once of that fact, stating the case or cases in which such appeals should be taken, and I will take appeals to the District Court.

Very respectfully,

John Embry

U.S. Attorney.

TRIPLICATE

CASH.

Voucher No. 11

FOR

TRAVELING EXPENSES

Second Quarter, 190 7

W. C. Kohlenberg.

$ 9.80

Paid in _____ or by Check No. 481460
Dated October 12, 1906;

DRAWN ON

Assistant Treasurer, U. S.,
St. Louis, Mo.

IN FAVOR OF

W. C. Kohlenberg.

State whether paid in cash or by check; if by check, give the
number and date of the check and the name of the bank or
institution upon which and in whose favor it is drawn.

****

(VOUCHER FOR ____Traveling Expense.____)

𝕿𝖍𝖊 𝖀𝖓𝖎𝖙𝖊𝖉 𝕾𝖙𝖆𝖙𝖊𝖘,

℟ W. C. Kohlenberg, _____, 𝒟𝓇.

DATE		Sub-voucher.	DOLLARS.	Cts.
1906				
Sept. 22,	Feeding and stabling team	1	2	80
Sept. 22,	Meals and lodging	2	7	00
			$ 9	80

NOTE:- Making a trip to Chandler, O. T., for
purpose of examining and transcribing accounts of
guardians of Indian minors in accordance with
directions contained in Office letter "Land"
68637-1906, dated August 17, 1906.

RECEIVED at __Sac and Fox Agency, Oklahoma,_____ October 12,_____, 190 6

of _W. C. Kohlenberg,_____ Supt. & Spl.Disb.Agt., U. S. Indian Agent,

_Nine and 80/100 ($9.80)_____ dollars in full of the above account.

W.C. Kohlenberg_____

I solemnly swear that the foregoing account is correct and just; " that the different charges in detail have been taken from
and verified by my memorandum; that the amount charged was actually paid; that no part of the journey charged for has been
made under any free pass on any railway, steamboat, or other public conveyance; that the number of days for which the same is
charged was necessarily consumed in unavoidable delays incident to travel, and the performance of the duty ordered or services
rendered; that the journey was performed by the shortest usually traveled routes under orders (copy annexed) or for the purpose

of _____See note above_____

_____; and that I have this____12th____day of____October_____, 190 6

actually paid the amount thereof, viz: ___Nine and 80/100 ($9.80)_____

dollars, and have taken claimant's receipt therefor in triplicate.

W.C. Kohlenberg_____
Supt. & Spl.Disb.Agt. U. S. Indian Agent.

Sworn to and subscribed before me this____24th____day of_____September_____, 190 6

Harry L. Elmslee_____
My Commission expires 10-11-08   ____Notary Public_____

Department of Justice.

Office of the United States Attorney.
District of Oklahoma.
Guthrie.

October 15, 1906.

W. C. Kohlenberg, Esq.,

    Supt. & Spl. Disb. Agent,

        Sac & Fox Agency, Oklahoma.

Dear Sir:-

    We send herewith bonds in Indian guardianship cases; and statement of Beadles and Sons for their commission. Some of these bonds will have to be signed by you. You will sign the bonds where necessary and file them and qualify as guardian.

            Very respectfully,

            John Embry

            U.S. Attorney.

TRIPLICATE

CASH.

Voucher No. ___18___

FOR

TRAVELING EXPENSES

___Second___ Quarter, 190_7_

John O. Arnold,

$ 3.45

Paid in _____ or by Check No. 481487

Dated OCT 19 1906

DRAWN ON

Assistant Treasurer, U. S.,

St. Louis, Missouri,

IN FAVOR OF

John O. Arnold

State whether paid in cash or by check; if by check, give the number and date of the check and the name of the bank or institution upon which and in whose favor it is drawn.

****

VOUCHER FOR TRAVELING EXPENSES
(OTHER THAN DISBURSING OFFICERS.)

The United States,

To _____ John O. Arnold _____ , *Dr.*

DATE		Sub-voucher.	DOLLARS.	Cts.
1906				
Sept. 10	Meals and feeding team	1		60
Sept. 11	Meals and lodging	2	1	50
Sept. 11	Meals and feeding team	3		60
Sept. 11	Feeding team.	4		75
			$ 3	45
	See Copy of Authority attached to			
	Voucher No 17- Second Quarter 1907			

Sac & Fox – Shawnee
1892-1909 Volume XII

I solemnly swear that the foregoing account is correct and just; * that the different charges in detail have been taken from and verified by my memorandum; that the amount charged was actually paid; that no part of the journey charged for has been made under any free pass on any railway, steamboat, or other public conveyance; that the number of days for which the same is charged was necessarily consumed in unavoidable delays incident to travel, and the performance of the duty ordered or services rendered; that the journey was performed by the shortest usually traveled routes under orders *(copy annexed)* or for the purpose of __serving guardianship notices, Indian minors__ and that where subvouchers are not furnished it was impracticable to obtain them.

__John O. Arnold__

Sworn to and subscribed before me this ___3rd___ day of _____October_____, 190 6

__Harry L. Elmslee__

My Commission expires 10-11-08 _____Notary Public_____

RECEIVED at __Sac and Fox Agency, Oklahoma,__ _____October 19_____, 190 6

of _____W. C. Kohlenberg,_____ ____Supt. & Spl. Disb. Agt.____, U. S. Indian Agent,

__Three and 45/100 ($3.45)__ _____dollars in full of the above account.

__John O. Arnold__

I certify, on honor, that the above account is correct and just, and that I have this _____19th_____ day

of ____October____, 190 6, actually paid the amount thereof, viz: ___Three and 45/100 ($3.45)__

_____dollars, and have taken claimant's receipt therefor in triplicate.

Dated at __Sac and Fox Agency, Oklahoma,__ } __W.C. Kohlenberg__

____October 19.____, 190 6 } __Supt. & Spl. Disb. Agt.__

Department of Justice.

RECEIVED OCT 25 1906 SAC & FOX AGENCY, OKLAHOMA.

Office of the United States Attorney.
District of Oklahoma.
Guthrie.

October 24, 1906.

W. C. Kohlenberg, Esq.,

Supt. & Spl. Disb. Agent,

Sac & Fox Agency, Oklahoma.

Dear Sir:-

Your letter of the 22nd instant received. So soon as Mr. McKnight, Assistant U.S. Attorney, can dispose of some court matters I shall have him take up the Payne County guardianship cases; and you can advise Judge

Smith that we will get to the matter just as soon as possible. The District Courts, seven in number, have been in session almost constantly; and it keeps us all very busy

Your statement of the 22nd instant calling my attention to publication fees and Attorney's fees in the guardianship matters at Chandler has been received. I shall refer this to Mr. Outcelt with direction that he follow the suggestions in your statement and see that all unearned fees are repaid by the parties liable, You understand, in as much as some of these people were former clients of mine, I am depending on your judgment and direction in these matters and furnishing Mr. Outcelt to advise you in all matters of law. I want these guardians, as well as all other guardians, and my former firm, if it appears that it was the beneficiary of any improper fee, to account for every penny due the wards regardless of who it affects and regardless of who might be required to make restitution of any moneys improperly paid out.

Very respectfully,

John Embry

U.S. Attorney.

Department of Justice.

RECEIVED
NOV 1 1906
SAC & FOX AGENCY,
OKLAHOMA.

Office of the United States Attorney.
District of Oklahoma.
Guthrie.

October 30, 1906.

W. C. Kohlenberg, Esq.,

Supt. & Spl. Disb. Agent,

Sac & Fox Agency, Oklahoma.

Dear Sir:-

Your letter of the 23rd instant transmitting bills of J.B. Beadles and Son for premiums on guardian bonds, has been received.

Beadles and son were to make these bonds at the following rates; $2.00 on $500.00 bonds; and for larger bonds, $3.50 on the first $1000.00; $2.30 on each additional $1000, up to $5000.00; and $1.00 per $1000 for all above $5000.00

I do not have the bonds before me now and can not say that the amount of bonds stated ae correct, but suppose they are.

You will ascertain if they are correct, and make your payments according to the above scheduled rates.

The claims filed appear to be according to the agreed rates.

I return herewith the statements sent us together with statements requested in your letter.

I also inclose statements of Sadie Engles[sic], Jno. Crane, Harry Crane and Thersa[sic] Crane.

Very respectfully,
John Embry
U.S. Attorney.

Inclosures.

****

ᚠred A. Wagoner,
Probate Judge.

Chandler, Oklahoma. Nov. 3, 1906.

Mr. W. C. Kohlenberg,

Sac and Fox Agency, O.T.

Dear sir:

Please find enclosed blank Bond in the Guardianship of Ira Walker. Send the same to Guthrie as soon as possible.   Also sign the Oath of Guardianship in the Crane, Ingalls, and Walker matter. Please return the Letters of Guardianship at your earliest convenience also send me some of your envelopes.

Yours truly,
Fred A Wagoner
Probate Judge

****

[Copy of Original] | [Transcription of Note]

Ira Walker

I fixed bond at 1000^{00} do not know whether that is to[sic] high or not the Pet alleges 500^{00} of Per. Prop and $150 income.

_____

Wagoner

SAMUEL SMITH, Probate Judge

O. C. LOWRY, Clerk

- OFFICE OF -

PROBATE JUDGE

PAYNE COUNTY

RECEIVED
NOV 9 1906
SAC & FOX AGENCY,
OKLAHOMA.

Stillwater, Oklahoma,   Nov. 7, 1906.

W. C. Kohlen^{b}erg,

Sac & Fox Agency, Okla.

Dear Sir:-

Replying to yours of the 5th inst. relative to any suit or suits which may be instituted against any Iowa or Sac & Fox Indian, will say that this office will at once inform yours.

In several guardianships of minor indians[sic] there are due costs, and as Mr. Foster, their guardian does not have the possession of the funds an is therefore unable to make payment I desire to know to whom these statements should be presented.

Yours very truly,

Samuel Smith,

Probate Judge.

𝔉reb 𝔄. 𝔚agoner,
𝔓robate 𝔍ubge.

Chandler, Oklahoma. Nov. 8, 1906.

Mr. Frank A. Thackery,

Shawnee, O. T.

Dear Sir:

Your letter of the 6th in reference to the Bonds in the Indian Cases in which you were appointed Guardian, will say.[sic] That the United States Attorney has forwarded the Bonds to me. They have all been approved and you are the Legal Guardian in each of those Cases. I will mail you in a few days the amount of the costs in each of said cases.

Yours truly,

Fred A Wagoner
Probate Judge

𝔚. 𝔑. 𝔐aben,

𝔓robate 𝔍ubge

Pottawatomie County,
Tecumseh,   Oklahoma.

𝔍. 𝔈. 𝔖impson,
Probate Clerk.

Feby. 1" 1907

Hon Frank A Thackery

Supt & Spl Disb Agt

Shawnee O.T.

Dear Sir:-

Refering[sic][sic] to our conversation a few days ago in regard to the guardianship matter, desire to advise that I have examined and the records and find that you have qualified in all of the cases mentioned, except the Vinson

case and in that one no final report or resignation has been filed   The costs
appear to have been paid by Miss Lunt.

Yours truly

JE Simpson
Clerk Probate Court

Ex-Judge Fifth Judicial District of Nebraska

ROBERT WHEELER,
ATTORNEY AND COUNSELOR

TELEPHONE { OFFICE, No. 112
RESIDENCE, No. 113

Ansd. 11-1906
TECUMSEH, OKLA.   Nov. 10/06.

Hon. Frank A. Thackery,

Shawnee, Okla.

Dear Sir:-

I wish to draw the papers in the two cases in Lincoln county[sic], in which
you are guardian, namely, Wah-tha-nah-keth-o-quah and Ah-che-tha-quah, and
then go up there and get the orders of sale, but I am at a loss to know what
statuatory[sic] grounds for making the sale I can allege. In the Wah-tha-nah-keth-
o-quah case, has the incompetent other lands that the money is needed to
improve?

Does he need the money for his support?

Does the land bring a reasonable interest on its value?

Will it be to the imcompetents[sic] interest to sell the land and place the
money at interest or invest it in productive stocks?

Give me as many statuatory grounds for make the sale as you can.

Also please answer the same questions as to the incompetent heirs in the
Ah-che-tha-quah case.

Yours very truly,

Robert Wheeler

I expect you had better have R. J. Benson and Jacob Scheidt each deposit about
$25. with you, to be used in paying court costs and advertising. That will be
about the sum needed in each case.

𝔇epartment of 𝔍ustice.

R E C E I V E D

NOV 14 1906

𝔒ffice of the 𝔘nited 𝔖tates 𝔄ttorney

SAC & FOX AGENCY,

𝔇istrict of 𝔒klahoma.

OKLAHOMA.

𝔊uthrie.

November 13, 1906.

W. C. Kohlenberg, Esq.,

Supt. & Spl. Disb. Agent,

Sac & Fox Agency, Oklahoma.

Dear Sir:-

Write me the facts in the case of Samuel Moore, guardian of Ruth and the other children, showing as nearly as you can the amount of money Moore received. I understand Moore is insane and has dissipated this estate. I want to prepare a petition for his removal as guardian and one for your appointment as his successor. Send me one of the blank forms for appointment of guardian in you[sic] county as we have none of the Lincoln County forms here.

Very respectfully,

John Embry

U.S. Attorney.

SAMUEL SMITH, Probate Judge

- OFFICE OF -

O. C. LOWRY, Clerk

R E C E I V E D

NOV 21 1906

PROBATE JUDGE

SAC & FOX AGENCY,

OKLAHOMA.

PAYNE COUNTY

Stillwater, Oklahoma,   Nov. 19, 06.

W. C. Kohlenberg,

Sac & Fox Agency, Okla.

Dear Sir:-

I herewith enclose you statements of the costs owing in the matter of the guardianship of Frank B. and Harry Davis and of Charles Mohee. Mr. Foster, Guardian of the above named minors advised me to present these statements to your office.

Yours truly,

Samuel Smith
Probate Judge.

****

IN THE **RECEIVED**	In the Matter of the guardianship
Probate Court of Payne County, 21 1906	of Charlie Mohee
Oklahoma Territory. SAC & FOX AGENCY, OKLAHOMA.	~~Plaintiff~~ minor
	vs.
Fees Earned Quarter Ending	
	~~Defendant~~

....................................190....

			Probate Judge's Fees	Sheriff's Fees
1905				
Jan	31	Filing & Recording Return of sale of the S.E. of S.W. 10-17-2 E. Payne County; certificate & seal to copy of said return	1 35	
"	"	Filing Recording Return of sal[sic] of the SE-NW-23-17-2 Lincoln County and certificate and seal to copy of same	1 35	
"	"	Filing & Recording Notice of sale and recording publishers affidavit and oath and seal to said affidavit of the sale of the SE of SW 10-17-2 Payne County	80	
"	"	Filing and Recording Notice of sale and recording publishers affidavit of notice of sale of the S.E. of N.W.-23-17-2 Lincoln County	55	
Feb	3	Filing Issuing & Recording Order for hearing return of sale of S.E. of S.W. 10-17-2 E Payne County	75	
"	3	Filing Issuing & Recording Order for hearing return of sale of SE of SW 23-17-2 E Lincoln Co	75	
"	18	Filing Issuing Recording Order confirming sale of abve[sic] tract of land, cert & seal to copy of same	1 65	
"	"	Filing & Entering Affidavit of posting notices of sale of above tract	15	
"	"	Filing issuing recording Order confirming sale of the SE of NW 10-17-2 Payne County, cert & seal to copy of same	1 65	

"	"	Filing & Entering Affidavit of posting notices of sale of above tract		15	
Apr	22	Cert copies of Letters of Guardianship		75	
Sep	11	" " " " " "		75	
Feb 1905	3	Issuing six notices of hearing return of sales of said described tracts of land @ 25¢ each		1 50	
		Advance publishing Co. publishing notice of sale.			7 00
		Chandler Tribune publishing notice of LincolnCo Tract			7 25
		Totals		12 15	14 25

TERRITORY OF OKLAHOMA ⎱ ss.
County of Payne, ⎰

I, ____Samuel Smith, Judge____ of the Probate Court in and for said County and Territory, do hereby certify that the foregoing is a true and correct statement of fees earned in the said cause as by the law allowed and to the persons thereto entitled, and that the same is true and correct.

Witness my hand and the seal of this Court, this ____19th____ day of ___November___ 190 6.

_____Samuel Smith_____
Judge of Probate Court.

DEPARTMENT OF THE INTERIOR RECEIVED

UNITED STATES INDIAN SERVICE   SAC & FOX AGENCY, OKLAHOMA.

Potawatomi Agency,

Hoyt, Kansas, November 19, 1906.

W. C. Kohlenberg,

Supt. & Spl. Dis. Agent,

Sac and Fox Agency, Oklahoma.

Sir:

Enclosed herewith I hand you check for $38.20 to pay probate court fees in the case of Wish-te-yah Lemont.

Very respectfully,

G. L. Williams
Supt. & Spl. Dis. Agent.

1 encl.
GLW:MEB.

𝔚. 𝔑. 𝔐aben,

𝔓robate 𝔍udge

𝔓ottawatomie 𝔆ounty,
𝔗ecumseh,   𝔆klahoma.

𝔍. 𝔆. 𝔖impson,
𝔓robate 𝔆lerk.

Ansd.

November 24/06

Hon Frank A. Thackery

Shawnee O.T.

Dear Sir:-

Enclosed I am sending you a list of the matters in which I find the Court has appointed you as guardian with amount of bond opposite each case.

I should have attended to this matter sooner but business has been pretty revoking and this is the first opportunity I have had to get out the list.

Yours very truly

J.E. Simpson
Clerk Probate Court

𝔉red 𝔄. 𝔚agoner,
𝔓robate 𝔍udge.

𝔆handler, 𝔆klahoma. Nov. 27, 1906.

Mr. W. C. Kohlenberg,

Sac and Fox Agency, O.T.

Dear sir:

You will find enclosed Letters of Guardianship in the Pearl Conger and Harriet and John Tohee Matters, which Oath of Guardian you will please sign and swear to it before a Notary Public and return the same to this Office as soon as possible. Also find enclosed the Bond in the Harriet and John Tohee matter I fixed the amount of the Bond in the sum of $1000.00 if that is not a sufficient amount you insert the correct amount and write me at once so I may change the Order. Full out this Bond, sign it, send it to Guthrie with instructions for it to be executed at once and returned immediately so that the same may be filed and placed of record.

Your communication of recent date in regard to the Holdings of the Department as to the sale of Minor '[sic] land has been received, and will say that I am not prepared at this time to give you my views upon the matter, but as soon as I have time to read it carefully, I will write you in full and give you my opinion.

Yours truly,

Fred A Wagoner
Probate Judge.

****

[Copy of Original]	[Transcription of Original]
	Harriet & John Tohee I made their bond $1000^{00} if that is not enough fix the amount yourself and write me the change. Fred Wagoner Amount O.K. W.C. Kohlenberg Supt & Spl Disb Agent

IN PROBATE COURT

COUNTY OF POTTAWATOMIE.

In the matter of the Guardianship of the Person
and Estate of

Frank Spybuck.

a **Minor/**

LETTERS OF GUARDIANSHIP OF MINORS.

Filed ...Dec, 2. "06. ....190....

W .N. Maben.
Judge of the Probate Court.

-----COPY ----

****

Letters of Guardianship of Minors.

Territory of Oklahoma, Pottawatomie County, S.S. -- COPY ---

THE TERRITORY OF OKLAHOMA, To all whom it may concern, and especially to _____

_____ Frank A. Thackery, _____ GREETING:

KNOW YE, THAT WHEREAS, Application has been made to the Probate Court of said County for the appointment

of a Guardian to __ Frank Spybuck. _____ aged ___ 18 _____ years,

_____ aged _____ years,

minor heirs of _____ deceased, and it appearing to the Court that it is necessary

to appoint a guardian to said _____ Minor, _____

_____

and the said _____ Frank A. Thackery, _____

having been approved for said trust by the Court and having given bond as required by law, which has been approved,

filed and recorded in said Court:

NOW, THEREFORE, Trusting in your care and fidelity, we have appointed, and do by these presents appoint you,

the said _____ Frank A. Thackery, _____ as such guardian, hereby authorizing and empowering you to

take and to have the custody of said minor ____ and the care of __ his ___ education and the care and management of

_ his _ estate until _ he _ arrive at the age of ___ Majority ___ or until you shall be discharged according to law.

And requiring you to make a true inventory of all the estate, real and personal, of the said ward ___ that shall come
to your possession or knowledge, and to return the same into the Probate Court within three months from the date of
these letters, or at any other time the Court shall direct, to dispose of and manage all such estate according to law, and
for the best interest of the ward ___ , and faithfully to discharge your trust in relation thereto, and also when required,
in relation to the care, custody and education of ward ____ to render an account on oath of the property, real and
personal, of the said ward ____ in your hands, and all proceeds and interest derived therefrom, and of the management
and disposition of the same, within one year after your appointment, and annually thereafter, and at such other times as
the proper Court shall direct, and at the expiration of your trust to settle your account with the Probate Court, or with

the ward __ , if _ he _ shall be of full age, or _ his _ legal representatives. And to pay over and deliver all the property,

real and personal, remaining in your hands or due from you on such settlement to the person lawfully entitled thereto.

IN TESTIMONY WHEREOF, We have caused the seal of our said Probate Court to be hereto affixed.

WITNESS, _____ W. N. Maben, _____ Judge of our said Court, at Tecumseh, in said County,

this __ 2" __ day of ___ Dec. 1906. ___ 190 __

_____ W. N. Maben, _____ Probate Judge

Filed Dec. 2" 1906. _____ W. N. Maben, _____ Probate Judge

(seal.)

231

_# 527._

IN PROBATE COURT

COUNTY OF POTTAWATOMIE.

In the matter of the Guarnianship of the Person....
and Estate of

.... Joseph Nona. ....

.... a   Minors.

LETTERS OF GUARDIANSHIP OF MINORS.

Filed .... Dec, 2. .... 190 .. 6

.... W .N. Maben. ....
Judge of the Probate Court.

-- COPY --

****

Territory of Oklahoma, Pottawatomie County, S.S.   -- COPY --

I, J. E. Simpson, Clerk of the Probate Court within and for said County and Territory aforesaid, do hereby certify

that ___the instrument hereto attached is a full, true and correct copy of Letters of guardianship, issued to Frank A. Thackery, as guardian,

~~is the duly appointed, qualified and acting Guardian of the estate of~~ _____

_____of Joseph Nona, a minor._____

as the same now appears of record in my office.

Witness my hand and official seal of said Court this S 28" day of ___May 1907.___ A.D. 190__

_____J. E. Simpson_____
Clerk of the Probate Court.

****

Exhibit "C"
Letters of Guardianship of Minors.

Territory of Oklahoma, Pottawatomie County, S.S.   --COPY---

THE TERRITORY OF OKLAHOMA, To all whom it may concern, and especially to _____

_____Frank A. Thackery,_____ GREETING:

KNOW YE, THAT WHEREAS, Application has been made to the Probate Court of said County for the appointment

of a Guardian to ___Joseph Nona,_____ aged _____ years,

_____ aged _____ years,

minor heir of _____Thos. Nona,_____ deceased, and it appearing to the Court that it is necessary

to appoint a guardian to said _____ minor heir._____

_____

and the said _____ Frank A. Thackery,_____

having been approved for said trust by the Court and having given bond as required by law, which has been approved, filed and recorded in said Court:

NOW, THEREFORE, Trusting in your care and fidelity, we have appointed, and do by these presents appoint you,

the said _____ Frank A. Thackery,_____ as such guardian, hereby authorizing and empowering you to

take and to have the custody of said minor ____ and the care of ___his____ education and the care and management of

__his__ estate until __he__ arrive at the age of ___Majority___ or until you shall be discharged according to law.

And requiring you to make a true inventory of all the estate, real and personal, of the said ward____ that shall come to your possession or knowledge, and to return the same into the Probate Court within three months from the date of these letters, or at any other time the Court shall direct, to dispose of and manage all such estate according to law, and for the best interest of the ward____, and faithfully to discharge your trust in relation thereto, and also when required, in relation to the care, custody and education of ward____ to render an account on oath of the property, real and personal, of the said ward____ in your hands, and all proceeds and interest derived therefrom, and of the management and disposition of the same, within one year after your appointment, and annually thereafter, and at such other times as the proper Court shall direct, and at the expiration of your trust to settle your account with the Probate Court, or with the ward__, if __he__ shall be of full age, or __his__ legal representatives. And to pay over and deliver all the property, real and personal, remaining in your hands or due from you on such settlement to the person lawfully entitled thereto.

IN TESTIMONY WHEREOF, We have caused the seal of our said Probate Court to be hereto affixed.

WITNESS, _____ W. N. Maben, _____ Judge of our said Court, at Tecumseh, in said County,

this __2__ day of ___Dec. 1906.___ 190__

_____ W. N. Maben, _____ Probate Judge

Filed Dec. 2 _____ 1906. _____ W. N. Maben, _____ Probate Judge

seal

IN PROBATE COURT

COUNTY OF POTTAWATOMIE.

In the matter of the Guardianship of the Person and Estate of

Etta King

Minor /

LETTERS OF GUARDIANSHIP OF MINORS.

Filed Dec. 2" ...... 1906 .... 190 ...

W .N. Maben.
Judge of the Probate Court

-- COPY --

Territory of Oklahoma, Pottawatomie County, S.S.   -- COPY --

I, J. E. Simpson, Clerk of the Probate Court within and for said County and Territory aforesaid, do hereby certify that ___ the instrument hereto attached is a full, true and correct copy of Letters of guardianship, issued to Frank A. Thackery, as guardian, of ~~is the duly appointed, qualified and acting Guardian of the estate of~~ _____

_____ Etta King; a minor. _____

as the same now appears of record in my office.

Witness my hand and official seal of said Court this **28"** day of **May 1907.** A.D. 190__

Seal.   **J. E. Simpson**
                                         Clerk of the Probate Court.

****

Exhibit "E"

Letters of Guardianship of Minors.

Territory of Oklahoma, Pottawatomie County, S.S.   --- COPY ---

THE TERRITORY OF OKLAHOMA, To all whom it may concern, and especially to _____

_____ Frank A. Thackery, _____ GREETING:

KNOW YE, THAT WHEREAS, Application has been made to the Probate Court of said County for the appointment of a Guardian to _____ **Etta King,** _____ aged _____ years,

_____ aged _____ years,

minor heirs of _____ **John C. King.** _____ deceased, and it appearing to the Court that it is necessary

to appoint a guardian to said _____ **Etta King   Minor** _____

_____

and the said _____ **Frank A. Thackery,** _____

having been approved for said trust by the Court and having given bond as required by law, which has been approved, filed and recorded in said Court:

NOW, THEREFORE, Trusting in your care and fidelity, we have appointed, and do by these presents appoint you,

the said _____ **Frank A. Thackery,** _____ as such guardian, hereby authorizing and empowering you to

take and to have the custody of said minor ___ and the care of _her_ education and the care and management of _her_

estate until _she_ arrive at the age of _**Majority**_ or until you shall be discharged according to law.

And requiring you to make a true inventory of all the estate, real and personal, of the said ward ____ that shall come to your possession or knowledge, and to return the same into the Probate Court within three months from the date of these letters, or at any other time the Court shall direct, to dispose of and manage all such estate according to law, and for the best interest of the ward ____, and faithfully to discharge your trust in relation thereto, and also when required, in relation to the care, custody and education of ward _____ to render an account on oath of the property, real and personal, of the said ward ____ in your hands, and all proceeds and interest derived therefrom, and of the management and disposition of the same, within one year after your appointment, and annually thereafter, and at such other times as the proper Court shall direct, and at the expiration of your trust to settle your account with the Probate Court, or with the ward __, if _she_ shall be of full age, or _her_ legal representatives. And to pay over and deliver all the property, real and personal, remaining in your hands or due from you on such settlement to the person lawfully entitled thereto.

IN TESTIMONY WHEREOF, We have caused the seal of our said Probate Court to be hereto affixed.

WITNESS, _____ W. N. Maben, _____ Judge of our said Court, at Tecumseh, in said County,

this __ 2" __ day of __ Dec. 1906 ____ 190 __

_____ W. N. Maben, _____ Probate Judge

Filed Dec. 2" 1906 190 __   _____ W. N. Maben, _____ Probate Judge
    seal.

1094

IN PROBATE COURT

COUNTY OF POTTAWATOMIE.

In the matter of the Guardianship of the Person
and Estate of

Willie Na-to-lo-ka

a Minor

LETTERS OF GUARDIANSHIP OF MINORS.

Filed ...... Dec 2" 190 6
    W. N. Maben
        Judge of the Probate Court.

CERTIFICATE OF COPY.

In the Probate Court of the Territory, in and for Pottawatomie County.

I, W. N. Mabeh, Probate Judge in and for the County and Territory aforesaid, do hereby certify the above and foregoing to be a full, true and complete copy of the __Letters of Guardianship__

__issued to Frank A. Thackery, as guardian of Willie Na-ta-lo-ka, minor__

----

as the same appears on file and of record in my office.

Witness my hand and the seal of said Court this ___2"___ day of __May__ ___190 6__

__J.E. Simpson__
Clerk Probate Court

****

Letters of Guardianship of Minors.

Territory of Oklahoma, Pottawatomie County, S.S.

THE TERRITORY OF OKLAHOMA, To all whom it may concern, and especially to _____

_____ __Frank A. Thackery,__ _____ GREETING:

KNOW YE, THAT WHEREAS, Application has been made to the Probate Court of said County for the appointment of a Guardian to ___ __Willie Na-to-la-ke[sic]__ _____ aged _____ years,

_____ aged _____ years,

minor heirs of ___ __Lizzie Wilson__ _____ deceased, and it appearing to the Court that it is necessary to appoint a guardian to said _____ __minor heir__ _____

----

and the said _____ __Frank A. Thackery,__ _____

having been approved for said trust by the Court and having given bond as required by law, which has been approved, filed and recorded in said Court:

NOW, THEREFORE, Trusting in your care and fidelity, we have appointed, and do by these presents appoint you,

the said _____ __Frank A. Thackery,__ _____ as such guardian, hereby authorizing and empowering you to

take and to have the custody of said minor ___ and the care of __his__ education and the care and management of __his__

estate until __he__ arrive at the age of __majority__ or until you shall be discharged according to law.

And requiring you to make a true inventory of all the estate, real and personal, of the said ward ___ that shall come to your possession or knowledge, and to return the same into the Probate Court within three months from the date of these letters, or at any other time the Court shall direct, to dispose of and manage all such estate according to law, and for the best interest of the ward ___ , and faithfully to discharge your trust in relation thereto, and also when required, in relation to the care, custody and education of ward_____to render an account on oath of the property, real and personal, of the said ward____in your hands, and all proceeds and interest derived therefrom, and of the management and disposition of the same, within one year after your appointment, and annually thereafter, and at such other times as the proper Court shall direct, and at the expiration of your trust to settle your account with the Probate Court, or with the ward_ _, if he___shall be of full age, or his__ legal representatives. And to pay over and deliver all the property, real and personal, remaining in your hands or due from you on such settlement to the person lawfully entitled thereto.

IN TESTIMONY WHEREOF, We have caused the seal of our said Probate Court to be hereto affixed.

WITNESS,_____ W. N. Maben,_____Judge of our said Court, at Tecumseh, in said County,

this__2"__day of___August_____190 6

_____ W. N. Maben,_____Probate Judge

Filed Dec 2" 190 6   _____ W. N. Maben,_____Probate Judge
Seal.

SAMUEL SMITH, Probate Judge   O. C. LOWRY, Clerk

- OFFICE OF -   RECEIVED
PROBATE JUDGE   DEC 25 1906
                                                SAC & FOX AGENCY,
                                                OKLAHOMA.
PAYNE COUNTY
Stillwater, Oklahoma,   Dec. 12, 1906.

W. C. Kohlenberg,

        Sac & Fox Agency, Okla.

Dear Sir:-

        John Foster, Guardian of Ben Hull Minor, has this day filed a petition asking for a sale of the real property belonging to his ward, and the matter has been assigned for hearing on the 28th day of Jan. 1907 at 9 o'clock A. M.

                                    Yours very truly,

                                    Samuel Smith
                                    Probate Judge.

HOFFMAN, ROBERTSON & CORDELL
ATTORNEYS AND COUNSELORS AT LAW
CHANDLER, OKLAHOMA.

ROY HOFFMAN
J. B. A. ROBERTSON
S. A. CORDELL

12--19--1906

Hon. W. C. Kohlenberg,

Supt. & Spl. Disb. Agt.,

Sac and Fox, O.T.

Dear Sir:-

We have referred your favor of the 17th in the guardianship matters to the Probate Judge and he thinks settlement should be made in open court. If you can be here on the 26th we will try to have all guardians present and turn over all money to you at that time. Please advise if it will be convenient for you to be here and close the matter up at that time.

Very truly,

Roy Hoffman

[The letter below was severely torn on the left side]

𝕱𝖗𝖊𝖉 𝕬. 𝖂𝖆𝖌𝖔𝖓𝖊𝖗,
𝕻𝖗𝖔𝖇𝖆𝖙𝖊 𝕵𝖚𝖉𝖌𝖊.

𝕮𝖍𝖆𝖓𝖉𝖑𝖊𝖗, 𝕺𝖐𝖑𝖆𝖍𝖔𝖒𝖆. Dec. 10   1906.

Mr. Frank A. Thackery,

Shawnee, O. T.

Dear Sir:-

The second year of my term of office is about to come to a close and it is necessary that all fees earned since the first of January, 1905, be paid as I am required to make a settlement with the County Commissioners on the first day of January next and pay to the County Treasurer all fees earned belonging to the county. It is impossible for me to make that settlement unless those who owe fees are prompt in payment.

I am enclosing herein a card which shows the total amount of fees due and owing by you to this date which amount you will either call personally and settle or mail to me a check, draft or postoffice[sic] money order on or before December the 20th, 1906. In making remittance [illegible...] personally or by letter please bring or mail the [illegible...] card. A Compliance with this request will be a [illegible...]avor to me.

[Illegible] that you will give this matter your prompt [illegible] and settle the same by the above mentioned date.

Your Obedient Servant,

Fred A Wagoner
Probate Judge.

𝔉𝔯𝔢𝔡 𝔄. 𝔚𝔞𝔤𝔬𝔫𝔢𝔯,
𝔓𝔯𝔬𝔟𝔞𝔱𝔢 𝔍𝔲𝔡𝔤𝔢.

𝔈𝔥𝔞𝔫𝔡𝔩𝔢𝔯, 𝔒𝔨𝔩𝔞𝔥𝔬𝔪𝔞. Dec. 10, 1906.

Mr. Frank A. Thackery,

Shawnee, O. T.

Dear sir:

In answer to your letter in reference to your making Bonds in Indian Gaurdain[sic] cases will say that under instructions of Hon. John Embry U. S. District Atty, Mr. Kohlenberg is making separate Bonds in each Indian Case in which he is appointed. It is my opinion under the law that that is necessary.

Yours truly,

Fred A Wagoner
Probate Judge.

DEPARTMENT OF THE INTERIOR

UNITED STATES INDIAN SERVICE

Pawnee Agency, Oklahoma. December 26, 1906.

Supt. W. C. Kohlenberg,

Sac & Fox Agency,

Oklahoma.

Dear Sir:

Will you kindly advise me as to whether or not you are now the legal guardian of Annie Eaves, the daughter of Lillie Carter. I have a lease payment to make to her and do not know to whom to make the check payable.

Very respectfully,

Geo. W. Nellis

GWN(S)   Supt. & Spl. Disb. Agent

#1306

IN PROBATE COURT

COUNTY OF POTTAWATOMIE.

In the matter of the Guardianship of the Person and Estate of

Thomas Sampson

Minors.

LETTERS OF GUARDIANSHIP OF MINORS.

Filed ...... Dec. 26" 1906

J.E. Simpson

Clerk Judge of the Probate Court

****

Letters of Guardianship of Minors.

Territory of Oklahoma, Pottawatomie County, S.S.

THE TERRITORY OF OKLAHOMA, To all whom it may concern, and especially to _.

_ _ _ _ _ _ _ _ _ _ _ _ _ Frank A. Thackery, _GREETING:

KNOW YE, THAT WHEREAS, Application has been made to the Probate Court of said County for the appointment of

a Guardian to _ _ Thomas Sampson _ _ _ _ _ _ _ _ _ _ _ _ _ _ aged _ _ 19 _ _ _ _ _ _ _ _ _ _ _ _years,

_ _aged_ _ _ _ _ _ _ _ _ _ _ _ _ _ _ _ years,

minor heirs of _ _ John Sampson _ _ _ _ _ _ _ _ _ _ _deceased, and it appearing to the Court that it is necessary

to appoint a guardian to said_ _ _ _ _ minor heir _

_ _

and the said _ _ _ _ _ _ _ _ _ _ _ _ _ Frank A. Thackery, _ _ _ _ _ _ _ _ _ _ _ _ _ _ _ _ _ _ _

having been approved for said trust by the Court and having given bond as required by law, which has been approved,

filed and recorded in said Court:

NOW, THEREFORE, Trusting in your care and fidelity, we have appointed, and do by these presents appoint you,

the said _ _ _ _ _ _ _ _ _ Frank A. Thackery, _ _ _ _ _ _ as such guardian, hereby authorizing and empowering you to

take and to have the custody of said minor _ ~~and the care of~~ _ _ _ _ ~~education~~ and the care and management of_ his _

estate until _ he _ _ _ arrive at the age of _ _ majority _ _ _ or until you shall be discharged according to law.

And requiring you to make a true inventory of all the estate, real and personal, of the said ward_ _ _ _that shall come

to your possession or knowledge, and to return the same into the Probate Court within three months from the date of

these letters, or at any other time the Court shall direct, to dispose of and manage all such estate according to law, and

for the best interest of the ward_ _ _ _, and faithfully to discharge your trust in relation thereto, and also when required,
_ _ _ _ management _ _ _ _ _ _ _ _ estate

in relation to the care, custody and ~~education~~ of ward_'s _to render an account on oath of the property, real and

personal, of the said ward_ _ _ _in your hands, and all proceeds and interest derived therefrom, and of the management

and disposition of the same, within one year after your appointment, and annually thereafter, and at such other times as

the proper Court shall direct, and at the expiration of your trust to settle your account with the Probate Court, or with

the ward_ _, if _ he _ _ shall be of full age, or_ his _legal representatives. And to pay over and deliver all the property,

real and personal, remaining in your hands or due from you on such settlement to the person lawfully entitled thereto.

IN TESTIMONY WHEREOF, We have caused the seal of our said Probate Court to be hereto affixed.

WITNESS,_ _ _ _ _ _ _ _ _ W. N. Maben, _ _ _ _ _ _ _ _ _Judge of our said Court, at Tecumseh, in said County,

this_ _ 26" _day of _ _ _ Dec _ _ _ 190_6

_ _ _ _ _ _ _ _ _ _ _ W. N. Maben, _ _ _ _ _ _ _ _ _ _Probate Judge

Filed_ Dec 26" _ 190 6 _ _ _ _ _ _ _ _ _ _ _ W. N. Maben, _ _ _ _ _ _ _ _ _ _Probate Judge

Seal.

DUPLICATE

$ 261 32/100 .... DEC 28 1906 ....., *190*..

𝕽eceibeð *of* FRANK A. THACKERY L.G. .... ~~U. S. Indian Agent,~~

...... Two hundred sixty-one and 32/100 .... *Dollars,*

~~consideration in deed, dated~~ .... , ~~190..., to~~

....

....................~~for~~..

....

WITNESS: Guy M. Salisbury   Her
...... Joseph Murdock .... Ah no tho tha[sic]... x ....
                                                                    mark

****

$108.75   DUPLICATE   Shawnee Indian Agency,
_____   Shawnee, Oklahoma, March 12, 1908.

Received of Frank A. Thackery, legal guardian (Superintendent &
Special Disbursing Agent) the sum of One hundred eight & 75/100 Dollars
($108.75) being annuity funds due me and paid to me for my support.

Witnesses:
                                                           her
__W.F. Dickens_____   _____Ah no tho the___x_____
__J Grecian_____   mark

****

$__.50___   DUPLICATE   U. S. Indian Agency,
                                     Shawnee, Okla.   6/15   1908.

Received of Frank A. Thackery, (Supt. & Spcl. Disb. Agent) Legal

Guardian of_____ Ah no tho the _____the sum of

_____ Fifty cents _____/100 Dollars

_____ for making Gdn Report _____.

Witnesses: _____

                            _____ J Grecian _____

_____

****

[Copy of Original Receipt]

DUPLICATE	**UNITED STATES INDIAN AGENCY**

$949 24   Shawnee, Okla., *July 17* – 190 *8*

Received of FRANK A. THACKERY (Supt. & Spcl. Disb. Agent), legal guardian

of *Ah-nah-tho-the* ———————————— the sum of

Nine hundred forty nine and 24/100 ———————— Dollars,

Checks Nos. 187-429-430 and 431

Witnesses *Joseph Murdock*
F. A. Thackery   *Ah Nah tho-the* her mark

[Transcription of above Receipt]

UNITED STATES INDIAN AGENCY

$949²⁴   Shawnee, Okla., July 17- 1908

Received of FRANK A. THACKERY (Supt. & Spl. Disb. Agent), legal
guardian of _____Ah-nah-tho-the_____the sum of
_____Nine hundred forty nine and 24/100_____Dollars,
___Checks Nos. 187-429-430 and 431_____

Witnesses ____Joseph Murdock_____
                                           her
                              Ah-Nah-tho-the___x_____
        F. A. Thackery_____   mark

****

[Copy of Original Receipt]

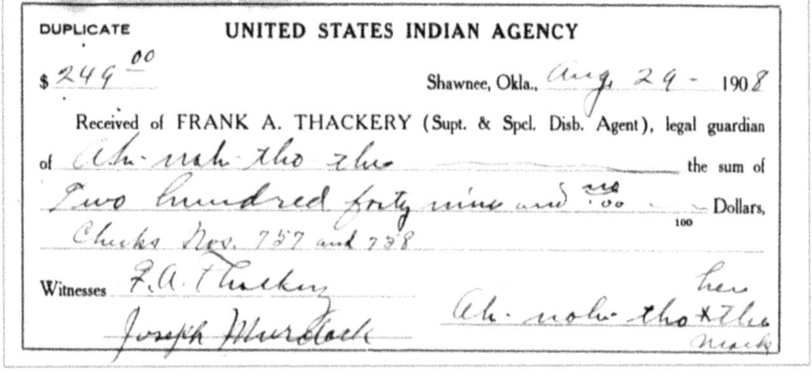

DUPLICATE	**UNITED STATES INDIAN AGENCY**

$249 00   Shawnee, Okla., *Aug. 29* – 190 *8*

Received of FRANK A. THACKERY (Supt. & Spcl. Disb. Agent), legal guardian

of *Ah-nah-tho-the* ———————————— the sum of

Two hundred forty nine and 00/100 ————— Dollars,

Checks Nos. 757 and 738

Witnesses *F. A. Thackery*
Joseph Murdock   *Ah-nah-tho-the* her mark

[Transcription of Receipt on Page 244]

UNITED STATES INDIAN AGENCY

249\underline{00}$ Shawnee, Okla., Aug. 29- 1908

Received of FRANK A. THACKERY (Supt. & Spl. Disb. Agent), legal guardian of _____ Ah-nah-tho-the _____ the sum of _____ Two hundred forty nine and no/100 _____ Dollars, ___ Checks Nos. 757 and 758 _____

Witnesses ___ F. A. Thackery ___

Joseph Murdock

her
___ Ah-Nah-tho-xthe ___
mark

---

an expenditure of 50$\underline{cts}$ 12-1 does not appear on this report, also data shows 1\underline{70}$ due you court cost which report shows 1\underline{70}$ expenditure over receipts.

DUPLICATE
$_{No}$
Final Report

In the Matter of the Estate of

.... guardianship of ....

...... Sho-we-na-qua ....   ~~Deceased~~

Incompetent

Report of Administrator.

Filed this_____day of_____190___.

County Judge.

****

GUARDIAN
REPORT OF ~~ADMINISTRATOR~~

State of Oklahoma, Pottawatomie County, S.S.

In the County Court in and for said County and State.

IN THE MATTER OF THE ESTATE OF

Sho-e-nah-quah   Incompetent

-- ~~Deceased~~

GUARDIAN
REPORT OF ~~ADMINISTRATOR~~

guardian

And now comes ___Frank A. Thackery___ the duly appointed, qualified and acting ~~administrator~~ guardian in the matter above entitled, and submits to the above named Court, h_ is _report as such ~~administrator~~ and respectfully asks the same to be approved.   DR.

12/26-06 Amt. received from U.S. (Annuity)	272	31
7/9-08 Recd. from Trustee a/c	1198	25

CR.   1470 56

12/27-06 Paid court costs & Letters	4	25		
" Men-ah-pe note	166	65		
" ward	101	41		
7/17-08 Do 273.94 224.31	498	25		
7/23-08 Do 475. 8/22220.	695	00		
9/5-08 Paid F.A. Thackery	5		1470	56

~~Balance in hands of Administrator~~

Dated this ___1st___ day of ___March___ A.D. 190_9_

___Frank A. Thackery___

___Frank A. Thackery___ being duly sworn on oath deposes and says that he is the duly appointed qualified and acting ~~administrator~~ guardian of the estate above named, and that the statements in the foregoing report are true.

___Frank A. Thackery___
~~Administrator.~~

Subscribed and sworn to before me this _11_ day of ___March___ 190_9_

My Commission Expires Sept. 15, 1917 ___Peter P. Ratzlaff___ ~~County Judge.~~
Notary Public

Above report filed and approved by me this _5_ day of ___Mch___ 190_9_

___E.D. Ressor___ County Judge.

DUPLICATE
No
Final Report

In the Matter of the Estate of

guardianship of

Me na mish   ~~Deceased~~

Incompetent

Report of ~~Administrator~~. Guardian

Filed this_____ day of_____ 190___.

County Judge.

****

REPORT OF ADMINISTRATOR

State of Oklahoma, Pottawatomie County, S.S.

In the County Court in and for said County and State.

IN THE MATTER OF THE ESTATE OF
ME-NA-MISH,

Incompetent.   FINAL **GUARDIAN**
REPORT OF ~~ADMINISTRATOR~~

~~Deceased~~

guardian

And now comes ___ FRANK A. THACKERY ___ the duly appointed, qualified and acting ~~administrator~~ in
the matter above entitled, and submits to the above named Court, h_ **is** _ final guardian report as such ~~administrator~~ and respectfully asks the
same to be approved.   DR.

AMOUNT RECEIVED FROM ALL SOURCES		
12/26/06, Received from U. S. (annuity)	261	33
5/14/05 Received from U. S. (annuity)	88	29
7/9/08 Received from Trustee a/c	1198	25
	CR.	1547.87

EXPENDITURES.		
12/27/06 Paid to ward,	261	33
5/15/07 Paid to ward,	78	29
5/16/07 Paid Pendleton, Abernathy & Howell,	10	00
7/15/08 Paid to ward,	334	25
7/24/08 Paid to ward,	864	00
		1547.87

~~Balance in hands of Administrator~~

Dated this ___ 1st ___ day of ___ March ___ A.D. 190 9

___ Frank A. Thackery ___

___ FRANK A. THACKERY ___ being duly sworn on oath deposes and says that he is the
guardian   incompetent
duly appointed qualified and acting ~~administrator~~ of the ~~estate~~ above named, and that the statements in the foregoing report are true.

___ Frank A. Thackery ___
GUARDIAN ~~Administrator.~~

Subscribed and sworn to before me this ___ 1st ___ day of ___ March ___ 190 9

My Commission Expires Sept. 15, 1917 ___ Peter P. Ratzlaff ___ ~~County Judge.~~
Notary Public

Above report filed and approved by me this __ 5 __ day of ___ Mch ___ 190 9

___ E.D. Ressor ___ County Judge.

C O P I E S .

No. 1   Dec. 29, 1906.

United States

     To A. T. & S. F. Ry.   Dr.

   For one first class passenger fare from Davenport, O. T. to

Stillwater, O. T., $1.21

     Received at Davenport, O. T., of W. C. Kohlenberg, Supt. & Spl.

Disb. Agt.   One and 21/100 Dollars ($121) in full of above account.

                (Signed)   C. S. Wilson, Agt.

===

No. 2   Dec. 30, 1906.
   United States
      To Hotel Youst,   Dr.
     For meals and lodging from supper Dec. 29, till after dinner Dec. 30, 1906.
                                 $2.00
     Received at Stillwater, Okla., of W. C. Kohlenberg, Supt. & Spl. Disb. Agt. Two
and NO/100 ($2.00) Dollars in full of above account.
                (Signed)   Youst Hotel,
                       Geo. T. Beard, Clerk.

===

No. 3.   Dec. 30, 1906.
   United States
     To A. T. & S. F. Ry.   Dr.

   For one first class passenger fare from Stillwater, O. T., to Davenport, O. T.

                                 $1.21

     Received at Stillwater, O. T., of W. C. Kohlenberg, Supt. & Spl. Disb. Agt.

One and 21/100 ($1.21) Dollars in full of above account.

                (Signed)   G. A. Hoke.

TRIPLICATE.

TRIPLICATE
CASH.

Voucher No. _____19_____

FOR

TRAVELING EXPENSES

_____2nd_____ Quarter, 190 7

$ 2\\ 50

Paid in _____ or by Check No. _416284_

DRAWN ON

Asst. Treas. St. Louis, Mo.

----

payable to the order of
IN FAVOR OF

_____Frank A. Thackery_____

State whether paid in cash or by check; if by check, give the
number and date of the check and the name of the bank or
institution upon which and in whose favor it is drawn.

****

Sac & Fox – Shawnee
1892-1909   Volume XII

(VOUCHER FOR .....Traveling Expenses.....*)*

The United States,

℁ ...Frank A. Thackery,................................., *Dr.*

DATE 1906.		Sub-voucher.	DOLLARS.	Cts.
	Traveling expense incurred by Frank A. Thackery, Supt. & Spl. Disbursing Agent, Shawnee Agency, Oklahoma, attending court at Tecumseh, Oklahoma, on Indian guardianship matters.			
Sept. 27	Dinner for self and Stenographer, at 50¢ ea.	1	1	00
	Feed for tam of horses, - - - - - - - - -	2		50
28	Dinner for self, 50¢; Feed for team, 50¢	3	1	00
	Total, - - - - - - - - - - - -		$ 2	50

RECEIVED at .....Shawnee, Oklahoma, December 31, 1906......................, 190...

of.........Frank A. Thackery, Supt. & Spl. Disbursing Agent........., U. S. Indian Agent,

.....Two and 50/100 - dollars in full of the above account.

.....Frank A. Thackery.....

I solemnly swear that the foregoing account is correct and just; that the different charges in detail have been taken from and verified by my memorandum; that the amount charged was actually paid; that no part of the journey charged for has been made under any free pass on any railway, steamboat, or other public conveyance; that the number of days for which the same is charged was necessarily consumed in unavoidable delays incident to travel, and the performance of the duty ordered or services rendered; that the journey was performed by the shortest usually traveled routes under orders *(copy annexed)* or for the purpose

of ...see caption.......... ; that where sub-vouchers were not furnished it was impossible to obtain them; and that

I have this ....31st.... day of .....December....., 190 6 actually paid the amount thereof, viz:

.....Two and 50/100 - dollars, and have taken

claimant's receipt therefor in triplicate.

.....Frank A. Thackery.....
Supt. & Spl. Disbursing Agent.

Sworn to and subscribed before me this....31st.... day of .....December....., 190 6

.....Walter F. Dickens.....
.....Notary Public.....

My Commission expires January 1, 1908.
Certificate on file in the Indian Office.

251

TRIPLICATE

CASH.

Voucher No. ___21___

FOR

TRAVELING EXPENSES

___2nd___ Quarter, 190 _7_

$ 8\\$^{75}$

Paid in ___ or by Check No. _416284_

DRAWN ON

___Asst. Treas. St. Louis, Mo.___

payable to the order of

IN FAVOR OF

___Frank A. Thackery___

State whether paid in cash or by check; if by check, give the number and date of the check and the name of the bank or institution upon which and in whose favor it is drawn.

****

(VOUCHER FOR ..... Traveling expense. ......)

𝕿𝖍𝖊 𝖀𝖓𝖎𝖙𝖊𝖉 𝕾𝖙𝖆𝖙𝖊𝖘,

𝒯𝑜 ... Frank A. Thackery, _____ , 𝒟𝓇.

DATE		Sub-voucher.	DOLLARS.	Cts.
	Traveling Expense incurred by Frank A. Thackery, Supt. & Spl. Disbursing Agent, Shawnee, Oklahoma, on a trip to Guthrie to consult with U.S. Atty., on official business relative to Indian guardianship matters.			
Nov. 22	To R. R. fare from Shawnee to Guthrie, Okla.	1	2	
	Dinner for self, -			50
	Buss[sic] fare fm. Burt hotel to Santa Fe R. depot.			50
	Shawnee, Oklahoma.			
	Buss[sic] fare from Santa Fe depot, Guthrie, to			
	Royal hotel. -			50
Nov. 23	To Board & lodging from Supper on 22nd, to breakfast on 23rd both inclusive, - - - - - - - - - - - - -	2	1	50
	Buss fare from Royal hotel to Sante Fe depot			50
	R.R. fare from Guthrie to Okla Cy. Oklahoma.	3		95
	Bussfare from Santa Fe depot to Lee hotel			25
	Dinner for self, Oklahoma Cy.	4		75
	Buss fare from Lee hotel to Rock Island depot			25
	R.R. Fare from Okla. Cy. to Shawnee, Okla.	5	1	05
	Total, - - - - - - - - - - - - -		$ 8	75

RECEIVED at ..... Shawnee, Oklahoma, December 31, 1906. _____ , 190 ...

of _____ Frank A. Thackery, Supt. & Spl. Disbursing Agent, _____ , U. S. Indian Agent,

_____ Eight and 75/100 - dollars in full of the above account.

_____ Frank A. Thackery _____

253

I solemnly swear that the foregoing account is correct and just; that the different charges in detail have been taken from and verified by my memorandum; that the amount charged was actually paid; that no part of the journey charged for has been made under any free pass on any railway, steamboat, or other public conveyance; that the number of days for which the same is charged was necessarily consumed in unavoidable delays incident to travel, and the performance of the duty ordered or services rendered; that the journey was performed by the shortest usually traveled routes under orders *(copy annexed)* or for the purpose of ___ see caption ___ ; that where sub-vouchers were not furnished it was impossible to obtain them; and that I have this ___ 31st ___ day of ___ December ___, 190 6 actually paid the amount thereof, viz:

___ Eight and 75/100 ------------------------------ dollars, and have taken claimant's receipt therefor in triplicate.

Frank A. Thackery
Supt. & Spl. Disbursing Agent.

Sworn to and subscribed before me this ___ 31st ___ day of ___ December ___, 190 6

Walter F. Dickens

My Commission expires January 1, 1908.   Notary Public
Certificate on file in the Indian Office.

DEPARTMENT OF THE INTERIOR

UNITED STATES INDIAN SERVICE

RECEIVED
JAN 7 1907
SAC & FOX AGENCY,
OKLAHOMA.

Sac and Fox School, Iowa.

Toledo, January 3, 1907.

W. C. Kohlenberg,

Supt. & Spl. Disb. Agt.

Sac and Fox Agency, Okla.

Sir:-

I have the honor to herewith enclose and transmit, Receipts signed by William and Nancy Davenport, also, by Stella Barker for the several amounts due them, as requested in your letter of the 20th. ultimo.

I have also sent the Receipt for the signature of Mr. S. C. Huber, guardian of Seba Davenport, to him, who will sign the same, and forward to you.

I have been appointed as Administrator of the estate of Lucy Thurman, deceased, and will send the necessary evidence, as soon as I can obtain the same from the clerk of the District Court of this County.

Very respectfully,

Wm G. Malin
Supt. & Spl. Disb. Agent.

COPY.

DEPARTMENT OF THE INTERIOR

Finance
113755/1906

UNITED STATES INDIAN SERVICE

Washington,   January 4, 1907.

The Superintendent,

Shawnee, School, Oklahoma.

Sir:-

Authority is hereby granted for you to expend $40.00, or so much thereof as may be necessary, in the open market purchase of one Jones improved current ledger, with 1000 ledgersheets[sic], two tabbed indexes, one two column open page cash book and one transfer binder, required in keeping accounts odf[sic] incompetent and minor Indians: as requested and for the reasons stated in your letter of the 27th ultimo. Payment therefor to be made from fees received from purchasers of Indian land in your hands.

Very respectfully,

C. F. Larrabee,
Acting Commissioner.

WAP(0)

DEPARTMENT OF THE INTERIOR

UNITED STATES INDIAN SERVICE

RECEIVED
JAN 21 1907
SAC & FOX AGENCY,
OKLAHOMA.

Sac and Fox School, Iowa.

Toledo, January 17, 1907.

W. C. Kohlenberg,

Supt. & Spl. Disb. Agt.

Sac and Fox Agency, Okla.

Sir:-

I have the honor to herewith enclose Receipts, signed by mark, by Emma Hunter, who came to my office this A. M. for this purpose.

I have made arrangements for her sister to come and sign the paper requesting your appointment as her guardian, and will forward the same to you as soon as accomplished.

Very respectfully,

Wm G. Malin

Supt. & Spl. Disb. Agt.

Letters of Guardianship of Minors.

Territory of Oklahoma, Pottawatomie County, S.S.   -----COPY-----

THE TERRITORY OF OKLAHOMA, To all whom it may concern, and especially to _____.

_____ Frank A. Thackery, _____ GREETING:

KNOW YE, THAT WHEREAS, Application has been made to the Probate Court of said County for the appointment of a Guardian to   Mah-ko the-quah   or _____ aged _____ years,

_____ Laura Sah-ah-peah, _____ aged _____ years,

-- aged _____ years,

minor heirs of _____ deceased, and it appearing to the Court that it is necessary to appoint a guardian to said ____ Minor _____

_____.

_____

and the said _____ Frank A. Thackery, _____

having been approved for said trust by the Court and having given bond as required by law, which has been approved, filed and recorded in said Court:

NOW, THEREFORE, Trusting in your care and fidelity, we have appointed, and do by these presents appoint you, the said _____ Franka[sic] A. Thackery, _____ as such guardian, hereby authorizing and empowering you to take and to have the custody of said minor___ and the care of her education and the care and management of

 her estate until she arriveS at the age of Majority or until you shall be discharged according to law.

And requiring you to make a true inventory of all the estate, real and personal, of the said ward___ that shall come to your possession or knowledge, and to return the same into the Probate Court within three months from the date of these letters, or at any other time the Court shall direct, to dispose of and manage all such estate according to law, and for the best interest of the ward ____, and faithfully to discharge your trust in relation thereto, and also when required, in relation to the care, custody and education of ward_____ to render an account on oath of the property, real and personal, of the said ward____ in your hands, and all proceeds and interest derived therefrom, and of the management and disposition of the same, within one year after your appointment, and annually thereafter, and at such other times as the proper Court shall direct, and at the expiration of your trust to settle your account with the Probate Court, or with the ward___, if she shall be of full age, or her legal representatives. And to pay over and deliver all the property, real and personal, remaining in your hands or due from you on such settlement to the person lawfully entitled thereto.

IN TESTIMONY WHEREOF, We have caused the seal of our said Probate Court to be hereto affixed.

WITNESS, _____ W. N. Maben, _____ Judge of our said Court, at Tecumseh, in said County, this __ 26" __ day of ___ January 1907 _____ 190 ...

_____ W. N. Maben, _____ Probate Judge

Filed __ Jan. 26" 1907 __ 190 __   _____ W. N. Maben, _____ Probate Judge

(seal).

Fred A. Wagoner,
Probate Judge.
Chandler, Oklahoma.

Feb. 12, 1907

Mr. Frank A. Thackery,

Shawnee, O. T.

Dear Sir:

Please find enclosed three certificates which you requested
Amount of charges is $1.50.

Yours truly,

Fred A. Wagoner
Probate Judge.

Pen ne ah kah qua	50
Wah pah nah ke quah	50
Pah nah ka quah	50
	$1⁵⁰

DIRECTORS { GEO M COURTS / ROB'T W SHAW / SEALY HUTCHINGS

GALVESTON, TEXAS, Feb. 16, 1907

U. S. Department of Interior, Indian Service,

Shawnee, Oklahoma

Bought of

CLARKE & COURTS

(INCORPORATED)

Manufacturing Stationers

CLARKE & COURTS BUILDING

NET 30 DAYS   NO DISCOUNT   W,F,FX   **FREIGHT PAID**

1 Jones Current Binder	111960	9.70
1 Jones Transfer Binder		6.30
2 Jones Indexes		3.20
1,000 Jones Loose Leaves		11.50
1 Cash Book	A-09225	4.10
		34.80

We hereby certify on honor that we have delivered the above specified goods to the Shawnee Indian Agency, Shawnee, Oklahoma, in good condition, and that we have received payment therefor as herein charged.

(Signed)   Clark & Courts

RW Shaw - Sec

ALL PRICES SUBJECT TO CHANGE WITHOUT NOTICE

WE MAKE THE BEST BLANK BOOKS ON EARTH

****

CERTIFICATE OF INSPECTION & COUNT.

I hereby certify on honor that I have carefully Inspected, and Counted, for the U. S. Indian Department, Shawnee, Oklahoma, one Jones current binder, one Jones Transfer binder, two Jones tabbed indexes, 1,000 ledger sheets and one Cash book, purchased of Clarke & Courts February 26th, 1907, and that I found same to be of first class quality, fully equal to the requirements of the service, and of full count.

Walter F Dickens

Financial Clerk.

TRIPLICATE
CASH.

Voucher No. _____16_____

FOR

TRAVELING EXPENSES

_____3^d_____ Quarter, 190_7_

_____Indian Guardianship matters_____

$ 16⁹⁵

Paid in_____or by Check No._529168_

DRAWN ON

Asst. Treas. St. Louis, Mo

payable to the order of

IN FAVOR OF

_____Frank A. Thackery_____

State whether paid in cash or by check; if by check, give the number and date of the check and the name of the bank or institution upon which and in whose favor it is drawn.

****

259

(VOUCHER FOR ..... Traveling Expenses. ..... *)*

𝔗𝔥𝔢 𝔘𝔫𝔦𝔱𝔢𝔡 𝔖𝔱𝔞𝔱𝔢𝔰,

𝒯𝔬 .... Frank A. Thackery .... , 𝒟𝓇.

DATE 1907.		Sub-voucher.	DOLLARS.	Cts.
Jan. 29	Supper at Burt hotel,			50
	Buss[sic] fare from Burt hotel to Rosck[sic] Island depot			25
	Ticket fm Shawnee to Okla. Cy. Okla.	1	1	05
	Buss fare fm Rock Island depot to Lee hotel			50
30	Board and lodging at Lee hotel, Oklahoma cy.	2	2	
	Buss fare from Lee hotel to Santa Fe depot			50
	Ticket fm. Okla. Cy. to Norman & return	3		95
	Buss fare from Santa Fe depot to Agnes hotel, Norman			50
	Messenger to locate Probate Judge,			50
	Bussfare from hotel to Santa Fe depot			50
	Bussfare from Santa Fe depot to Lee hotel			50
31	Board and lodging at Lee hotel, Okla. Cy.	4	2	
	Bussfare fm. Lee hotel to Frisco depot			50
	Ticket fm. Okla. Cy. to Chandler, Okla. and ret.	5	2	65
	Buss fare fm. Frisco depot to St. Cloud hotel,			50
	Bussfare fm. Frisco depot to Lee hotel, Okla. Cy.			50
Feb. 1	Lodging and breakfast, Lee hotel Okla.	6	1	50
	Buss[sic] fare fm. Lee hotel to M.K. & T. depot			50
	Ticket fm. Oklahoma city to Shawnee, Okla.	7	1	05
	Total, - - - - - - - - - -		$16	95

RECEIVED at .. Shawnee, Oklahoma, ... February 20, 1907. .... , 190 ...

of .... Frank A. Thackery, ... Supt. & Spl. Disbursing Agent, ..., U. S. Indian Agent,

..... Sixteen and 95/100 .... dollars in full of the above account.

..... Frank A. Thackery ....

I solemnly swear that the foregoing account is correct and just; * that the different charges in detail have been taken from and verified by my memorandum; that the amount charged was actually paid; that no part of the journey charged for has been made under any free pass on any railway, steamboat, or other public conveyance; that the number of days for which the same is charged was necessarily consumed in unavoidable delays incident to travel, and the performance of the duty ordered or services rendered; that the journey was performed by the shortest usually traveled routes under orders *(copy annexed)* or for the purpose

of .... Visiting County Courts on Indian Guardianship matters ....

.... ; and that I have this .. 20th ... day of ..... February .... , 190 7.

actually paid the amount thereof, viz: ..... Sixteen and 95/100 ....

dollars, and have taken claimant's receipt therefor in triplicate.

..... Frank A. Thackery ....
Supt. & Spl. Disbursing Agent.

Sworn to and subscribed before me this ____20th____ day of _____February_____, 190 7

_____Walter F. Dickens_____

My Commission expires Jan. 1, 1908
Certificate on file in the Indian Office.

_____Notary Public_____

Any disbursing or other officer of the United States or other person who shall knowingly present, or cause to be presented, any voucher, account, or claim to any officer of the United States for approval or payment, or for the purpose of securing a credit in any account with the United States, relating to any matter pertaining to the Indian Service, which shall contain any material misrepresentation of fact in regard to the amount due or paid, the name or character of the article furnished or received, or of the service rendered, or to the date of purchase, delivery, or performance of service, or in any other particular, shall not be entitled to payment or credit for any part of said voucher, account, or claim; and if any such credit shall be given or received, or payment made, the United States may recharge the same to the officer or person receiving the credit or payment and recover the amount from either or both, in the same manner as other debts due the United States are collected; PROVIDED, That where an account contains more than one voucher the foregoing shall apply only to such vouchers as contain the misrepresentation; AND PROVIDED FURTHER, That the officers and persons by and between whom the business is transacted shall be presumed to know the facts in relation to the matter set forth in the voucher, account, or claim; AND PROVIDED FURTHER, That the foregoing shall be in addition to the penalties now prescribed by law, and in no way to affect proceedings under existing law for like offenses. That, where practicable, this section shall be printed on the blank forms of vouchers provided for general use. (Act March 1, 1883 § 8, 22 Stat. 451; Ace July 4, 1884, § 8; Cir. 113 Ind. O.)

CASH
TRIPLICATE
Voucher No. __28__

OPEN-MARKET PURCHASE

_____3ᵈ_____ Quarter, 190 7

_____ Loose Leaf Ledger Outfit _____

$ 34⁸⁰

Paid in _____ or by Check No. __529171__

DRAWN ON

__Asst. Treas. St. Louis, Mo__
payable to the order of
IN FAVOR OF

_____ Clarke and Courts _____

State whether paid in cash or by check; if by check, give the number and date of the check and the name of the bank or institution upon which and in whose favor it is drawn.

****

VOUCHER FOR OPEN MARKET PURCHASES.

THE UNITED STATES,

To .... Clarke & Courts .... , Dr.

DATE OF PURCHASE.		DOLLARS	CENTS
1907 Feb. 26	To 1 Jones Current Binder	9	70
	1 Jones Transfer Binder	6	30
	2 Jones Indexes	3	20
	1,000 Jones Eureka Leaves	11	50
	1 Cash Book	4	10
	Total, - - - - - - - - - -	$ 34	80
	XXXXXXXXXXXXXXXXXXXXXXXXXXXXXXXXXXXX		
	We hereby certify that we have delivered the above specified goods to the Superintendent and Special Disbursing Agent, Shawnee School, Oklahoma, in good condition, and that we have received payment therefor as herein charged.		
	Per		
	Proposals received and attached to original voucher.		
	Clarke & Courts - $34.80		
	F. P. Burnap Sta. & Ptg. Co., - - - - - - - - - - - - - - - - 35.65		
	Geo. D. Barnard & Co., - - - - - - - - - - - - - - - - - 40.35		
	Prepaid expenses receipt attached to original		

Received at .... Shawnee, Oklahoma, February 26, 1907. .... 190 ... .

of ..... Frank A. Thackery, Supt. & Spl. Disbursing Agent. .... U. S. Indian Agent,

... Thirty four & 80/100 - .... Dollars,

in full of the above account.   Clarke & Courts

.... RW Shaw Secty ....

I CERTIFY, on honor, that the above account is correct and just; that the articles therein named were required for immediate use ... keeping proper record of Indian Guardianship ... accounts.

that there is no contract for the delivery thereof; that authority for the purchase is shown by letter from the Commissioner of Indian Affairs dated ... January 4th, 1907. ... ,190..., a copy of which is hereto attached; that the articles were purchased at .. Galveston[sic], Texas .... of the person named in the original invoice of purchase annexed hereto, and delivered to me at ... Shawnee Indian Training School .. on the .26th. day of ... February ..., 190 7 ., and that the same appear on my Return of Property for the .3rd... quarter, 190 ... .

I FURTHER CERTIFY that the prices charged therefor are reasonable, and the lowest for which

they could be obtained, and that I have actually, this __26th__ day of _____February___ , 19__,
paid the amount thereof, viz: _____Thirty four & 80/100 - - - - - - - - - - - - - - - - dollars,
and have taken the claimant's receipt therefor in triplicate.

                                    ___Frank A. Thackery_____

Dated at__Shawnee, Okla. Feb. 26, 1907__, 190___   Supt. & Spl. Disb. Agent*dian Agent.*

C O P I E S .

No. 1   Jan. 9th, 1907.
United States.
  To St. Louis & San Francisco Ry.   Dr.
  One first class passenger fare from Stroud, Oklahoma to Chandler, Okla.,
                                                        $0.50
  Received at Stroud, Oklahoma, of W. C. Kohlenberg, Supt. & Spl. Disb. Agt
Fifty Centy,   (%0.50) in full of above account.
                          (Signed)   J. A. Weeks,

No. 2   Jan. 10, 1907.
United States to
  St. Cloud Hotel,   Dr.
  For meals and lodging from supper Jan. 9, till after breakfast Jan. 10, 1907.
                                                        $1.50
  Received at Chandler, Oklahoma, of W. C. Kohlenberg, Supt. & Spl. Disb. Agt.
One and 50/100   ($1.50) Dollars in full of above account.
                          (Signed)   St. Cloud Hotel,
                                     Jack Shaffer.

No. 3   Jan. 10, 1907.
United States
  To St. Louis & S. F. Ry.   Dr.
  One first class passenger fare from Chandler, O. T. to Davenport, O. T.,
                                                        $0.26
  Received at Chandler, O. T. of W. C. Kohlenberg, Supt. & Spl. Disb. Agt.,
Twenty six cents ($0.26) in full of above account.
                          (Signed)   A. D. Necomber,

No. 4   Jan. 10, 1907.
United States
  To A. T. & S. F. Ry   Dr.
  For one first class passenger fare from Davenport, O. T. to Guthrie, O. T.
                                                        $1.51
  Received at Davenport, Okla., of W. C. Kohlenberg, Supt. & Spl. Disb. Agt
One and 51/100   ($1.51) Dollars in full of above account.
                          (Signed)   C. S. Wilson.

No. 5   Jan. 11, 1907.
United States
    To Royal Hotel,   Dr.
    For meals and lodging from after Supper. Jan 10, till after dinner Jan. 11, 1907.
                                        $1.50
    Received at Guthrie, Oklahoma, of W. C. Kohlenberg, Supt. & Spl. Disb. Agt
One and 50/100 ($1.50) Dollars in full of above account.
                         (Signed)   Royal Hotel
                                Per W. R. B.

No. 6   Jan. 11, 1907.
United States
    C. R. I. & Pac. Ry.   Dr.
    For one first class passenger fare from Guthrie, O. T., to Chandler, O. T.
                                          $1.14
    Received at Guthrie, O.T., of W. C. Kohlenberg, Supt. & Spl. Disb. Agt.,
One and 14/100 ($1.14) in full of above account.
                         (Signed) H. L. Melenacker,

No. 7   Jan. 12, 1907.
United States.
    To St. Cloud Hotel,   Dr.
    For meals and lodging from supper Jan. 11, 1907, till after supper Jan. 12, 1907.
                                        $2.50
    Received at Chandler, Oklahoma, of W. C. Kohlenberg, Supt. & Spl. Disb. Agt.,
Two and 50/100 ($2.50) Dollars in full of above account.
                         (Signed) St. Cloud Hotel, J. Shaffer.

No. 8   Jan. 12, 1907.
United States
    To St. Louis & San Francisco Ry.,   Dr.
    For one first class passenger fare from Chandler, Okla. to Stroud, Oklahoma,
                                        $0.50
    Received at Chandler, Oklahoma, of W. C. Kohlenberg, Supt. & Spl. Disb. Agt.,
Fifty Cents ($0.50) in full of above account.
                         (Signed) A. D. Macomber[sic].

DEPARTMENT OF THE INTERIOR

UNITED STATES INDIAN SERVICE

Sac and Fox School, Iowa.

Toledo, February 15, 1907.

W. C. Kohlenberg,

Superintendent,

Sac and Fox Agency, Okla.

Sir:-

Please find certified copy of the appointment of S. C. Huber as guardian of Seba Davenport as per request.

I also wish to enquire, as to the nature of the evidence of my appointment as Administrator of the estate of Lucy Thurman, required by you. Upon being so informed, I will transmit the necessary information in the case.

Leases for the signature of Jim Scott received to-day. Will obtain the said signature as soon as possible, and return the same to you.

Very Respectfully,

Wm G. Malin
Superintendent.

Department of Justice.

Office of the United States Attorney.
District of Oklahoma.
Guthrie.

Anadarko, Oklahoma, January 12, 1907.

W. C. Kohlenburg[sic], Esq.,

Superintendent,

Sauk and Fox Agency, Oklahoma.

Dear Sir:

I should be pleased to have you advise you[sic] of the filing of petitions for the appointment of yourself as guardian of certain Indian minors in Payne county just as soon as you have them ready.

Very respectfully,

[Illegible] E. McKnight
Assistant U. S. Attorney.

Department of Justice.

—

**Office of the United States Attorney.
District of Oklahoma.**
Guthrie.

Anadarko, Oklahoma, February 19, 1907.

W. C. Kolenbrug[sic], Esq.,

Sac and Fox Agency, Oklahoma.

Dear Sir:

Answering your letter of the 13th inst., relative to the guardianship cases of your agency, beg to say that I thought we would be able to dispose of those matters last week but the work piled up on us to such an extent that I was unable to reach you. It may be the latter part of next wekk[sic] I will be able to get to Stillwater, if so I will phone to you.

Very respectfully,

[Illegible] E. McKnight
Assistant U. S. Attorney.

DEPARTMENT OF THE INTERIOR,

Finance
16967/1907   United States Indian Service,
4 enclos.

Washington.   February 21, 1907.

The Superintendent,

Sac and Fox School, Oklahoma.

Sir:

Authority is hereby granted you to settle an indebtedness amounting to $28.53, incurred during the Second and Third Quarters, 1907, for traveling and incidental expenses on official business, and for telephoning: as requested and for the reasons stated in your letter of February 14, 1907, and as evidenced by the vouchers herewith returned for completion and file with your accounts; payment therefore to be made from "Contingencies Indian Department, 1907", $27.03, in your hands, and "Telegraphing, Transportation, etc., Indian Supplies, 1907", $1.50.

Very respectfully,

(Signed)　　Frank M. Conser,

WAP/RS.　　　　　　　　　　　　　　　　Chief Clerk.

TRIPLICATE

CASH.

Voucher No. _____21_____

FOR

TRAVELING EXPENSES

_____Third_____ Quarter, 190_7_

_____W. C. Kohlenberg,_____

$ 11.01 _____

Paid in _____ or by Check No. 483273
Dated February 25th, 1907;

DRAWN ON

Assistant Treasurer, U. S.,
_____St. Louis, Mo._____

IN FAVOR OF

_____W. C. Kohlenberg._____

State whether paid in cash or by check; if by check, give the
number and date of the check and the name of the bank or
institution upon which and in whose favor it is drawn.

****

(VOUCHER FOR _____ Traveling Expense. _____)

𝕿𝕳𝖊 𝖀𝖓𝖎𝖙𝖊𝖉 𝕾𝖙𝖆𝖙𝖊𝖘,

℀   W. C. Kohlenberg, _____,   𝒟𝓇.

DATE 1907		Sub-voucher.	DOLLARS.	Cts.
Jan. 9	R. R. fare Stroud, O. T. to Chandler, O. T.,	1		50
Jan. 9	Bus fare from Depot to Hotel (raining)			25
Jan. 10	Meals and lodging, Jan. 9th & 10th,	2	1	50
Jan. 10,	R. R. fare from Chandler, O.T. to Davenport, O.T.	3		26
Jan. 10	Telephone from Davenport O. T. to Agency,			25
Jan. 10	Dinner,			35
Jan. 10	R. R. fare from Davenport, O.T. to Guthrie, O.T.	4	1	52
Jan. 10	Supper,			50
Jan. 11,	Meals and lodging, Jan. 10th, & 11th,	5	1	50
Jan. 11	R. R. fare Guthrie, O. T. to Chandler, O. T.	6	1	14
Jan. 12	Meals and Lodging, Jan. 11 & 12th	7	2	50
Jan. 12	Telephone, Chandler O. T. to Agency,			25
Jan. 12	R. R. fare, Chandler O. T., to Stroud, O. T.	8	--	50
			$ 11	01

Trip to Chandler, O. T., settling guardianship case of Jane Butler,
Sac and Fox Indian; and to Guthrie, O. T. to consult with U. S. Attorney
relative to cerrtain[sic] points before closing same.

RECEIVED at __ Sac and Fox Agency, Oklahoma, _____ February 25th, _____, 190 _7_
of _____ W. C. Kohlenberg, _____ Supt. & Spl. Disb. Agt. _____, U. S. Indian Agent,

_____ Eleven and 01/100 ($11.01) _____ dollars in full of the above account.

W.C. Kohlenberg _____

I solemnly swear that the foregoing account is correct and just; * that the different charges in detail have been taken from and verified by my memorandum; that the amount charged was actually paid; that no part of the journey charged for has been made under any free pass on any railway, steamboat, or other public conveyance; that the number of days for which the same is charged was necessarily consumed in unavoidable delays incident to travel, and the performance of the duty ordered or services rendered; that the journey was performed by the shortest usually traveled routes under orders *(copy annexed)* or for the purpose of _____ See note above _____

_____ ; and that I have this ___25th___ day of _____February_____, 190 7

actually paid the amount thereof, viz: __Eleven and 01/100 ($11.01)__

dollars, and have taken claimant's receipt therefor in triplicate.

_____W.C. Kohlenberg_____
Supt. & Spl. Disb. Agt. *U.S. Indian Agent.*

Sworn to and subscribed before me this _____14_____ day of _____February_____, 190 7

_____Harry L. Elmslee_____

My Commission Expires 10-11-08   _____Notary Public_____

TRIPLICATE

CASH.

Voucher No. _____24_____

FOR

TRAVELING EXPENSES

_____Third_____ Quarter, 190 7

_____W. C. Kohlenberg,_____

$ __5.42__

Paid in _____ or by Check No. __483276__
Dated February 25th, 1907;

DRAWN ON

Assistant Treasurer, U. S.,
_____St. Louis, Mo._____

IN FAVOR OF

_____W. C. Kohlenberg._____

State whether paid in cash or by check; if by check, give the number and date of the check and the name of the bank or institution upon which and in whose favor it is drawn.

****

(*VOUCHER FOR* _____Traveling Expense_____)

𝕿𝖍𝖊 𝖀𝖓𝖎𝖙𝖊𝖉 𝕾𝖙𝖆𝖙𝖊𝖘,

𝕿𝖔   W. C. Kohlenberg,   𝒟𝓇.

DATE		Sub-voucher.	DOLLARS.	Cts.
1906.				
Dec. 29,	R. R. fare from Davenport, O. T. to Stillwater, O. T.	1	1	21
Dec. 29	Bus fare from Depot to Hotel & Return (raining)			25
Dec. 29	Telephone message from Stillwater O. T., to			
	John Foster, Cushing, O. T. relative to filing final			
	report in guardianship cases			20
Dec. 29	Telephone from Stillwater, O. T. to Albert			
	Kenworthy, Perkins, O. T., rel. filing final report in			
	guardianship cases.			15
Dec. 30,	Telephone and ,messenger fees on message from			
	Stillwater, O. T. to Agency, O. T. for team			40
Dec. 30	Meals and lodging, Dec. 29th and 30th,	2	2	00
Dec. 30	R. R. fare, Stillwater, O. T. to Davenport, O. T.	3	1	21
	See Copy of Authority attached to Voucher No 21		$ 5	42
	Third Quarter 1907			
	Trip to Stillwater, O. T., at request of Assistant U. S. Attorney			
	to take up guardianship matters in Payne Co.,			

RECEIVED at __Sac and Fox Agency, Oklahoma,__   February 25th, 1907, __, 190__

of _____ W. C. Kohlenberg, _____ Supt. & Spl. Disb. Agt. _____ ~~U. S. Indian Agent~~,

____ Five and 42/100 ($5.42) _____ dollars in full of the above account.

W.C. Kohlenberg

I solemnly swear that the foregoing account is correct and just; * that the different charges in detail have been taken from and verified by my memorandum; that the amount charged was actually paid; that no part of the journey charged for has been made under any free pass on any railway, steamboat, or other public conveyance; that the number of days for which the same is charged was necessarily consumed in unavoidable delays incident to travel, and the performance of the duty ordered or services rendered; that the journey was performed by the shortest usually traveled routes under orders *(copy annexed)* or for the purpose

of _____ See note above _____

_____ ; and that I have this ___25th___ day of _____February_____ , 190 7

actually paid the amount thereof, viz: ___Five and 42/100 ($5.42)_____

dollars, and have taken claimant's receipt therefor in triplicate.

_____W.C. Kohlenberg_____
Supt. & Spl. D~~isb. /Agt. Agent~~

Sworn to and subscribed before me this_____14____ day of _____February_____ , 190 7

_____Harry L. Elmslee_____

My Commission expires 10-11-08   _____Notary Public_____

DEPARTMENT OF THE INTERIOR

UNITED STATES INDIAN SERVICE

Sac and Fox Agency, Oklahoma,

February 26, 1907.

Jennie Harper,

Paden, I.T.

Dear Madam:

I am advised by Superintendent Thackery, of Shawnee, that you are the legal guardian of Jesse Chisholm. We have a very small amount in this office due Jesse Chisholm as one of the heirs of Popo Stanley and Mattie Stanley. We would appreciate it if you would advise us of the present address of your ward. A short time ago we wrote Jesse at "Peyton, I.T." The letter has this day been returned to this office, marked "No such post-office in state named".

Very respectfully

W.C. Kohlenberg,
Sup. & Spl. Dis. Agent.
Per   John R.T. Reeves
Financial Clerk.

Mr. W.C. Kohlenberg,
Sac and Fox Agency,
Oklahoma.

271

Dear sir:- Mr. Sam. B. Davis of this place is the Legal Guardian of
Jessie Chisholm, and Jessie"s[sic] address is PADEN, I.T.

Yours truly,

Paden I.T. March-1st-07.

Jennie Davis
nee Harper

NO. __1242__

IN PROBATE COURT,

County of Pottawatomie.

In the Matter of the Estate of

Meah-ah-quot

~~Deceased.~~

Incompetent

CITATION.

Filed the ____ day of _____ 190 ___

_____
Judge of Probate.

_____
Attorney for Petitioner.

*I hereby certify the within to be a true copy of the
original citation, now in my possession with all the
indorsements thereon.*

This _____ day of _____ 190 ____

W A Grace
Sheriff.

By A D King

Under Sheriff

****

CITATION.

Territory of Oklahoma,
Pottawatomie County,

In the Probate Court in and for Pottawatomie County, Territory of Oklahoma.

In the matter of the___ Guardianship of Wish-ah-quot Incompetent _____

The Territory of Oklahoma

To___ Frank A Thackery _____ Greeting:

WHEREAS, Letters___ of Guardianship _____

were on the___ 14 ___ day of ____ Aug _____ A.D. 190_7_, issued out of said Probate

Court to _____ you as guardian of the estate of _____

of ____ Meah-ah-quot Incompetant[sic] person _____ deceased.

AND WHEREAS,__ The said Incompetent person has filed his motion this

day to have you discharged on the grounds that he is capable of transacting his

business affairs and managing his Estate. _____

You are, therefore, hereby notified and cited to be and appear before said Probate Court at a regular term
thereof to be holden at the Probate Court Room in Tecumseh, in said County of Pottawatomie, on the

_5_ day of _____ March _____ A. D., 190_7_, at the hour of _2_ o'clock_P_M of

said day, then and there to _____ answer said motion _____

AND FURTHER, to do and perform what shall then and there be ordered and
adjudged by said court in said matter. And hereof fail not.

WITNESS. The Judge of the Probate Court and the

[SEAL]   seal thereof affixed at Tecumseh, in said County of

seal   Pottawatomie, this__27__day of ____ Feby _____ 190_7_

_____ W N Maben _____
Probate Judge.

ROBERT WHEELER,
ATTORNEY AND COUNSELOR

Brief sent to J. H. Maxey Jr.
3-27-1907

TECUMSEH, OKLA. Mar. 1/07.

Hon. Frank A. Thackery,

Shawnee, Okla.

Dear Sir:-

Enclosed find a letter from Judge Harper and my reply, copy, also copy of the brief I filed with the judge.

I am firmly of the opinion that Judge Harper alone has jurisdiction where the land lies wholly in Oklahoma county, and I want if possible to satisfy him so that he will assume jurisdiction in the cases we have in that county.

I believe I have said all to him that I can say profitably, and, as we talked some days ago, if you can go to Oklahoma City soon and get some good strong attorney in whose opinion the judge has confidence to assist in these cases, we may get him to hold our way.

If you do this, you may leave the judge's letter and the copy of my brief with the attorney you angage[sic]. But ask him to return the brief to me ahen[sic] he is through with it.

Yours very truly,

Robert Wheeler

****

ROBERT WHEELER,
ATTORNEY AND COUNSELOR

Copy

TECUMSEH, OKLA. Mar. 1/07.

Judge, Wm. P. Harper,

Oklahoma City, Okla.

Dear Judge:-

Your favor of the 28, ult. concerning the guardianship case received, and I want to thank you for holding these matters in abeyance and writing me. It is

274

an important question, involving as it does the title to real estate, and I am sure all of us want to be right.

    I will communicate with Mr. Thackery, and we will determine as soon as possible what course we will take. In the mean time I trust you will not file the cases, but allow them to rest as they are until you hear from us further.

Yours very truly,

Robert Wheeler

No. 1   March 1st, 1907.

United States

    To St. Louis & S. F. Ry.   Dr.

For one first class passenger fare from Stroud, O. T. to Chandler, O. T., and return.

                                        $0.90

    Received at Stroud, O. T., of John R. T. Reeves, Financial Clerk, Ninety cents ($0.90) in full of above account.

(Signed)   J. A. Weeks.

No. 2   March 1st, 1907.

United States

    To J. F. D. Walker,   Dr.

For feeding and stabling team at noon March 1st, 1907........$0.50

Received at Stroud, O. T., of John R. T. Reeves, Financial Clerk, fifty cents ($0.40) in full of above account.

TRIPLICATE

CASH.

Voucher No. _____43_____

FOR

TRAVELING EXPENSES,

(OTHER THAN DISBURSING OFFICERS.)

_____Third_____Quarter, 190 7

_____John R. T. Reeves,_____

$ 1.65 _____

Paid in_____or by Check No. 483363

Dated March 25th, 1907;

DRAWN ON

Assistant Treasurer, U. S.,
_____St. Louis, Mo._____

IN FAVOR OF

_____John R. T. Reeves._____

State whether paid in cash or by check; if by check, give the number and date of the check and the name of the bank or institution upon which and in whose favor it is drawn.

****

VOUCHER FOR TRAVELING EXPENSES
(OTHER THAN DISBURSING OFFICERS.)

The United States,

To .... John R. T. Reeves, ... *Dr.*

DATE		Sub-voucher.	DOLLARS.	Cts.
1907				
March 1	R. R. Fare from Stroud, O. T. to Chandler, O. T.,			
	and return	1		90
March 1	Feeding and Stabling team at noon March 1, 1907	2		50
March 1	Lunch for self, noon March 1st, 1907			25
			$ 1	65

See copy of Authority attached to Voucher No. 42

Third Quarter 1907

I solemnly swear that the foregoing account is correct and just; * that the different charges in detail have been taken from and verified by my memorandum; that the amount charged was actually paid; that no part of the journey charged for has been made under any free pass on any railway, steamboat, or other public conveyance; that the number of days for which the same is charged was necessarily consumed in unavoidable delays incident to travel, and the performance of the duty ordered or services rendered; that the journey was performed by the shortest usually traveled routes under orders *(copy annexed)* or for the purpose of Collecting Mortgage belonging to estate of Indian minor ; and that where subvouchers are not furnished it was impracticable to obtain them.

John R.T. Reeves

Sworn to and subscribed before me this 13th day of March , 190 7

W.C. Kohlenberg

Supt. & Spl. Disb. Agt.

RECEIVED at Sac and Fox Agency, Oklahoma, March 25th, , 190 7 of W. C. Kohlenberg, Supt. & Spl. Disb. Agt. , U. S. Indian Agent,

One and 65/100 ($1.65) dollars in full of the above account.

John R.T. Reeves

I CERTIFY, on honor, that the above account is correct and just, and that I have this 25th day of March , 190 7 , actually paid the amount thereof, viz:

One and 65/100 ($1.65) dollars, and have taken claimant's receipt therefor in triplicate.

Dated at ___ Sac and Fox Agency, Oklahoma. ⎫
_____ March 25th, _____ , 190 7 ⎬   W.C. Kohlenberg
Supt. & Spl. Disb. Ag~~t. S. Indian Agent~~

W. N. Maben,

Probate Judge

Pottawatomie County,
Tecumseh,   Oklahoma.

RECEIVED

MAR 15 1907

SAC & FOX AGENCY,
OKLAHOMA.

J. E. Simpson,
Probate Clerk.

Tecumseh OT
Mch 13-1907

Hon W.C. Kohlenberg
   Supt and Spl Disb Agt
   Sac and Fox, O.T.

Dear Sir:-

I have prepared and have ready for filing my final report and resignation as guardian of Brown heirs, but before the Court will accept the same the costs will have to be paid and as I have never received any monies I respectfully ask that you send me a check to cover the amount ($14^{05}) and when this is done the court advises me he will accept my resignation and approve you as guardian.

This cost in part was incurred by the former guardian Mr. L. T. Sammons and remain at this time unpaid

Judge Maben holds that the now acting guardian should pay all costs incurred to date.

When you send me the check to cover the amount I will send you a blank form for your appointment as guardian.

Yours truly
J.E. Simpson

IN PROBATE COURT

IN AND FOR THE COUNTY OF POTTAWATOMIE AND TERRITORY OF OKLAHOMA.

1.30 P.M., March 16, 1907.

Case

Number 1252.

In re Guardianship of Pom-me-home-nah, alias Pom-me hone-wah.   Plaintiff appeared by his attorneys, C. G. Cutlip and E. E. Hood.   Frank A. Thackery, Guardian appeared in person and by his attorney, John Embry, U. S. Attorney, whereupon the following proceedings were had:

W. L. Ducker sworn as stenographer:

Application for removal of guardian withdrawn on account of the discrepancy of the name of the Indian as given in the application and the name of the Indian in fact.

I., W. L. Ducker, being first duly sworn, depose and say that the above and foregoing is a complete and correct statement of the proceedings in the above case.

Subscribed and sworn to before me this   day of   , 1907.

IN PROBATE COURT

IN AND FOR THE COUNTY OF POTTAWATOMIE AND TERRITORY OF OKLAHOMA.

Case Number-----1259.

John Garrett, and   )
)
Wah-ko-nash-ka-ka ,   )
)
(or Henry Bentley), Plf.   )
)
)   In re Removal of Guardian.
        vs.   )
)
Frank A. Thackery,   )
)

279

Legal Guardian of the)
)
person and estate of)
)
Wah-ko-na\h-ka-ka[sic] (or)
)
Henry Bentley) , Deft.)

Case called pursuant to continuance, at 1:30 P. M., March 16, 1907, Plaintiff appeared in person and by his attorneys, C. G. Cutlip and E. E. Hood.   Defendant, Frank A. Thackery, appeared in person, and by his attorney, John Embry, U. S. Attorney, whereupon the following proceedings were had.

On application of E. E. Hood, attorney for John Garrett, the motion herein filed by John Garrett to have the guardian removed is withdrawn:

The Court: It is hereby ordered that this action shall proceed in the name of Wah-ko-nash-ka-ka, (or Henry Bentley-Plaintiff, vs. Frank A. Thackery, Guardian, Defendant.

Henry Bentley.

Henry Bentley, called on behalf of himself, being first duly sworn testified as follows:

DIRECT EXAMINATION by Mr. Hood:

Q.   State your name to the Court.

A.   My name is Henry Bentley.

Q.   How old are you, Henry?   A. 25.

Q.   25?   A. Yes sir.

Q.   How old?   A.   25.

Q.   25?   A. Yes sir.

Q.   Did you ever attend school?   A.   Yes sir.

Q.   What school did you attend?   A.   Carlisle, Pa.

Q.   Carlisle, Pa.?   A.   Yes sir.

Q.   How many years were you in school at Carlisle?

A.   I was there four years and a half.

Q?[sic] When did you leave school?

A.   It was in 1902 when I left school.

Q.   Can you read and write?   A   Yes sir.

Q.   The English language?

A   Yes sir, I can read pretty fair.

Q.   Thoroughly understand it?

A.   Yes sir I can understand it.

Q.   Are you able Henry to transact your own business affairs?

A.   Yes sir, I am.

Q.   Have you ever requested that Mr. Thackery be appointed your guardian?

A.   No sir, I never have.

Q.   Was any notice ever served on you that Mr. Thackery had made application to be appointed your guardian?

A.   They just gave me a paper while I was in jail at the time.

Q.   Where is that paper now?

A.   I got it in my truck over there yet.

Q.   Where was[sic] you at the time the paper was given you?

A.   In jail here.

Q.   In jail here?   A.   Yes sir.

Q.   Was you ever taken out of jail and brought to the Probate Court here on the time on which you were cited to appear?

A.   No sir, they didn't take me out at all. I was looking for them, but they never done it.

Q.   The notice was served on you while you was in jail?

A.   No sir, They never read it to me or nothing.

Q.   It was given to you while you was in jail was it, Henry?

A   Yes sir. They gave it to me there.

Q.   What jail was you confined in when you received this notice?

A.   In the County Jail.

Q.   Here in Tecumseh?   A.   Yes sir.

Q.   Was that on a Territorial or United States charge.[sic]

A   Territorial.

Q.   Territorial?   A.   Yes sir.

Q.   How long did you remain in jail after you received the notice.[sic]

A.   They gave it to me July 10th-- about four months.

Q.   Do you desire at this time that Mr. Thackery shall continue as your guardian.[sic]

A.   No sir.

Q.   Have you any personal property at this time, Henry?

A.   What's that?

Q.   Have you any personal property outside of your land at this time?

A.   No not here.

Q.   Do you own any personal property, Henry, I don't mean your land, just any personal property. Do you own any?

A.   Do I own any?

Q.   Do you, yes?

A.   Yes, On my sister's place, part of it.

Q.   What is the nature of your personal property, just wearing apparel and such as that.

A.   Therr[sic] was only wearing apparel, that is all.

Q.   You do not own any horses do you?

A.   Who? me?   [sic] No.

Q.   Cows?   A.   No.

Q.   Any live stock of any kind?   A.   No.

Q.   The time you was in jail up there and this notice was served on you, you owned some land in this county?   A.   Yes sir.

Q.   Where is that located?

A.   Over east of McLoud.

Q.   Over east of McLoud?

A.   Two miles east of McLoud on the lake about.

Q.   Henry, do you desire to sell that land?   A.   Yes sir.

Q.   You desire to go to the Republic of Mexico.   A.   Yes sir.

Q. When do you want to go?

A. Any time when I get through with this case.

Q. Any time when you get through with this case?   A. Yes sir.

Q. And you are staying here now for the purpose of getting this guardian removed, are you?   A. Yes sir.

Q. Are there any improvements on that land up there of yours?

A. No sir.

Q. What amount of money do you receive from it a year?

A. Fifteen dollars.

Q. Fifteen dollars?   A. Yes sir.

Q. And that land you desire to sell do you?   A. Yes sir.

CROSS EXAMINATION by Mr. Embry.

Q. You have contracted to sell the land have you, Henry?

A. Yes sir.

Q. Whom to?   A. Conine.

Q. Who, Dr. R. C. Conine?   A. Yes sir.

Q. How much is he to give you for it?   A. $700.00

Q. $700.00?   A. Yes sir.

Q. What is that land worth, Henry?

Mr. Cutlip: We object, it is alleged in the application to be worth $800.00.

Q. What is that land worth, Henry?   Your[sic] know what it is worth.

A. I have been getting fifteen dollars a year from the land.

Q. Now, Henry, Mr. Thackery has been putting most of the rent in improvements on the land has he not?

A. I don't know whether he has or not.

Q. Haven't you been looking at your farm to see how it was getting along and being improved.

A. I know there was nothing being done on my farm.

Q. Well, have you an interest in any other farm?

A. Yes I have-- interest in another another[sic] farm, but there is nothing but a long house there. They promised they would put up a better house there when they got the lease.

Q. When did you make the lease, Henry? A. 1905.

Q. Has there been any breaking done on the land since then.

A. Yes, they broke the land all right.

Q. Why don't you stay on that land and work it? You are big and stout.

A. I don't want to.

Q. What have you been working at to earn anything the past year?

Objected to as incompetent, irrelevant and immaterial.

Objection overruled.

Q. What have you been doing for the past year, Henry, to earn any money?

A. Gambling around.

Q. Gambling around?

A. Yes, that is the only way I get my money to get my clothes.

Q. That is where your farm would go to if you got the money out of it?

A. No sir.

Q. What would you do with it. A. Keep it.

Q. Keep it? A. Yes, and buy what I need.

Q. When did you do a day's work for which you received wages, Henry?

Objected to as incompetent, irrelevant and immaterial.

Question withdrawn.

Q. You say you want to go to Mexico? A. Yes sir.

Q. What do you want to go to Mexico for?

A. All Kickapoos go to Mexico after a while. That is why I want to go there.

Q. Now if you had this money do you know anything you could invest it in? A. Yes sir.

Q. What?

A. Well, what I need when I go to Mexico. I need that money over there because I do not have any money over there.

Q. What will you do with that money over there?

A. Buy me horses.

Q. What would you want of horses?

A. Oh, ride them around.

Q. You would not want them to work or anything of that kind?

A. Why of course I would want them to work with.

Q. Have you ever worked here during your twenty-five years?

A. Of course I have been working.

Q. How long is it since you worked any?

A. Well I was working yesterday.

Q. For whom?   A. What?

Q. For whom were you working yesterday.

A. For whom?

Q. WHO did you work for yesterday.

A. Joe Whipple's.

Q. How many days have you worked for Joe Whipple?

A. Just two days.

Q. You know you were going to be a witness here today?

A. Yes sir. That is the reason I came.

Q. And that is the reason you worked for Joe Whipple, so you could testify to it that you had worked?

A. Yes sir. I work there most of the time when I can get a job.

Mr. Embry: I do not believe I would care to resist the removal of the Guardian of this Indian.

Mr. Cutlipp[sic]:   We ask that the order be made then.

The Court: I will not make the order just now.

I, W. L. Ducker, being first duly sworn, depose and say that the above and foregoing is a complete and correct statement of the testimony in the foregoing case as faithfully reported by me in shorthand, and correctly reduced to writing.

Subscribed and sworn to before me this   day of   , 1907.

IN PROBATE COURT

IN AND FOR THE COUNTY OF POTTAWATOMIE AND TERRITORY OF OKLAHOMA.

Case Number-----1242

J. R. Jacobs, and	)	
Henry Smith, (or	)	
Mesh-ah-quot, Plf.	)	
	)	IN RE REMOVAL OF GUARDIAN.
vs.	)	
Frank A. Thackery,	)	
Legal Guardian of the	)	
estate of Mesh-ah-quot, Deft.	)	

Case called pursuant to continuance at 1:30 P. M., March 16, 1907, Plaintiff appeared by his attorneys, C. G. Cutlip and E. E. Hood. Defendant, appeared in person and by his attorney, U. S. Attorney, John Embry, whereupon the following proceedings were had.

E. E. Hood, counsel for J. R. Jacobs withdraws his said application in this case.

It is hereby ordered by the Court that this action hereafter proceed under the name of Mesh-as-quot, or Henry Smith, Plaintiff, vs. Frank A. Thackery, Guardian, Defendant.

Comes now the defendant, Frank A. Thackery, and objects to any testimony on this application in that it does not state facts sufficient to authorize removal of the guardian.

It is the order of the Court that in this case the order appointing Frank A. Thackery guardian of Henry Smith or Mesh-ah-quot be, and the same is hereby revoked and set aside.

I. W. L. Ducker, being first duly sworn, depose and say that the foregoing is a correct statement of the proceedings had in the above entitled case, Mar. 16, 1907.

_____

IN PROBATE COURT

IN AND FOR THE COUNTY OF POTTAWATOMIE AND TERRITORY OF OKLAHOMA.

1.30 P. M., March 16, 1907.

Case

Number 1252.

In re Guardianship of Pom-me-home-nah, alias Pom-me hone-wah. Plaintiff appeared by his attorneys, C. G. Cutlip and E. E. Hood. Frank A. Thackery, Guardian, appeared in person and by his attorney, John Embry, U. S. Attorney, whereupon the following proceedings were had:

W. L. Ducker sworn as stenographer:

Application for removal of guardian withdrawn on account of the discrepancy of the name of the Indian as given in the application and the name of the Indian in fact.

I., W. L. Ducker, being first duly sworn, depose and say that the above and foregoing is a complete and correct statement of the proceedings in the above case.

_____

Subscribed and sworn to before me this   day of   , 1907

_____

[Copy of Original Letter]

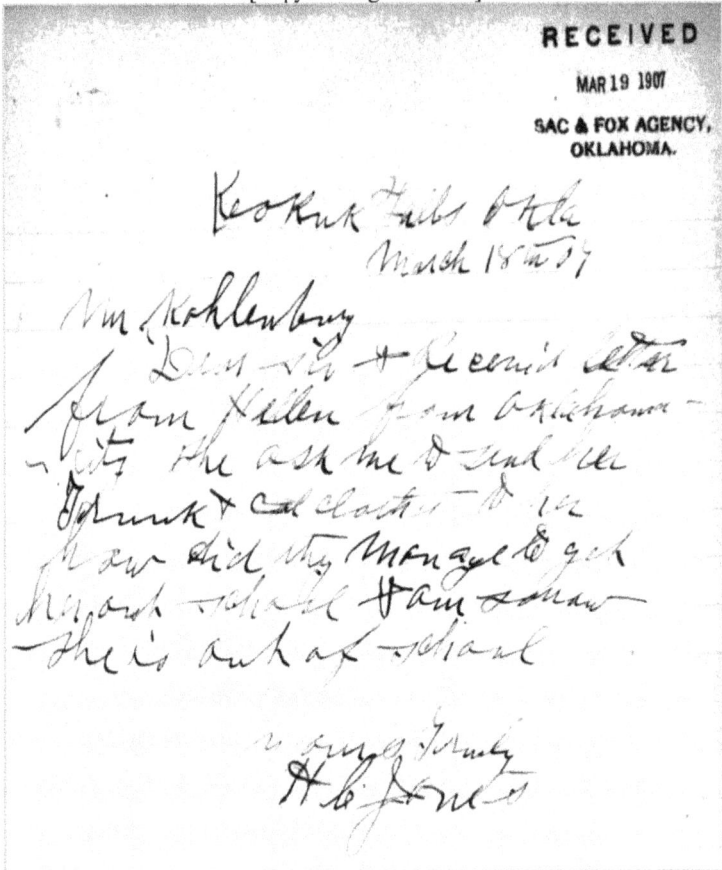

RECEIVED

MAR 19 1907

SAC & FOX AGENCY,
OKLAHOMA.

[Transcription of above letter]

RECEIVED
MAR 19 1907
SAC & FOX AGENCY,
OKLAHOMA.

Keokuk Falls Okla
March 18th 07

Mr Kohlenburg[sic]

   Dear sir   I Received letter from Hellen from Oklahoma City   She ask me to send her Trunk and ~~eal~~ clothes to her   how did thy manage to get her out school I am sorrow she is out of school.

Yours truly
H C Jones

Tecumseh O. T. July 15/07

Mr. F. A. Thackery
Shawnee O. T.

Dear Sir

Enclosed please find note, of Anna and Phil Cuellar 153\frac{73}{}$ They said for you to deduct same from money due Anna Cuellar

Respectfully Yours
M. H. Wagner

****

U. S. Indian Agency,

Shawnee, Okla., July 19, 1907.

Mr. M. H. Wagner,

Tecumseh, Okla.

Dear Sir:

I am in receipt of your letter of the 15th instant with the note against Anna and Philemon Cuellar, amounting to $153.73 inclosed as stated.

When Mr. Cuellar receives money through this office his attention will be called to this note.

Very respectfully,

Supt. & Spl. Disb. Agent.

WLD.

Misc.

Cy. I.G.

DEPARTMENT OF THE INTERIOR

UNITED STATES INDIAN SERVICE

RECEIVED
MAR 27 1907
SAC & FOX AGENCY,
OKLAHOMA,

Quapaw Agency, Indian Territory,

Wyandotte, I.T.,   March 25, 1907.

Supt. W. A[sic]. Kohlenberg,

    Sac & Fox Agency, Oklahoma.

Dear Sir:

    Acknowledging the receipt of your letter of 22nd instant requesting information concerning money in my hands due Rosa Hurr- (it is assumed that you mean Rosa Wolf) - you are respectfully advised that Rosa Wolf's father died at this agency on Aug. 14, 1906, having to his credit, under my control, about $652, moneys derived from the sale of inherited Indian land. The amount has been increased at the rate of $1.64 per month, accrued interest, and will so continue until paid.

    I understand that Rosa is the sole heir and have so advised the Indian Office. I understand that she will be of age soon in which case the money may be paid to her if she is competent to care for it. If otherwise it will be paid her at the rate of $10 per month. As soon as I am advised by the Office what disposition to make of the fund I shall inform Rosa, through your office.

                Very respectfully,

                    Horace B Durant
                    Superintendent.

Please advise me if I am correct about the name.

****

DEPARTMENT OF THE INTERIOR

UNITED STATES INDIAN SERVICE

RECEIVED
MAR 27 1907
SAC & FOX AGENCY,
OKLAHOMA.

Supt. W. A. Kohlenberg. 2 .

wrote 2/27/07

Later:
R.

I am in receipt to-day of a letter from Joel Delonais, of Sacred Heart, Oklahoma, who states that he the legal guardian of Rosa Wolf, and making inquiry in regard to the allotment left by her father in this agency.

Have you any advice in regard to the appointment of a legal guardian of this girl? What necessity is there for such an expense to her and the estate? Is the guardian a responsible person and capable?

I shall be glad to act on any suggestions you may offer as to the disposition of the funds and estate coming to Rosa.

Very respectfully,

Horace B. Durant

Rosa's Mother was allotted near Tecumseh.   Superintendent.

****

Sacred Heart, Oklahoma.

RECEIVED
APR 15 1907
SAC & FOX AGENCY,
OKLAHOMA.

April 11, 1907.

Mr. W.C. Kohlenberg,

Supt. & Spec'l. Dsbg. Agent,

Sac and Fox Agency,

Okla.

Dear Sir:-

In answer to your letter of the 28 ult. I will say that I was appointed Legal Guardian of Rosa Wolf by the Probate Court of Pottawatomie County, about five years ago, Wm. H. Pendleton being Probate Judge at the time. I have no funds whatever under my control, belonging to said ward. All the land belonging to said ward has been leased for improvements, and the time has not expired on the leases yet.

I do not know anything about the estate this ward inherited from her father, James Wolfe. Her own 80, and her mothers'[sic] 160 acres have been leased for improvements. I do not know any such name as Rosa Hurr.

The Rosa Wolf I refer to, is the daughter of James Wolf, and Ellen Shop-way-tuck.

Very respectfully,

Joel Delonais

NOTICE:

NOTICE IS HEREBY GIVEN that in pursuance of an order of the County Court of the County of Noble, State of Oklahoma, made on the 14th day of March, A. D., 1908, in the matter of the estate of Mary Dupee, minor, the undersigned as guardian of the said Mary Dupee, minor, will sell at public auction, to the highest bidder or bidders, for cash, at the Sac and Fox Agency, Oklahoma, on May 4th, 1908, at twelve o'clock non, the following:

An undivided two forty-fifths (2/45) interest in the South half of the North-West Quarter, Section Nineteen, Township Seventeen, North of Range Three, East of the Indian Meridian in Oklahoma.

Also an undivided two fifteenths (2/15) interest in the North half of the North West Quarter, Section Nineteen, Township Seventeen, North of Range three East of the Indian Meridian in Oklahoma.

The two forty-fifths interest above described represents the share by inheritance of the said Mary Dupee, minor, in the allotment on one Hot-chi-see, a deceased allottee of the Iowa Tribe of Indians in Oklahoma, and the two fifteenths interest represents the share of said minor in the allotment of one Muc-cum-pem-pe, a deceased allottee of the Iowa Tribe of Indians.

For the information of prospective bidders the following information is submitted:

The undivided interests above referred to will be sold in conjunction with the remaining interests. That is each allotment will be sold separately in its entirety, in accordance with the rules and regulations prescribed by the Department of the Interior regulating the sale of deceased Indian's allotments.

All bids must be in the hands of the undersigned by twelve o'clock on the daye[sic] named; each bid must be sealed and the envelope marked "Bid for Indian land to be opened May 4, 1908". Description of the land must not be noted on outside of envelope. All bids must be accompanied by certified

check for not less than twenty five percent of amount bid. Bids containing cash in lieu of certified check will not be received, or considered.
For further information apply to,

WC Kohlenberg

Supt. & Spl. Disb. Agt
Sac and Fox Agency, Oklahoma.
Guardian of Mary Dupee

GUARDIANSHIPS: HEIRSHIPS: & ETC.

+++++++++++++++++++++++++

ITEM NO.

1 -   CERTIFICATE OF HEIRSHIP FILES WITH LEASE ROLL FOR THE FIRST QUARTER 1907.

9 -   A CERTIFICATE OF HEIRSHIP IN THE MATTER OF THE ESTATE OF KE-AH-KO-PIT, HERETO ATTACHED, MARKED EXHIBIT "A".

18 -   A CERTIFICATE OF HEIRSHIP IN THE MATTER OF THE ESTATE OF KA-SE-CA, DEC., IS ATTACHED TO THE APPROVED LEASE.

22 -   A CERTIFICATE OF HEIRSHIP IN THE MATTER OF THE ESTATE OF TILDA SULTUSKA, DECEASED IS ATTACHED TO THE ORIGINAL COPY OF APPROVED LEASE.

LETTERS OF GUARDIANSHIP/ FRANK A. THACKERY, L. GDN., OF HILDA, LOUISE, GEORGE A. ANN, AND JEROME SULTUSKA, HEREUNTO ATTACHED, MARKED EXHIBIT "B".

24 -   A CERTIFICATE OF HEIRSHIP IN THE MATTER OF THE ESTATE OF JIM BULLFROG,
26   DECEASED IS ATTACHED TO THE ORIGINAL COPY OF THE APPROVED LEASE.

28   LETTERS OF GUARDIANSHIP IN THE MATTER OF THE GUARDIANSHIP OF FRANK A. THACKERY, L. GDN. OF ALLEN LONGHORN HERETO ATTACHED MARKED EXHIBIT "C".

33 -   A CERTIFICATE OF HEIRSHIP IN THE MATTER OF THE ESTATE OF WINNIE MARK ROLETTE, DEC., IS ATTACHED TO ORIGINAL COPY OF LEASE.

35 -   A CERTIFICATE OF HEIRSHIP IN THE MATTER OF THE ESTATE OF JOHN KING, DEC., ATTACHED TO THE ORIGINAL COPY OF THE APPROVED LEASE.

41 -   A CERTIFICATE OF HEIRSHIP IN THE MATTER OF THE ESTATE OF WAH-KEE-NAH, DEC., ATTACHED TO THE ORIGINAL COPY OF THE APPROVED LEASE.

60 -   THIS LEASE SIGNED BY SHAWNEE LITTLE BEAR, L. GDN. CHARLEY LITTLE BEAR, A CERTIFICATE IN THE MATTER OF THE MAJORITY OF CHARLEY LITTLE BEAR, IS HERETO ATTACHED, MARKED EXHIBIT "D".

67 -   A CERTIFICATE OF HERISHIP[sic] IN THE MATTER OF THE ESTATE OF THOMAS WASHINGTON, DECEASED, IS ATTACHED TO THE ORIGINAL COPY OF THE APPROVED LEASE.

88 -   LETTERS OF GUARDIANSHIP IN THE MATTER OF WILLIAM C. ROBINSON, L. GDN., OF EDGAR CREEK ARE ATTACHED TO THE ORIGINAL COPY OF THE APPROVED LEASE.

91   A CERTIFICATE OF HEIRSHIP IN THE MATTER OF THE ESTATE OF HARRY BRADY, DEC., IS ATTACHED TO THE ORIGINAL COPY OF THE APPROVED LEASE.

113 -   LETTERS OF GUARDIANSHIP IN THE MATTER OF THE GUARDIANSHIP OF FRANK A. THACKERY, L. GDN. OF WAH-QUE-TAH-NO-QUAH, WERE FILED WITH THE OFFICE IN LETTER DATED SEPTEMBER 18, 1908.

ITEM NO.

114 &

115   LETTERS OF GUARDIANSHIP IN THE MATTER OF THE GUARDIANSHIP OF FRANK A. THACKERY, L. GND., OF QUEN-NEP-PE-THOT AND KISH-KE-TON-O-QUAH, INCOMPETENTS, WERE FILED WITH THE OFFICE IN LETTER DATED SEPTEMBER 18, 1906.

119 &

120 -   SEE REMARKS TO NOS. 24 & 26, WHICH APPLY.

124 -   A CERTIFICATE OF HEIRSHIP IN THE MATTER OF THE HEIRSHIP OF LILLY FOREMAN, ATTACHED TO THE ORIGINAL COPY OF THE APPROVED LEASE.

151 -   A CERTIFICATE OF HEIRSHIP IN THE MATTER OF THE HEIRSHIP OF LIZZIE WASHINGTON, DECEASED, IS ATTACHED TO THE ORIGINAL COPY OF THE APPROVED LEASE.

157 -   A CERTIFICATE OF HEIRSHIP IN THE MATTER OF THE HEIRSHIP OF CLARRISSA SHINCIS IS ATTACHED TO THE ORIGINAL COPY OF THE APPROVED LEASE.

165 -   LETTERS OF GUARDIANSHIP IN THE MATTER OF THE GUARDIANSHIP OF FRANK A. THACKERY, L. GDN., OF AH-KO-THE WERE FILED WITH OFFICE IN LETTER DATED SEPTEMBER 18, 1906.

198 -   A CERTIFICATE OF HEIRSHIP IN THE MATTER OF THE HEIRSHIP OF WILLIAM SHAWNEE, DECEASED, IS ATTACHED TO THE APPROVED COPY OF THE APPROVED LEASE.

199 -   A CERTIFICATE OF HEIRSHIP IN THE MATTER OF THE HEIRSHIP OF SALLY FOREMAN, DECEASED, IS ATTACHED TO THE ORIGINAL COPY OF THE APPROVED LEASE.

202 -   A CERTIFICATE OF GUARDIANSHIP IN THE MATTER OF THE GUARDIANSHIP OF FRANK A. THACKERY, L. GDN. OF PE-AH-CHE-THOT, OR BURT PE-AH-CHE-THOT, HEREUNTO ATTACHED MARKED EXHIBIT "E".

225 -   A CERTIFICATE OF HEIRSHIP IN THE MATTER OF THE HEIRSHIP OF WAH-CUT-TAH-PEA-SE, DECEASED, IS HEREUNTO ATTACHED MARKED EXHIBIT "F".

228 -   LETTERS OF GUARDIANSHIP IN THE MATTER OF THE GUARDIANSHIP OF FRANK A. THACKERY, L. GDN. OF ME-NA-MISH WERE FILED WITH OFFICE IN LETTER DATED SEPTEMBER 18, 1906.

250 -   A CERTIFICATE OF HEIRSHIP IN THE MATTER OF THE HEIRSHIP OF EVA FRENCH, DEC., IS ATTACHED TO THE ORIGINAL COPY OF THE APPROVED LEASE.

267 -   THERE WAS NO APPROVED LEASE ON THIS ALLOTMENT.

274 -   A CERTIFICATE OF HEIRSHIP IN THE MATTER OF THE ESTATE OF DICK ELLIS IS ATTACHED TO THE ORIGINAL COPY OF THE APPROVED LAESE[sic].

275 -   A CERTIFICATE OF HEIRSHIP IN THE MATTER OF THE ESTATE OF MAYTHAH-PEA-SCA-CA, DECEASED, WAS FILED WITH MY LEASE ROLL FOR THE FIRST QUARTER, 1907, ENDED SEPTEMBER 30, 1906, MARKED EXHIBIT "D".

276 -   A CERTIFICATE OF HEIRSHIP IN THE MATTER OF THE HEIRSHIP OF JOE LONGHORN, DECEASED, IS ATTACHED TO THE ORIGINAL COPY OF THE APPROVED LEASE/

279 -   THE REMARKS TO NO. 274 APPLY.

280 -   A CERTIFICATE OF HEIRSHIP IN THE MATTER OF THE HEIRSHIP OF JERRY WILSON, DECEASED, IS ATTACHED TO THE ORIGINAL COPY OF THE APPROVED LEASE.

304 -   LETTERS OF GUARDIANSHIP IN THE MATTER OF THE GUARDIANSHIP OF JAMES S. SLOAT, LEGAL GUARDIAN OF LA*LA*GE-PEA-SKE-KA, AND LA-LA-GE-PEA-SE, MINORS, ATTACHED TO THE ORIGINAL COPY OF THE APPROVED LEASE.

313 -   A CERTIFICATE OF HEIRSHIP IN THE MATTER OF THE GUARDIANSHIP OF FRANK A. THAVKERY[sic], L. GDN. OF THOMAS SAMPSON, MINOR, HEREUNTO ATTACHED MARKED EXHIBIT "G".

"Exhibit A"

Territory of Oklahoma
                      ss
Pottawatomie County

Shawnee Okla., March 30, 1907.

We, Henry Murdock and Me-na-mish, being first duly sworn on oath depose and say, that we were well acquainted with Ke-ah-qua-pit (Ke-ah-k-pit) during his life time, that he died in the year 1899 and left his father, Wah-sko-ta-a-tah as his sole heir at law, that said Wah-sko-ta-a-tah died in the year 1904, and left the following heirs: Qua-ye, aged about fifty years, wife; Ah-no-tho-the daughter, aged 25 years; Nah-she-pe-eth, daughter aged 23 years; Ma-ko-the-quah, daughter, aged 22 years; and Cha-cha-ko-the-wa (John Snake) son, aged 20 years; and Py-a-tho, daughter aged about 19 years; that said Qua-you died on the 4th of March 1906, leaving as he only heirs Py-atho, her only child by Wah-sko-ta-a-tah, and Me-she-kah-tah-no aged about 35 years, an only son by a former husband.

We further swear that we have no interest whatever in the above estate

_____Henry W. Murdock_____

_____me na mish_____

Subscribed to in my presence and sworn to before me this 30th day of March, A. D., 1907.

~~My commission expires Jan. 2, 1907~~.

_____

Notary Public.

My commission expires Jan. 2, 1907.
Certificate on file in Indian Office.

"Exhibit B"

Letters of Guardianship of Minors.

Territory of Oklahoma, Pottawatomie County, S.S.

THE TERRITORY OF OKLAHOMA, To all whom it may concern, and especially to _____.

_____ Frank A. Thackery, _____ GREETING:

KNOW YE, THAT WHEREAS, Application has been made to the Probate Court of said County for the appointment of a Guardian to __ Anna Suttuska _____ aged _____ years,

_____ Louisa Suttuska _____ aged _____ years,

_____ Hilda Suttuska _____ aged _____ years,

_____ Jerome Suttuska _____ aged _____ years,

_____ And George Suttuska _____ aged _____ years,

minor heirs of __ Hilda Suttuska _____ deceased, and it appearing to the Court that it is necessary to appoint a guardian to said ____ minor heirs _____

_____

_____

and the said _____ Frank A. Thackery, _____

having been approved for said trust by the Court and having given bond as required by law, which has been approved, filed and recorded in said Court:

NOW, THEREFORE, Trusting in your care and fidelity, we have appointed, and do by these presents appoint you, the said _____ Frank A. Thackery, _____ as such guardian, hereby authorizing and empowering you to take and to have the custody of said minorS_ and the care of _their_ education and the care and management of _their_ estate until _they_ arrive at the age of _Majority_ or until you shall be discharged according to law.

And requiring you to make a true inventory of all the estate, real and personal, of the said ward S_ that shall come to your possession or knowledge, and to return the same into the Probate Court within three months from the date of these letters, or at any other time the Court shall direct, to dispose of and manage all such estate according to law, and for the best interest of the ward S_ , and faithfully to discharge your trust in relation thereto, and also when required, in relation to the care, custody and education of ward S_ to render an account on oath of the property, real and personal, of the said ward S_ in your hands, and all proceeds and interest derived therefrom, and of the management and disposition of the same, within one year after your appointment, and annually thereafter, and at such other times as the proper Court shall direct, and at the expiration of your trust to settle your account with the Probate Court, or with the ward S , if they shall be of full age, or their legal representatives. And to pay over and deliver all the property, real and personal, remaining in your hands or due from you on such settlement to the person lawfully entitled thereto.

IN TESTIMONY WHEREOF, We have caused the seal of our said Probate Court to be hereto affixed.

WITNESS, W. M[sic]. Maben, Judge of our said Court, at Tecumseh, in said County, this 2 day of Dec 190 6

W. M. Maben, Probate Judge

Filed Dec 2 190 6

W. M. Maben, Probate Judge

(Seal.)

****

In the Probate Court of the Territory, in and for Pottawatomie County.

I, J. E. Simpson Cler,[sic] in and for the County and Territory aforesaid, do hereby certify the abive[sic] and fore going to be a full true and complete copy of the Letters of guardianship of issued to Frank A Thackery as guardian Anna Suttuska et al Minor heirs of Hilda Suttuska Decd

as the same appears on file and of record in my office.

Witness my hand the seal of the said Court this 23rd day of April 1907.

J E Simpson
pRO[sic] Probate Clerk

"Exhibit D"

POTTAWATOMIE COUNTY
                    S S:
TERRITORY OF OKLAHOMA

IN THE MATTER OF THE MAJORITY OF CHARLEY LITTLE BEAR, AN ABSENTEE SHAWNEE INDIAN.

* * * * * * * * * * * * * * * * * * * *

WE, SHAWNEE LITTLE BEAR, AND BETSEY LITTLE BEAR, HUSBAND AND WIFE, OF LAWFUL AGE, BEING FIRST DULY SWORN ON OATH DEPOSE AND SAY, THAT CHARLEY LITTLE BEAR IS OUR LAWFUL SON; THAT HE WAS BORN ON THE 29TH DAY OF MARCH, 1885, AND THAT HE IS NOW IN HIS 22ND YEAR, AND THEREFORE HAS REACHED THE

AGE OF MAJORITY AND IS LAWFULLY INTITLED[sic] TO TRANSACT ANY AND ALL OF HIS BUSINESS AFFAIRS FOR HIM

SELF, AND FURTHER AFFIANTS SAYETH NOT.

WITNESSES.

	his
Mary Bullfrog	Shawnee Little Bear ___X mark
W. F. Dickens .	Betsey Little Bear ___X mark her

SUBSCRIBED AND SWORN TO BEFORE ME THIS __16__ DYA[sic] OF MARCH, 1907.

MY COMMISSION EXPIRES JAN. 1ST, 1908.   _____Walter F. Dickens_____
CERTIFICATE ON FILE IN THE INDIAN OFFICE   NOTARY PUBLIC.

POTTAWATOMIE COUNTY
                              S S:
TERRITORY OF OKLAHOMA

                                    I MARY BULLFROG BEING FIRST DULY SWORN ON OATH DEPOSE
AND STATE, THAT I HAVE CAREFULLY AND TRULY INTERPRETED THE ABOVE AFFIDAVIT TO SHAWNEE LITTLE BEAR,
AND BETSEY LITTLE BEAR, AND THAT THEY EACH OF THEM FULLY UNDERSTAND THE MEANING AND PURPORT OF
SAME; THAT I READ AND WRITE THE ENGLISH LANGUAGE, AND THAT I SPEAK AND FULLY UNDERSTAND THE
SHAWNEE INDIAN LANGUAGE.

                                    _____Mary Bullfrog_____.

SUBSCRIBED AND SWORN TO BEFORE ME THIS __16__ DAY OF MARCH, 1907.

MY COMMISSION EXPIRES JAN. 1ST, 1908.   _____Walter F. Dickens_____
CERTIFICATE ON FILE IN THE INDIAN OFFICE   NOTARY PUBLIC.

"Exhibit E"
Letters of Guardianship of Minors.

Territory of Oklahoma, Pottawatomie County, S.S.

THE TERRITORY OF OKLAHOMA, To all whom it may concern, and especially to _____

_____ Frank A. Thackery, _____ GREETING:

KNOW YE, THAT WHEREAS, Application has been made to the Probate Court of said County for the appointment of

a Guardian to ____ Pe-ah-che-that _____ aged _____ years,

____ And   M-she-ka-pot _____ aged _____ years,

_____ aged _____ years,

minor heirs of _____ deceased, and it appearing to the Court that it is necessary

to appoint a guardian to said ____ Minor heirs _____

_____

and the said _____ Frank A. Thackery, _____

having been approved for said trust by the Court and having given bond as required by law, which has been approved,

filed and recorded in said Court:

NOW, THEREFORE, Trusting in your care and fidelity, we have appointed, and do by these presents appoint you, the said _____ Frank A. Thackery, _____ as such guardian, hereby authorizing and empowering you to take and to have the custody of said minor S ___ and the care of their ___ education and the care and management of their __ estate until they __ arrive at the age of __ Majority ___ or until you shall be discharged according to law.

And requiring you to make a true inventory of all the estate, real and personal, of the said ward S ___ that shall come to your possession or knowledge, and to return the same into the Probate Court within three months from the date of these letters, or at any other time the Court shall direct, to dispose of and manage all such estate according to law, and for the best interest of the ward S ___ , and faithfully to discharge your trust in relation thereto, and also when required, in relation to the care, custody and education of ward S ___ to render an account on oath of the property, real and personal, of the said ward S ___ in your hands, and all proceeds and interest derived therefrom, and of the management and disposition of the same, within one year after your appointment, and annually thereafter, and at such other times as the proper Court shall direct, and at the expiration of your trust to settle your account with the Probate Court, or with the ward S __ , if they ___ shall be of full age, or their ____ legal representatives. And to pay over and deliver all the property, real and personal, remaining in your hands or due from you on such settlement to the person lawfully entitled thereto.

IN TESTIMONY WHEREOF, We have caused the seal of our said Probate Court to be hereto affixed.

WITNESS, _____ W. M[sic]. Maben. _____ Judge of our said Court, at Tecumseh, in said County, this _7_ day of __ Feby _____ 190 7

_____ W. M. Maben, _____ Probate Judge

Filed _Feby 7_ ___ 190 7   _____ W. M. Maben, _____ Probate Judge

(Seal.)

****

In the Probate Court of the Territory, in and for Pottawatomie County.

I, W. N. Maben, Probate Judge J. E. Simpson Clerk in and for the County and Territory aforesaid, do hereby certify the above and foregoing to be a full, true and complete copy of the Letters of guardianship issued to Frank A Thackery as guardian of Pe-ah-che-that et al Minors

as the same appears on file and of record in my office.

Witness my hand and the seal of the said Court this 23rd day of _Apl_ 1907.

_____ J E Simpson _____
Probate Judge Clerk

"Exhibit F"

SHAWNEE INDIAN AGENCY, SHAWNEE OKLAHOMA:

MAR 30 1907 1907.

We,   Henry Murdock   , and   Me na mish   ,

Each of lawful age, having been duly sworn each for himself deposes and sys that he

was well acquainted with ___Wah-cut-tah-peah-she,_____ Mexican Kickapoo Allottee

No.___164____, during his lifetime; that he died in the year of 1895, at the age of four

(4) years, leaving his Father,___KE-SHO-KAH-ME,_____as his only surviving heir.

___Ke-sho-kah-me_____died in the year of 1900, and left as his only surviving heirs,

__MAH-NAH-THE-QUAH, (Wife), WAH-PE-KE-CHE, (Son),_____

PAH-KE-CHE-MOKE (Daughter), and HENRY BENTLY[sic](Son);_____

We further swear that we have no interest in the above estate.
Witnesses.

------------------------------------   ____Henry W. Murdock_____

------------------------------------   _____Me na mish_____

Subscribed and sworn to before me this___30___day of___March___1907.

My Comm. exps.__1 '08___   _____Walter F. Dickens_____
cert on file.   Notary Public.

"Exhibit G"

Territory of Oklahoma ⎫
                      ⎬ ss
Pottawatomie County ⎭

I J. E. Simpson Clerk of the Probate Court in and for
said County and Territory do hereby certify that Frank A Thackery
is the duly appointed, qualified and acting guardian of Thomas
Sampson a Minor as the same now appears of record in the Office.

Witness my hand and the official seal of said Court at
Tecumseh O.T. on this 22" day of April 1907

J. E. Simpson
Clerk Probate Court

303

www.ingramcontent.com/pod-product-compliance
Lightning Source LLC
Chambersburg PA
CBHW032101040426

42336CB00040B/625